BEYOND LAKE TITICACA

by

ANGELA CACCIA

HODDER AND STOUGHTON

64175

Printed in Great Britain for Hodder and Stoughton Limited, St. Paul's House, Warwick Lane, London, E.C.4 by The Camelot Press Limited, London and Southampton

If there is no other work for the people, force it to move a hill from one place to another. For so there shall be peace in the Kingdom.

Inca Huayna Capac

We came here to serve God, and to get rich.

Bernal Diaz del Castillo,
Conquistador

God there may be, but the *gringo* always beats him.

Bolivian saying

And we shrug our shoulders at death, as at life, confronting it in silence, or with a contemptuous smile.

Octavio Paz

The *campesinos* are as impenetrable as stones. When one talks with them, it seems as if, in the depths of their eyes, they are only mocking.

Ché Guevara

Preface

A<small>T THE END</small> of 1963 my husband, who was at that time a member of H.M. Foreign Service, was posted to La Paz, in Bolivia.

As so often when an event of great consequence in one's life takes place, we were ill-prepared. We knew nothing about South America, and no Spanish. All our background reading and language studies had to be done on the journey out.

But we had just spent more than a year behind the Iron Curtain. From the gloom of central Europe this was like a step into some wild romance. We entered light-heartedly into this new phase in our lives: it seemed a great adventure.

Dwarfed perhaps by the giants of the immense continent, Bolivia is in fact more than twice the size of Spain. Her terrain is extraordinarily complicated, embracing some of the highest peaks of the Andes, huge tropical forests threaded by the headwaters of the Amazon, thick, sub-tropical woodland and swamps, the forests of the Gran Chaco known as Green Hell, and finally the great high plateau round Lake Titicaca.

The population is small, under four million people, over seventy-five per cent of whom live on the plateau, the *altiplano*, in a rigorous, hostile climate. The problems of communication are immense: many towns are only reachable from the outside world by air; there are miles of roads, and miles of navigable riverway, but these rarely connect with each other. Seasonal floods transform vast areas of the country into swamps: in Trinidad, in the dry season, boats lie about incongruously, tied to gateposts or trees, waiting for the next rains. Railways are few and often unreliable. Landslides and sudden storms destroy, in minutes, the work of months on roads and bridges.

7

It is a place where, in the mid-twentieth century, man is still the inferior force, pitted against the vast, inscrutable, overpowering persona of nature. In places he has come to terms with her, but the struggle is constant, and any pause will tilt the balance against him.

It is easy to disappear in country like this. Ché Guevara's was far from the first band of guerillas to roam the province of Santa Cruz. Guevara not only misjudged the Indians, and chose the wrong group of people to "work" with his revolutionary promises, he also chose the wrong terrain and quite failed to realise the true nature of the Bolivian forests. The area of his choice was bigger than the whole of Cuba, the population very sparse, decimated by plague, and probably sick to death of all guerillas. The story of Guevara's months in the wild is a pathetic record of the struggle against nature. They ran out of rations, had to live on wild fruit and what they could shoot, and all too quickly succumbed to obvious tropical diseases; men drowned in flooded rivers, and equipment was lost in whirlpools. Long before the Bolivian army caught up with them, the terrain had taken its toll. And the Indians they met were as inscrutable as the landscape. Guevara's capture was in effect the victory of Green Hell herself.

This power of the natural world in Bolivia both frightened and fascinated me: the brave, isolated efforts of men, their flowering and decay, and the way nature closed in again.

In the Beni, near Brazil, on the river Madre de Dios which flows down into the Amazon, lies Cachuela Esperanza, a settlement where one man, not very long ago, made a huge fortune out of rubber and Brazil nuts. He built a grand house, a hospital, a theatre, and imported doctors and singers from Europe. But in the next generation the fortune was gambled away, and now the buildings are decaying, and the jungle creeping back to hide it all.

There are many such places, and of all, perhaps, Potosí, the city of silver, has the strangest story. Like some wild dream of man's folly and time's caprice it haunts me still. And I am haunted, too, by all that vast, secret world of peaks and forests, by the lonely wastes of the high plateau, and the "cold candelabra of those high solitudes of snow".

Contents

List of Illustrations

from photographs by David Caccia

BOLIVIA

10°S

B R A Z I L

N

PANDO

Rio Madera

Guayará Mirim
Guayaramerin

PERU

Rio Madre de Dios

Rio Beni

LA PAZ

BENI

Rio Mamore

Rio Itenez Guaporé

15°S

TITICACA

Coroico

Trinidad

COCHABAMBA

Rio Chapare

Rio Grande o Guapay

Copacabanca

La Paz
Tiahuanacu

SANTA CRUZ

Cochabamba

Santa Cruz

Roboré

Oruro

Porto Suarez
Corumbá

ORURO

L. POOPO

Sucre

Camiri

20°

Potosi

PACIFIC

CHILE

POTOSI

CHUQUISACA

Rio Paraguay

PARAGUAY

Tarija

TARIJA

Bermejo

Antofagasta

Rio Pilcomayo

25°S

OCEAN

ARGENTINA

International Boundaries

Provincial Boundaries

0   50   100   200
Miles

12

I

Journey to the Andes

To arrive in La Paz by air is too sudden, the change too abrupt from the blare and hum, the smell of diesel and paper and disinfectant of the big international airports. One comes too swiftly from the flashing lights, the whirl and rumble of big cities with people always on the move, into this high dry plateau where movement itself takes on a different dimension.

Thirteen-and-a-half thousand feet above sea-level is so high that one's reactions cannot be imagined beforehand. The air, so thin, only just over half as heavy with oxygen as at sea level, slows down one's system and actions at first, almost as if, at an opposite extreme, it were water.

People walk from the aircraft dazed, almost conscious of putting one foot in front of the other. For some, there are even dangers in arriving so suddenly. Strong men have been known to set off at a run just to show they feel nothing, only to collapse after a few yards, and babies have turned blue on arrival and been rushed away for doses of oxygen.

The airport, when I knew it, had a ramshackle air of neglect and desolation. The few jets that roared and bumped down its one long dirt runway seemed gigantic intruders from another more stream-lined and efficient realm. A large board straddled the view, proclaiming that this was the highest international airport in the world. It rattled in the thin breeze and little eddies of dust formed miniature whirlwinds beneath its struts. Two llamas tethered to a post stared haughtily at a few bystanders. From the other side of the building a gravel road wound away out of sight across a brown plain towards the jagged white peaks that fringed the horizon.

I once flew into La Paz from Peru, in a tiny aeroplane which had

13

to wind its way up through gaps in the Andes, tilting one way and another as the dark masses loomed towards us like great mouths open for prey. The wings seemed constantly about to crunch on some rocky spike, and in a brief instant, looking down through thin cloud, I saw our shadow far below, tiny and crumpled like a fallen moth on the brown rocks.

Our arrival in La Paz then seemed miraculous, and the tossing, bird's-eye view we had of this remote world made the history of its conquest, first by the Incas, and then by a handful of Spanish soldiers, seem even more astonishing. For these were victories not just over people, but over the place itself, and neither was complete. The struggle with the place continues still.

I always felt that this airborne arrival on to the high plateau was too swift, and that to come in overland, either by bus, bumping along the plain, and on to the ferry across Lake Titicaca, or by train, as we did, somehow made the place more real.

Our first journey to Bolivia from England was a very long one, for before taking the train we spent weeks on the sea, in a small Italian ship bound from Naples to Santiago. This gave us time to try to adjust to the New World, to learn the language, and avoid what the Americans called the "transcultural neurosis". And a series of mishaps before we even left Europe gave us full warning of our vulnerability.

We left London one chill December day and travelled to Barcelona by separate routes, I by air with our new baby, and David, my husband, by train with the luggage.

"I feel sorry for this baby," declared the monthly nurse as she bid me good-bye. "Poor little thing, going out to the back of beyond with two such scatter-brained irresponsible parents." The packing-up process had worn down her nerves, and she had so worn down mine that I had no reply.

I was as anxious and ignorant as any new mother. The baby, Alexander, was only a few weeks old. I kept him in a little rush basket and fussed over his feeding and washing, and worried incessantly how he would stand the journey and the altitude. I was terrified to leave him for an instant, as I thought him so beautiful that someone would be sure to steal him. This made having meals, and checking-in luggage and tickets very muddled and exhausting. My fears were groundless. Porters, stewards, American ladies, all set my heart pounding by admiring the baby, but no one even tried to steal him. And he stood the journey far better than his parents.

A prelude to any service abroad is a study of the post report, which tries to give concise information about the nature of life wherever it may be. The domestic section of the La Paz post report was full of dire warnings: we must take every possible equipment for the two years of our stay, and expect to lose about a third of it on the way. Our heavy luggage, consisting of china and glass and linen, and an enormous supply of consumer goods, from tomato ketchup to soap powder, went by cargo boat. I later decided that this part of the post report must have been written by a very urban supermarket addict, for none of these goods was really necessary. Admittedly aspirin in La Paz cost about 10s. a bottle, but so did the products of Mr. Boots in our luggage by the time they got there.

We were taking with us on the passenger ship two years' supply of clothing for all three of us, and a huge miscellany of extras, such as cotton-wool and toothbrushes, which the urban housewife had warned us would be unobtainable or too expensive. They filled a great many cases and trunks, several of which were old hand-me-downs and did not lock properly. We were being very optimistic.

All these David loaded on to the train at Victoria, and in Paris they were trundled across from the Gare du Nord to the Gare de Lyons in a lorry kindly provided by the Embassy.

At the Spanish border, David was met by the local travel agent who was charming and talkative, and arranged everything. The señor must worry about nothing, he declared, as he, the agent, personally, had seen the luggage on to the right train.

So we all arrived safely in Barcelona, but the luggage did not. In his still halting Spanish, David made frantic telephone calls to the travel agent, who swore each time more ardently that he had, with his own eyes, seen the luggage leave. Then he found the luggage, confessed, protested, swore again that this time he had sent it. But it still did not arrive. For two days, David met the trains in vain. Even after we had boarded the ship he made hourly journeys to the station, refusing to believe our fate. Half-an-hour before the ship was due to leave, we sat in our cabin, muffled in our heavy winter tweeds, adding up in despair the things we had with us to last a six-week sea voyage across the equator. I have never been good at packing. For ourselves we had only nightclothes besides what we wore; there were a few clothes for the baby but no food. David had seventy-five ties, I had nine hats, and between us we had 240 stiff white paper envelopes.

A posse of ship's officers, sympathetic to our crisis, hovered about the door of our cabin.

"What can I do about food for the baby?" I cried, "We shall have to get off the ship."

"We can find food for the baby, señora," volunteered a dapper young officer, and sent messages to ask the chef. But the chef replied that he had no baby food on board: could the baby eat vegetables, perhaps, or bread, or *ensalada verde*?

"But he has no teeth," I wailed. "And anyway, what can we wear?" I pointed to our clothes.

"But we are all in this ship one family, señora," the Captain had joined in by now. "For sure some of the other señoras will be able to lend you some clothes, they will be kind."

But although there were other señoras about, all of them were small and dark and Latin; I was like a giant beside them. So, five minutes before the ship sailed, we decided to disembark. It was too late to pack up the bits and pieces by now strewn about the cabin; we simply took the baby with his little Moses basket and his case of clothes, and while the other officers threw up their hands and exclaimed to the Virgin-mother, the Captain himself locked our cabin door and sealed it with a piece of red tape and a small lead seal. The ship's horn blew.

"We'll see you in Tenerife," David said to the officers, and full of misgiving they glowered, as if to say, "You'd better turn up after all this trouble, or we'll keep your luggage, hats, envelopes and all."

I felt quite ashamed at our lack of resolution. Or was it reckless-ness? I pictured them asking what had become of the famous British stamina, that these people were not prepared to face the tropics in their tweeds. We went sheepishly down the gangway and back to the hotel.

Our luggage arrived that afternoon, but it took two days to persuade the customs office to let us "fiddle" with it. However, we managed at last to open a few cases under the interested gaze of the dock-hands in an enormous grey goods yard. We took out a few essentials, leaving the rest to follow us by the next ship, and, heavily overweight by now, flew to Madrid and thence to the Canaries.

We reached Tenerife exhausted, late at night, and asked a taxi-driver to take us to a good hotel. His choice was an enormous place with marble staircases and halls, and verandahs shaded by lazy palm trees. We changed into some other crumpled clothes, and ate dinner in a stupor in a dining-hall full of waiters and dazzling lights and elderly couples in evening dress. There was a band somewhere in the distance, playing old, out-of-date tunes.

We woke in the morning to realise that it was Christmas day. Breakfast was on the verandah, where the elderly couples of the night before sat in silence, immaculately dressed in light, uncreased tropical clothes, reading newspapers and munching toast. The palm tree fronds waved and clattered in a light breeze, and the mountains in the distance were deep blue. Waiters in white suits walked about soundlessly on the rush matting.

Our cane chairs squeaked loudly, and I felt we were being studied from behind the newspapers. I had a sudden wave of misery, at the incongruity of it all, the isolation of our Christmas, and the unknown perils that I imagined lay ahead of us.

After a while, most of the elderly couples got up and left, and one man stopped at our table.

"Have you just arrived?" he asked.

David said, "Well, yes, we have."

The man grunted, and thought for a bit. "Did you get off all right? Dreadful shambles, wasn't it? Are you all right for clothes, by the way? If you aren't the British Consul's the one to contact. Man

B

named Fox. Very kind and competent. I must say, everyone has been most extraordinarily kind—very kind indeed."

We agreed, mystified, that everyone was kind, and said that we had enough clothes and did not think we need trouble the British Consul.

"Well, he was very good to me," the man went on, "he gave me these—this shirt, and the shorts I've got on. Don't fit all that well, but they're not too bad, and I'm so large I suppose I'm lucky to get anything. Now he's going to fix my papers, but of course he's rushed off his feet, poor man. Are you leaving by boat?"

David was beginning to enjoy this strange conversation. Yes, he said, we were leaving by boat, in fact he hoped the boat would leave this afternoon.

"Well, you're quite lucky then—got everything in order? Dreadful business, isn't it? Absolute disgrace! How long did you spend in the water?"

It took some time for us to explain that we had not been in the water at all, but arrived, quite simply, by air, and for him to explain that he had been shipwrecked. He had been on a Greek liner, a luxury cruiser bound for the Canaries with a load of English passengers all paying large sums to escape the winter. A fire had broken out in the engine-room, and the polyglot crew, with no one language common to all of them, had panicked. Even the captain had quite lost his head and told passengers to jump into the sea.

"It's lucky I'm so strong," said our friend, "I spent six hours in the water. Most people of my age—I'm seventy-two, you know—wouldn't have survived that. Fortunately the water was quite warm. They tried to push me off you know—just said, 'Jump in and swim', disgraceful lot they were, and of course some of the poor suckers did swim for it. I don't know how many were drowned. And half the crew took the lifeboats, they were pushing the passengers away. It was worse than the war.

"Well, I climbed down a ladder into the water and hung on at the bottom. I could see the flames and thought I'd just jolly well hang on until I could see if the ship really was going to go down. And after all those hours, I climbed up the ladder a bit, and called and waved, and an Indian ship sent a boat off—and here I am. There are quite a lot of us, and half of the others don't know what has happened to their friends or families. Disgraceful affair."

I was appalled. Several times that day we were taken for survivors, and given further alarming accounts of the disaster. We telephoned the port constantly but there was no sign of our ship, and I viewed the coming voyage with increasing trepidation. But the ship arrived, white and gleaming, at sunset, and we were greeted as old friends by the officers, who unsealed our cabin with a flourish, and wished us "*Feliz Navidad*".

From then on the voyage was uneventful. We slept long hours and struggled with our Spanish. The grey, lazy equatorial days passed quickly. We reached the New World, and the ship began to call at ports.

Caracas, in lush and beautiful country, was an untidy city, full of huge, half-finished buildings. As we drove down a boulevard of flowering trees a burst of gunfire shattered the air, and we saw a man standing in a garden, firing a machine-gun into a flower-bed.

"He is just bored," remarked the friend who was driving us round. "It's Sunday." And he took us on to have lunch in a garden full of orchids, with parrots in the trees.

We walked around notorious Cristobal at night, down one alley after another of sleazy-looking night-spots. It was very dirty and ramshackle and smelt of hot-dogs and refuse. Beautiful negresses swung down the streets in thin, clinging cotton dresses, and the policemen all carried tommy-guns.

And we walked around the Canal-zone of Panama, past old houses with thick, neatly-mown lawns and borders of canna lilies, and the spruce little offices of the American police, standing below rows of gigantic palm trees. It all seemed very calm, modern and well-organised as we slid through the canal with twelve Canal-zone officers to take us through at a dollar a ton. The canal seemed so neatly sliced through the wild continent; sometimes the lawns came right down to the water's edge. There was no jungle here, no room for snipers. In fact we were almost the last ship to pass through before the whole area was engulfed in a revolution and the canal closed for a period the length of which no one could predict.

Down the Pacific coast we sailed now, past Guayaquil, grey and steamy, and Callao, the desert port for Lima. The crowds of passengers thinned, and the remainder took on the slightly jaded, dejected air that people wear at the end of a voyage.

The weather changed as we reached the Humboldt current, the flying-fish disappeared, and the grey, silken water became blue and choppy. The coastline changed too, from rolling green jungles to huge cliffs, and then an endless line of mountains. We would lean on the deck ledges, watching through the haze that always gives land seen from the sea such an air of mystery and desirability, straining to make out details behind the mist where the Andes soared up like huge teeth against a cloudless sky.

We landed at Antofagasta. As I was waiting to disembark an elderly Chilean leant on the rails with me, watching the cranes unloading cargo.

"Where are you going now?" he asked. "You are not staying in Antofagasta?"

"No, we're going up to La Paz in the train," I said.

"La Paz? Ha! You'd better be careful. They eat the *gringos* up there." (*Gringo* in Latin America is a foreigner, usually English or American; the word is in common use, though in context it can still have its original sting, as a term of contempt.)

The British Consul in Antofagasta came on board to meet us. We had arrived rather early, he said, and anyway the railways were a bit disorganised, so we would have to wait for the train. It was not going to leave until Saturday. As today was Tuesday we had to stay somewhere, so he took us to a huge, half-finished luxury hotel on the edge of the sea. It had lounges and halls slung out on concrete buttresses over the rocks, with walls of glass to show the view across an enormous blue bay to a line of pink and purple mountains.

Below the building thundered the great Pacific breakers, crashing over a jagged little promontory to fill a swimming-pool cut in the rocks. *Mestizo* fishermen picked their way over the mussels and flung heavy lines into the water, and thousands of sea-birds, white gulls, and black cormorants with vicious beaks, wheeled and flapped about the air all day, cawing and screeching, and plummeting into the waves.

Our room was at the back, looking out over the town, a muddle of sun-cracked buildings dwarfed and menaced by the desert which rose beyond them into a horseshoe of spectacular red-gold hills that shimmered and gleamed in the sun.

I walked around the town, and thought it rather a sad place. Everywhere the smell of fish and guano was very strong. But there were some big, dignified old buildings, and, surprisingly, an English church, and a small square with pepper and eucalyptus trees, a few dusty beds of zinnias, and benches where old men sat asleep, oblivious of the noise of shoe-shine boys or an old squeaky barrel-organ.

The Consul was a happy man. He was a Scot, and still had his strong accent although it was so long ago now—1912—that he had come out to Chile as a young engineer to work on a copper mine in the Atacama desert.

He had lived in a tent for years, he told us, and knew what the rough life really was. It had been a struggle for everything then, and the people of Antofagasta did not know what comfort they lived in now, with the good coast road to Santiago, and fresh water brought down by pipeline from the Andes 120 miles inland.

The Consul lived now in retirement in Antofagasta, in an old house smothered with flowers, with his Chilean wife and children, of whom he was extremely proud. One son was a Member of Parliament in Santiago, and others were at University there. Several grandchildren lived with the old man, and they took us swimming at a club some miles down the desert coast, where we surfed, and sat in deck-chairs sipping fizzy drinks and watching the youth of Antofagasta at play.

"There's not very much to do," the Consul admitted. "Not many people like you come through. Of course there are lots of goods that have to be seen to, and one has to be on good terms with the port authorities. And then there are episodes—young English sailors you know—very rough and drunk sometimes. They go round the town and start shouting and beating things, and get arrested and put in prison.

"What happens then?" we asked.

"Well, I usually leave them there a couple of days until they've sobered up and had a bit of a lesson. Then I go and talk it over with the chief of police, who is a good friend of mine . . ."

We all laughed. I pictured him dealing with the police and the sailors, with the port authorities, the railways, the Chilean business-men, or the tough miners from the interior: always with the same skill and tact, gay and amused, but also detached and quite firm. I thought him the epitome of what a consul should be.

On Saturday morning we went to the station. The railway had been built years ago by the British, at great cost of life, and still had the air of a pioneering enterprise. There was a makeshift muddle of tin sheds and goods trucks, a few cramped passenger carriages, and some very cut-throat-looking passengers. After a short struggle up and down the crowded platform, we found our carriage, a small compartment with two narrow bunks one above the other, a great deal of Victorian curled ironwork and decorative effects, and a tiny washroom at one end. No water could be got from either tap or flush, and the stench was overwhelming. We piled our suitcases in, thereby leaving ourselves no alternative between lying prone on the bunks and standing in the corridor.

"Beware of pickpockets," warned the Consul, and as a parting benediction introduced us to one of his friends, the English railway manager, who happened to be travelling on the train too.

"He will look after you, I'm sure," and he pushed his way through the crowd, waving his panama hat as the train drew slowly out with the guards peeling joy-riders off its steps and doorways.

The English railway manager was riding up to La Paz on a tour of inspection. His carriage, which was hooked on to the end of the train, was old, but very comfortable. It had two bedrooms, a bathroom with a shower and boiling hot water, and a kitchen with sinks, pots and pans, and a roaring furnace that served for a stove. Right at the back was a little observation room where he could sit and watch the railway tracks unfold endlessly and the world disappear. And all this he had entirely to himself. After the stench and clutter in our little compartment it seemed a place of untold luxury.

The manager was more than kind. He took us under his wing and under his roof. The baby spent most of the journey on a bunk in one

bedroom, while we sat in luxury in the observation car, showered
in the manager's shower, and ate large meals prepared by his
personal cook.

The line began to climb at once, up into the foothills, and soon
we were in the completely dead landscape of the Atacama desert.
Sparse vegetation, with dry grass and bushes, gave way to lifeless
hills of reddish pebbles. The double railway track ended, and with it
an illusion of safety—that one could somehow await a downcoming
train and reach the sea again. Even the two engines pulling us uphill
seemed to puff after this with a greater fatality.

The red rubble merged into grey pebbles and shale, mounds and
valleys with black shadows stretching to the horizon, like the
charred remnant of some giant prehistoric bonfire.

Red and grey dust already whirled everywhere. It filled our throats
and noses and stuck to our eyelids. We poured out drinks and the
dust made rims on the glasses as we drank, and our fingertips left
little dustless patches. In some anxiety, I shut the baby firmly into
the manager's bedroom, sealed doors and windows, and even
covered his basket so that it was surprising he did not smother.

Night fell in a wild dust storm with scarlet and gold eddies hanging
like torn rainclouds in the sky, and a huge golden moon rose above
the shale as we trundled slowly up towards a gap in the hills ahead.

As we made our way back to our carriage to bed, shaking and
lurching with the train, we could see our rocking reflections in the
windows, and beyond them the moonlight on the slopes glittered
like a sea swarming with tiny fish: I felt myself suddenly a Jonah,
hurtling through the bright shoals into the jaws of the whale.

I wedged the baby's basket firmly between the bunk ladder and
my hatbox, and climbed into bed.

I woke terrified, as though I had dreamed, but remembering
nothing. The blood pounded in my throat and echoed in my head,
and however deep I breathed I still gasped for breath again. I felt
giddy and sick, and shivered with the sudden cold. So this was the
altitude, I thought—we must be in Bolivia by now.

The train had stopped at a siding. I pushed up the slatted shutter
beside me and looked out. It was about three in the morning, and
the air was piercingly cold and thin. One small electric light bulb

lit the platform, and in its jolting light, squinting through my tiny window, I could see a crowd of people, not Spaniards or *mestizos* but small people with mongoloid faces, *café au lait* skins, and narrow, tilted eyes. There were men muffled against the cold in coats or ponchos, and high knitted caps with spaniel-ear flaps down the sides; and several of them were carrying guns. At the back, there were a few women in shawls and bowler hats, all carrying heavy bundles. It was so cold, and half dark, and I noticed no colours, everything seemed greyish khaki, like the light itself, and the cement of the building.

In a babble that grew louder as the guard marched about blowing his whistle, they pushed and tore their way into the train, and our carriage rocked and crashed until our departure settled us all once more into the familiar deafening rattle.

By breakfast time the new passengers had settled in the corridor, and found or forced places for all their bundles of clothes, food, plates, spoons, children and livestock. To reach our friend, we had to manœuvre ourselves and the baby over all these and sacks of potatoes, chickens, and three sheep.

All day we drew slowly across a vast plateau, gazing at the stubbly grass, the bland, pale sky, and the dust storms that would suddenly puff across the plain. Sometimes long, low, flat-topped hills broke the flat line of the horizon, and as the sun climbed higher shimmering sheets of water, a hazy pinkish brown, appeared in the far distance. If one stared or blinked they seemed to move, and hover, grow bigger, or fade in colour.

"Look," I said the first time, "water!"

"Not at all," the manager was a matter-of-fact man, "they're mirages. Like the Sahara, you'd die before you found any water over there."

The air was terribly dry, and the sun beat down with such brilliance that we wore our sunglasses even with the curtains of the carriage drawn. After breakfast we drank tea, then orange-juice, then beer, and it was the same after lunch. But our thirst was un-quenched, our lips cracked, and our hands hissed if we rubbed them together as if they would ignite. At sidings we would get out and shuffle through the dust to walk under a few pepper trees, while our friend did a short tour of inspection, and the train took on water and even more passengers.

Sipping his beer as the train clanked on stilts for miles across a salt pan, or the huge white cone of a peak in Chile rose above the horizon and sank again below it, the manager talked about his life, about the days of the pioneers, the mines in the Atacama desert, and the little British railway colony in La Paz. He was sentimental about La Paz, its beauty and remoteness, and thought it a far gayer place than Antofagasta. He wished he lived up there.

"You will see it first at night—that's the best way."

When at about four in the afternoon another white peak began to rise slowly above the grassland, he sighed lovingly, "Illimani—the spirit of La Paz, always changing. People love the mountain. So do I. It's fantastic, magical—and frightening too."

Later, in the sunset, more peaks appeared, looming larger until the darkness before moonrise hid them. And suddenly we found ourselves there, clinging to the edge as the plateau cut away beneath us into a vast gorge, deep blue and mazed with lights, glittering down below us and out of sight. As the train plunged down into it, whistling and wheezing along hairpin bends through groves of eucalyptus trees, we could see in flashes between trunks and foliage, the stars, dazzlingly bright, and Illimani, enormous now, gleaming coldly as the moon rose, bleak, powerful and remote. It was like a brief flash of some truth about how our life would be in this high eyrie in the mountains—yet I could not discern more than this, it was only an impression of something strong but elusive which both drew and frightened me.

And then at once we clattered into the station, all unpainted cement and corrugated iron, with no platform, and many odd, bulky goods carriages standing about. There were friends to meet us, and we bundled everything into their Land-Rover, and drove at a terrifying pace down bending, dusty streets, very rough and ill-lit, then hurtled down wide boulevards lined with trees, and some steep, dark avenues.

A room had been booked for us at a small *pensión*, and we arrived to find a plump señora waiting to greet us. She rhapsodised and worried over the baby, calling him *chiquitito*, and *pobrecito* to have endured such a journey and urged us not to go up the stairs too quickly. We dragged ourselves and our possessions slowly up to the first floor, hardly hearing her stream of explanation and instructions, bewildered by the finality of our arrival at our strange destination, and wondering what this new chapter in our lives would bring.

II

The High City

OUR ROOM HAD a double bed which we soon discovered was built too short and too narrow for our teutonic stature, a little corner for the baby, and a bathroom where the water came cold out of the tap, and was heated by an apparatus like an old-fashioned toaster which one lowered into the water until it reached the required temperature. The señora explained the use of this heater with voluble warnings about its danger. We must never put our hands into the water while the heater was in, or we should die at once:

"*Muerte! Terrible!*" Her tone suggested that she had witnessed several such accidents. We must take it out by the rubber handle—so—and she had stuck several notices on the wall to remind us: "*Atencion* Danger of *Muerte!*" with a skull and crossbones of her own composition.

"Yes, yes, we quite understand, señora," we said, and at once I saw myself lying on the bathroom floor amid a heap of washing, my life cut short by this dreadful electrocution-kit.

However, we got used to the bathroom, and even to the bed, despite the discomfort of trying to sleep lying diagonally across it. And the room had one great compensation, which was its balcony: it had an enormous view over trees and roof tops across blue-green valleys and slopes to the brooding white bulk of Illimani. Waking at dawn, moving about tending the baby, lolling about at midday, leaning on the balcony ledge in a daydream or in the chill evening, by daylight or moonlight and starlight, each as dazzling in its way —there was never an hour passed without some glimpse of this view. It was a constant feast of beauty, an excitement, and a refuge from discomfort, insecurity and loneliness.

27

The other inhabitants of the *pensión* were all Americans. There were a couple of Texan advisers in the U.S. Aid programme, who wore bright checked shirts and told long, slow jokes; an air force pilot, a doctor, and a few itinerant businessmen. There was also Luiz, who worked for the U.S. Information Service, and his wife, both of them fresh from Berkeley University in California. We would sit in their room sometimes, eating popcorn and listening to records, while they bemoaned the dearth of culture and good films in La Paz.

The *pensión* became a little centre for our lives, a familiar haven from the strange world outside. We met at breakfast, lunch and dinner, and gradually built up, like a jig-saw, a peculiar picture of Bolivian life, a picture which, at first, we had little means of supplementing, as David, busy organising a new department in the Embassy, seldom left the Chancery, and I seldom left the *pensión* for several weeks while we were acclimatising.

There were two main topics of conversation at table: politics and *pensión* food. It was a time of great unrest in the country, and we lived in daily expectation of a revolution. One of the Texans said:

"You folks just don't know the dangers we Americans have to face here in these underdeveloped countries. . . . Here we are, pouring our dollars into this place, and what do we get? Corruption and incompetence. And we get kidnapped. Do you know Mrs. Cristal in the house next door?"

"The one with the pet llama that eats all the rose-bushes," interrupted his wife.

"Yeah, well, her husband was kidnapped. She's had a rough time, that kid. Bob Cristal went with a Dutchman up to a school on the *altiplano* (the high plateau). They were gonna have a big ceremony to donate a lot o' dollars for developin' the school and payin' for a big new hall they just built. You know what they done? Took 'em prisoner.

"Boy, there was some trouble. They got the Ambassador out there, diplomatic protests, even President Johnson made a speech about it. Okay, they got 'em out, but only after four days sittin' in that hall being guarded by a lot o' *chola* women with machine-guns. And the *cholas* also had sticks o' dynamite hidden under their skirts, and told 'em that if they tried to get out, they'd blow the place up first." (In much of Latin-America, the word *chola* means a half-breed, or an Indian who has become "Europeanised". But in Bolivian usage it means the opposite, one who has not discarded the Indian language or dress, and far from being contemptuous, tends almost to convey affection, or even compliment, particularly in the diminutive, *cholita*. Moreover, since the 1953 revolution, the term *Indio* has taken on an insulting sense, and the Andean peasants prefer to be known as *campesinos*, countrymen.)

The Texans had an air of Wild-West frontier bravado about them. They grumbled about trips they had to do to far-flung villages in tiny aeroplanes which seemed constantly to be getting lost over Brazil and landing at last with only three minutes' petrol left. And yet they loved the Bolivian pilots for their reckless confidence, and related admiringly how they would fly in thick cloud down narrow mountain gorges, with only a stop-watch and compass to guide them.

"Five seconds this way—click—five seconds another way—click, and they sure know how to do it. Two seconds wrong and boy, you're into the mountain."

All Bolivia seemed to be swarming with Americans. Not in vain had President Kennedy once said that it was the most important country on the whole southern continent. There were the U.S. Embassy, the U.S. Information Service, the U.S. Army mission, the U.S. Air Force mission, and U.S. Aid, not to speak of the Peace Corps, and the education missions and religious missions, though most of the latter were scattered about in remote villages and their members rarely seen in La Paz itself.

Down the road from the *pensión* was an enormous U.S. store, the P.X., where American housewives could do their shopping and buy goods in familiar U.S. packages.

Next to the P.X. were the houses of two political leaders in the thick of the present unrest. Both men were candidates in the forthcoming vice-presidential elections. The older of these two was a strikingly handsome man, half Arab, very left-wing, and the darling of the tin-miners who were a powerful force in the country and a law unto themselves. Soon after our arrival this leader was expelled from the main political party, accused both of being behind the kidnapping incident, and being involved in a drug-running scandal.

The younger leader was a general of the air force (a very small air force, consisting, we were told, of some four Mustangs and a little flock of very old cast-offs from the wartime stores of other nations). This general was a colourful and popular figure, with a high rating in *machismo*, that untranslatable word so widely used in South America. *Machismo* embraces a whole range of attitudes about male behaviour, a cult of masculinity which may seem to an outsider to be carried to absurd proportions. In this one word are included all the qualities taken for granted about the male, his superiority, his strength and energy, his pride, his virility, his valour, his success as a womaniser, a romantic, a lover and a master. All these would add to the image of a true *caudillo*, or hero-leader.

But the General had other attributes as well: he was ruthless, and brave to the point of recklessness. There was a story that to show the proficiency of the air force, he had arranged an air display, the highlight of which was a parachute jump. Fourteen brave young men jumped, but the parachutes of several failed to open, as the air at that altitude above the *altiplano* was so thin, and the planes could not fly very high above the ground. Their deaths were passionately lamented by the next day's newspapers, and blame laid squarely upon the General, who reacted at once. He summoned the journalists who had berated him, bundled them into a jeep, whirled them up to the *altiplano*, and into an aeroplane, which promptly took off. They flew over La Paz a few times, looping the loop to make the journalists really frightened, and then the General suddenly opened the hatch and jumped out. His parachute opened perfectly, he made an immaculate landing, and was waiting to greet the journalists when they returned, green and unsteady, to the airport.

"You see, gentlemen," he said with a shrug, "it is quite simple, there is nothing to it."

It was well known that he had never jumped before, so his reputation rocketed. He conducted a flamboyant electioneering campaign for the vice-presidency, but having spent on it some 100,000 dollars (had they been kindly provided by the Americans, we wondered), he stood down at the last minute, claiming that the elections were being rigged.

It was perhaps incongruous that these two rivals should live next door to one another. But they were said to have a most convenient arrangement whereby if the house of one were stoned by an angry mob, shot at, or otherwise attacked, he could quickly hop over the fence into the shelter of his neighbour's abode.

The night after we arrived, an explosion shook our *pensión* in the small hours of the morning, and at breakfast we heard that a bomb had gone off in the house of the left-wing leader. Fortunately, he was away campaigning in a town 600 kilometres away, but some journalists at once found other reasons for his absence, and accused him of blowing up his own dining-room to attract sympathetic votes.

A few nights later we were woken by sand and pebbles thrown at our window, meant for the U.S. air force sergeant, who was called to fly the young General out of the country. The next day's newspapers carried a colourful story: the General had been "saying goodnight to his sister by the light of the moon" when he was shot at by a would-be assassin. Fortunately, he was wearing his uniform and medals, and the bullet hit one of the medals. He was somewhat wounded, however, and, convinced that his enemies were still after him, he insisted on being treated at American expense in Panama.

Upon the food in the *pensión* all the inmates vented their feelings of loneliness, frustration or homesickness. Almost every meal was greeted with a chorus of disgust, and none of the array of sauces and ketchups from the P.X. seemed able to improve the standard or the taste. One day we all agreed to try to improve matters, and I spent several laborious hours trying to translate some wholesome English recipes into comprehensible Spanish. Even the dictionary failed me at times, and I had to resort to hieroglyphics. The señora had to be won round with much tact and careful confession of our own eccentricities, and at last for the sake of peace, and the prospect of fewer rejects being smartly returned through the kitchen door, she agreed diffidently to have a try.

The result of all our labours appeared at the table one day in the form of an innocent steak-and-kidney pie of a texture which would have delighted Mrs. Beeton. The air force sergeant took one sniff

and left the room declaring he would not be served "Turks' food".
In the ensuing consternation most of the pie returned to the kitchen,
where the señora and her pigtailed maids consumed it with relish,
and swore they would make an even greater effort in future.

Outside this little world, our lives moved slowly. It took us both
some time to become adjusted to the altitude. People said we would
gradually start to breathe more deeply, that the Indians themselves
had enormous lungs. Everyone had different complaints about the
altitude's effects: one slept badly, another could not take alcohol,
panted constantly, or forgot everything. Certainly we seemed to
spend most nights tossing, with pounding hearts, though it was the
moon too which caused this, shining so brightly that I often awoke
as if someone had shone a blazing light inches from my face. We
suffered from constant indigestion, and dreadful wind. I became quite
tight on even a small glass of gin, and almost any other drink made
me feel ill. But gradually most ailments wore off, or we became so
used to them that we did not notice, and did not remain aware,
either, that we had less energy or enthusiasm than before. The slower,
less vital pace became our way of life in the altitude, and as everyone
else was similarly afflicted, we had no norm against which to measure
ourselves.

At times we felt very miserable and isolated. I read Gilbert
Highet's *Poets in a Landscape*, and tried to lose myself in the world of
Horace and Juvenal, which was so much more familiar in a way, so
civilised and secure, and so far from this wild, beautiful place, and
the people whose languages and ways of thought we saw no hope of
understanding. We imagined ourselves sometimes back in Europe,
with the cold, foggy winters, and our old friends; and in Prague,
which had been our last post.

We would sit and talk about the life we had led in Czechoslovakia, the tensions and isolation of the Iron Curtain, the grey
stones and grey faces, the matchless baroque of Bohemia and the
Hapsburg Empire. We remembered the terrible frozen enclosure of
winter, and the voluptuous summers, with apple, pear and cherry,
lilac and chestnut all bursting at once into bloom, and the little
hilltop villages with green-onion-domed churches peeping over the
treetops, and fairy castles perched on the crags above pine-fringed

Altiplano

La Paz from Villa Victoria

Doña Josefa

Magdalena with Miguelito José

Pablo

lakes. At first we longed to return there. But gradually we saw it was really the familiarity that we loved and longed for.

Despite my motherly qualms, the baby flourished. I grew confident enough to leave him sometimes in the care of the señora, who was constantly amazed that he wore so few clothes, and that those he did wear belied his sex—"señorita", she would tease him, as she showed him off to her friends in his English lawn dresses.

I began to explore La Paz. I was afraid, at first, of these strange, different people, of the stories of violence, death, and brutality, of the *mestizos*, of the Spanish Bolivians, with their *orgullo* (pride), and *machismo*, and *caudillos*, and other such unfamiliar concepts. And I was afraid of the Indians, the men in the buses who smelt so strongly of dirty clothes, drink and excrement, and spoke in high, soft voices; and the women with their long black pigtails tied neatly back with wool, and their mute, staring black almond-eyes. I was afraid of the policemen in the Nazi-style helmets which accentuated their mongoloid features, and of the cringing beggars; and of the abject resignation to poverty which I saw everywhere.

Yet it was a peculiar kind of fear, because the faces soon became familiar, and as I worked at the language my greetings or questions produced responses. With custom, fear recedes. I recognised after a while my uneasiness about the Indians, about the sullen, remote nature which I could not hope to penetrate. And I saw that it was the place itself that I feared, with at the same time curiosity and wonder. The mountains already had me in thrall.

Was it perhaps their violent beginnings, their comparatively recent breakthrough in the history of the earth that gave the Andes such an air of contemptuous, merciless impenetrability? Still unconquered they seemed, viciously hiding their secrets from the puny scratchings of man. I had not seen the Himalayas but in Africa and in Europe I had been in high mountains, sometimes as a climber, pitted against the rock, when their power was overwhelming. However, no other place I knew was on such a scale of desolation as this, of exclusion, almost derision, of human effort. Of course, we could say to ourselves, other people had been everywhere, seen all of this before, but here the vistas across peaks and ravines gave an uncanny feeling that one was nevertheless the first to be there, and entirely

c

alone. In the dark that night of our arrival, it had felt as if we were the first to come into the remote blue gorge, to look up alone at the peaks with fascination, awe and terror.

I began to read: books about the Incas, and their predecessors the Nasca, the Chimu, the Mochica, the Chavin; about the Peru of the *conquistadores*, and the empire of rapacious Spain. New names became familiar: Prescott, Bingham, von Hagen, Posnansky, Tello; Pizarro, Garsilasco de la Vega, Guaman Poma de Ayala; Macchu Picchu, Cuzco, Tiahuanaco, Potosí. They crackled through my head. I would go to sleep in a half-dream about the Inca Manco Capac and his rooms full of gold, and ceremonies where he baptized his people in sacred water brought from Tiahuanaco on the shores of Lake Titicaca, filling a font with the maize-beer, *chicha*, which spouted into channels running all over the town so that the people drank and danced for days. And all this became muddled in my dreams with poems from my childhood, of Chimborazo and Cotopaxi and Popacatapetl and the Mayas and Aztecs and Quezcoatl, and I found myself moving through the mountains in processions of ochre-skinned people dressed in parrot-feather capes of blue and gold, and the king passed by on a palanquin, with his gold headdress, like a pharaoh's, glinting in the sun; his barge struck out from the reedy shore of a lake, and disappeared across the bright water, leaving only ripples of light which spun across my eyes until I turned away blinded, and awoke under the blaze of the moon.

The lake upon which I dreamed the Inca was there in reality: on the *altiplano* above La Paz lay Titicaca, unplumbed and unpredictable, an inland sea caught in the plain that spread bleakly for miles around it, between containing ridges of the Andes. Mankind had no visible roots here layered back into pre-history. Even what there was of more recent date was fragmentary and as yet unexplained. At Tiahuanaco, near the lake, there were the ruins of an ancient city, its origins shrouded in time and legend; pottery of a classic purity, and skilled stonework had shown it to have been the centre of a widely-spread culture. But much beyond this was still conjecture, and anything else had been erased, eroded or washed away by a nature which then returned to its own desolate self unscathed.

Only the Incas had managed to achieve some permanence here,

and a brief glory, with their sun-god empire among remote, road-strung peaks. Their precision of mind, and genius for social organisation, and also their toughness of body and spirit, must have been phenomenal, to conquer the Andes as they did. I read critics who tried to place the Incas, or rate them in some anthropological scale, who pointed to their lack of cultural "product"—no writing, no tradition of poetry, drama and song, no philosophers or teachers. But life in the high Andes, I thought, did not lend itself to this, nature was too merciless, the struggle too constant, for the leisure that is a prelude to creative thought. The sun was a ruthless tormenting god, burning, but not giving enough heat even for a siesta. The air was too thin for the expenditure of great physical energy on anything much more than survival. And drinking, in the absence of the grape, was a prelude to oblivion, not gaiety or wit.

The studies of the Incas filled me with dismay—the rigidity of their society, the dictatorship, the imposition of a way of life even to forcing a new language on to people, was such a grim acknowledgement of the struggle to survive. They appeared through the filters of time as an amazing but grim people, and this grimness, a gloomy taciturnity and sullen acceptance of life, seemed to survive in their descendants, the Aymhara and Quechua-speaking Andean Indians whom we met all about us.

And yet the beauty of the place constantly astounded us. In the mornings, woken early by the sun, we would go out on the balcony to look up at Illimani, the blinding white and deep blue shadows of its snows, and the foothills, blue and green now as it was the rainy season. We had a pair of field-glasses, and would lean on the parapet studying all the contours. The air was so clear and thin, it was amazing how far one could see. The green foothills below Illimani were miles away, yet with the naked eye one could easily pick out fields, trees and small isolated farmhouses or sheds, while the glasses would show more detail, people or animals, roofs and doorways.

It was a strange landscape, this city—the muddle of undistinguished houses spilling about the great bowl-like gorge; the enclosing cliffs, the brooding peaks. David described it as a curious mixture of Leonardo da Vinci rocks, Douanier Rousseau trees, and odd bits of Bournemouth or cheap French seaside hotels.

Up on the *altiplano*, where there was only the airport and an untidy muddle of railway goods yards, one could walk right to the edge of the cliffs and look at the layout of the city. It was very large (with a population of some 350,000). The cliffs were sandy and eroded, sharp and gullied, and one came upon them so suddenly it was as though a giant hand, long ages ago, had ripped open a gash between the plain and the mountains. This had softened somewhat, into a series of enormous dips, slung between the cliffs and the peaks, each lower than the last like huge curved steps, and joined by steep gullies, sloping and jutting away until no longer visible from the plateau itself.

The sides of the gorge were so steep that even going down a main road was often like negotiating a mountain pass, and the levels of the main avenue presented constant vistas where the road seemed to end abruptly in a misty abyss before the blue-green walls of Illimani. One slowed down in astonishment to find another valley or fold of the mountainside appear.

The descent from the airport began with a straight stretch of tarred road cut into the sides of the cliff. Just before the first hair-raising slopes and hairpin bends began, one passed a concrete and iron platform slung out over a gaping drop: this displayed the corpse of a car which had gone over the edge a couple of years before, bent, mangled and rusted almost beyond recognition, and flanked by large notices bearing skull and crossbones and other warnings of death.

"*Atencion! Cuidado! La velocedad lo conducira al cementerio!*" ("Attention! Take Care! Speed will drive you to the cemetery!") one would read, and just have time to brake and change into low gear for the perilous descent, or to stop and let a large lorry grind its way past uphill. (Almost the only law of the country which everyone obeyed without fail was the unwritten one that uphill traffic had the right of way—a rule it could be suicidal to transgress.)

The reverse of other cities, where the rich tend to build ever higher up the mountain, La Paz had its slums on the fringe of the *altiplano*— a spill of small Indian houses built like those on the plateau itself of mud bricks, covered perhaps with mud plaster, roofed with the traditional thatch, or with corrugated iron. This was Villa Victoria, where all revolutions were said to begin. Here only the main road down the mountain was paved, tarred or cobbled. For the rest, the streets were rough and raw, some passable by a lorry or Land-Rover or other strong vehicle, others simply narrow alleys where only men or llamas could pass, picking their way over the gullies worn by rain and refuse. Most of these streets had no names; it was a confusing and sinister place. Somewhere up here was a home for blind children where I would go, later on, with the Ambassadress, to give food and clothing. And among some factories lay the remains of the early railway settlement. The club, still in use, was very incongruous now, with its lawns and gardens still kept up, and a little cluster of houses with red corrugated iron roofs, long verandahs, and tatty bougainvillaea struggling against the cold and dust.

Past all these one tossed and hurtled on the descent to the city, past the stations where lorries arrived from the lowlands, past markets and a few derelict hotels. Past the fire station too; there were never any fires to put out, the altitude being what it was, and the air so lacking in oxygen, but the two large red fire-engines were very useful in political troubles, when they were taken out, loaded with soldiers and hoses, to deal with the mobs.

One usually emerged breathless into the Plaza San Francisco below the large and beautiful church of that name, a focal point after which the city divided roughly into two parts, one side Indian, the other Spanish.

Beyond this plaza the main road became straight, and evened out into the Prado, a wide, flat boulevard with trees and flowers, tourist shops and antique shops, restaurants and cafés, the university and a luxury hotel. Here in the afternoons people would walk up and down, sit on the benches in the sun, or at the tables of the pavement bars, watching the world go by and always keeping an eye open for a pretty girl—as in any Spanish town.

The division of Spanish from Indian was somewhat arbitrary, as the barriers were social and economic rather than racial, but nevertheless, to walk in different directions from the Prado, took one into two quite different worlds.

The Spanish town had a regular layout of streets and squares.

Here was the Plaza Mayor with its trees and statues, the Cathedral and the President's palace, and the large, anonymous stone buildings of government ministries. This side of the town were the embassies and banks and law courts, *bureaux de change*, post office, and cinemas. The Teatro Municipal was here, crumbling and derelict and covered in graffiti, its halls and corridors apparently more in use as a public latrine than as a meeting-place for the cultured in search of entertainment. Tucked away in a little square on its own was the flower market where one could buy every day fresh flowers which were brought up overnight from the fertile lowland valleys: roses, lilies and daisies, sweet peas, carnations or amaryllis, in bunches or twined into bouquets or wreaths.

Here too were the offices of the businessmen, and the cafés where they met to gossip and do business, and where pressmen or a few diplomats would sit and wait, sipping endless cups of black coffee, for information, confidences, or opportunities to influence.

And then there were the shops, sweet shops and pastry shops and delicatessens, photographic shops, and a few special importers who stocked German and English china and other goods at prohibitive prices to cover the cost of transport and losses *en route* to La Paz. But mostly they were a maze of little shops, which stocked anything from baby clothes to screwdrivers, where buying a knife or a lemon-squeezer could take as long as half-an-hour. There were tourist shops selling little silver replicas of Indian houses, fishes or the rush boats of Lake Titicaca, and other more expensive ones selling the same things in Bolivian gold. There were fur-dealers with rugs, mats and coats made from alpaca pelts, and a few coats, hats and cravats of vicuña, incredibly soft and very precious and expensive, as while llama and alpaca, similar animals, could be domesticated and kept in large herds, the vicuña was shy and wild, and always died in captivity, and had to be hunted in danger and solitude in the high mountains.

There were Japanese traders, selling motor-cars, china, saucepans, little paper parasols, and pearls which could be bought by the string, or singly with much care and biting to test them.

And there were a few antique dealers who never failed to fascinate. Two of them, known as Nuñes Rico and Nuñes Pobre were brothers, and people said that the rich brother had better things but was more of a rogue, and that the poor one was more honest but less successful; but we found that every now and then they would exchange goods with each other, and so they must have been in league in any case. They had beautiful things: heavy chests and pieces of furniture, intricately carved, or painted and decorated with gold, and pictures of saints and madonnas in heavy and intricate gold frames; all of these must have come from churches or monasteries, and had probably been made by Indian workmen under the tuition of priests. They had a heavy, solid Spanish look, but also a barbaric quality and simple, naïve crudity. We would walk about fingering things and longing to possess them, and wondering how they would fit into our surroundings once we were back in England where they might look too crude and dark—or too magnificent. Everything was very expensive, and when we protested and started bargaining the brothers would take out heavy volumes on the colonial furniture of Argentina and Peru, and show us pictures of pieces in museums exactly like those we wanted to buy, and tell us that this was the last source of treasures of the colonial epoch.

They had a great deal of silver too, and though they protested that the Spaniards had taken all the good silver, and that the rich families had gone off with whatever was left, when they showed us what they had, it seemed that there was a good deal left still, for they had beautiful ornaments and sconces and church pieces and jewellery. They had all sorts of domestic silver too, because it was once, if one was rich, much easier to come by than porcelain; so the rich families had eaten off silver and washed off it, they had had plates and mugs made of silver, silver washing-bowls and ewers, and large, solid silver chamber-pots.

Here in the Spanish town the *avenidas* (avenues) all ran along the contours of the hills, and one looked down each of them, along narrowing flanks of dark buildings at the stupendous bulk of Illimani. The *calles* (streets) all ran down the slopes, cobbled and irregular, so steep that in a car one had to change into the lowest gear, and on foot one tottered and stumbled and leant backwards to stop slipping, and only once made the mistake of wearing high heeled shoes to go shopping.

The other side of the Prado and the Plaza San Francisco, in the Indian town, the streets were even narrower and steeper, with cobbles less regular, or with no cobbles at all. The layout was more mediaeval, more like what one can see now in an Arab *medina*. It was not unlike Fez, in Morocco, I sometimes thought, where each alley has its occupation, and different sorts of people inhabit different quarters of the town.

Here each street had its own trade or character, which sometimes made shopping much more straightforward. The road up from the Plaza San Francisco ran past a row of ironware shops selling zinc baths and buckets, ropes, nails, hammers and saws. These were always very busy and prosperous, as Bolivians were adept at making useful things out of odd bits and pieces, and one had to push one's way into the shops, through customers, onlookers, and optimistic pedlars who set out their trays of wares at the door, offering needles and scissors, cottons, silks and elastics and other small essentials.

The street of the carpenters was very aromatic, for the most popular local wood was cedar, and one could get rather badly-made boxes, chests, cupboards and desks made to order if one was prepared to wait weeks and months for their completion, and return endlessly to hang about the workshop protesting through the veils of scented sawdust.

There was a street of beds, and one of mattresses and pillows; another of saucepans and pottery and everything for the kitchen— blue, easy-to-chip enamel pots and enormous ladles for soup, and pottery bowls of all shapes and sizes, very coarse and irregular and always painted in the same soupy browns and khaki green. In one dark, narrow alley there were goldsmiths and silversmiths, working the Bolivian gold that came up from panning sites among the cataracts and wild rivers in the mountains, and the silver from the mines.

The potato sellers had their own street, so did the charcoal sellers, and another lane had shops all selling flour and sugar which households bought by the sack; and lard and oil, and methylated spirits for igniting paraffin stoves. Everything was displayed on the pavement, or hung on the walls to persuade people to buy, and every shop-owner or pedlar called and cajoled passers-by.

The streets of clothes were the most difficult to pass through, for the goods were hung out on strings, and even poles, right into the street, and it was impossible to walk past them without bobbing down into the gutter among the lorries, donkeys or llamas, or brushing and knocking the clothes themselves. Coats, shirts, overalls, blue jeans, mackintoshes, Wellington boots, all hung in rows, smelling of rubber and canvas, and warm, cheap cotton. Men's clothes and women's were separate—and the women's clothes occupied a long precipitous street sloping back towards the Plaza. There was row upon row of skirts and petticoats in every imaginable colour, in cottons and brocaded silks; there were blouses with wide necks, and frilled elbow-length sleeves, shawls of cotton, wool, alpaca, vicuña or silks and brocades, all with long fringes; rows of shoes, all for very small feet, and dyed in colours to match the shawls and skirts—green, red and lilac. And endless dozens of bowler hats, again in a dazzling variety of colours, were piled one above the other into columns up to five feet high or more. (This fashion for headgear was supposed to have been started by an enterprising German from Hamburg more than a century ago. He must have made a tidy fortune, as the hat was now a uniform across the whole span of the Andes—lorryloads of bowlers, contraband or no, made their way up from Argentina, where factories were trying to cash in on this Indian infatuation.)

Somewhere up here was the black-market—in fact in almost any of the streets one might find contraband goods—and the thieves' market where it was said one could find a good many things that had been burgled—and buy back one's own if it came to that.

And in a dark alley, conspicuous after the flamboyant clothes' market, and shaded by the high walls of San Francisco itself, was the market of magic. Within earshot of bells and chanting and the Christian message, was this row of little shops, each kept by a very old, bent woman, and the wares stretched out on trays and wooden counters along the pavement were dried seed-pods, sticks and grasses, little pieces of rock and gnarled wood, and brilliant coloured powders. Some I could recognise as spices or dyes, others not, and questions never produced any answer as the women spoke no Spanish. They would try to explain in their own language, or by pointing to the head, the eyes, or the stomach, to indicate remedies for some ailment. The place smelt musty, and sometimes putrid, for there were also skinned carcases of small rats and guinea-pigs, and the dried foetuses of llamas, pathetic little wizened things, stillborn perhaps, ripped untimely from their mothers' wombs, or taken from dead animals. I did manage to discover about these that they were very important if anyone built a house, and must be buried under the first corner completed, when they would bring good luck and good health to the occupants, and safety from attack by man, beast or weather. But it was an eerie place, and sinister, and filled me with childish fears of evil spells.

On down the Prado and the main Avenida, beyond and below the Spanish and Indian cities, the suburbs spread out over the slopes. At Miraflores there was a barracks, a large hospital, and the football stadium, and a few restaurants, night-clubs and cinemas. The houses were often perched on the edge of precipices above the gorge where the river ran. Sopocachi had more comfortable villas, some embassy residences, and tree-lined avenues.

The lowest suburbs were like separate villages. Obrajes lay some two miles down the gorge, reached by only one road, tortuous with hairpin bends, bridges over the river, and sandy cliffs. In heavy rains the cliffs often collapsed, tossing huge boulders across the road and into the gorge below. With its sudden descent into shadow over rushing water, and fringes of low-bending eucalyptus trees, the place was a sniper's ideal, and when the President, in this time of unrest, came up from his house in the lowest valley, he rode in a bullet-proof car, with blaring sirens and an escort of steel-helmeted police on snorting motor-bicycles.

For two miles further below Obrajes, the road bumped past a few small houses, their walls for ever festooned with blue-flowered plumbago, a petrol station, and then down a narrow cutting beside the river with smallholdings flanking the water. Round a corner, hidden till then by cliffs, lay Calacoto, a long valley scattered with modern houses, and an avenue running straight for miles to disappear in some brown hillocks.

Here the President lived, and a number of Cabinet ministers and diplomats, and Americans who declared that they would rather endure the long journey up to the city and have the compensation of a couple of thousand feet knocked off the altitude. The houses were mostly modern villas of undistinguished design, each barricaded behind a wall or high hedge with strong gates always kept locked, for all Bolivians believed in fortifying themselves, whether against neighbours, mobs or mad dogs.

III

The House in the Valley

O NCE ACCLIMATISED, WE began to take more part in the diplomatic round in Laz Paz. Bolivia was a member of the United Nations Security Council, and everyone at the Chancery was kept very busy putting over the British point of view to Bolivian politicians and journalists, drawing up long, simplified histories and diagrams of such unheard-of places as the Yemen or Indonesia, to explain our policy and try to persuade the Bolivians to support us in New York.

I donned hat and gloves and made my first formal call on the Ambassadress, and was drawn into the round of diplomatic duties—the cocktail parties and lunches and tea parties, and visits to convents and schools and prisons and homes, and the obligatory membership of the *Sociedad de las Damas Diplomaticas*. These ladies met frequently to discuss their favourite charities, hold long complicated elections for new honorary officials, and equally long arguments about their coming money-raising efforts. The meetings were always crowded, and very hot as no one ever seemed to want the windows open, so one sat perspiring and dizzy, sipping Coca-Cola and passing about little trays of cheese-cake, straining to understand the Spanish of the German, French, Italian, Japanese or Argentine ladies who all spoke at great speed with vastly different accents. The money-raising efforts were much the same as these meetings, except that there were sometimes men too, cake and alcohol instead of fizzy drinks, and raffles or compulsory bridge instead of speeches.

Our Land-Rover, we heard, had arrived in South America but was still a long way away, lying on the docks in a Peruvian port. We must be patient as there was a strike at the port, and on the railway too, so nothing was likely to get done for some time.

44

Meanwhile we got about in taxis, which were quite cheap, and very ramshackle, and rattled along frighteningly fast; and in the local buses, the *colectivos*, which were far older and more ramshackle, and often broke down halfway up the mountain. These were always crowded with very pungent old men, barefoot children, and women with large bundles, and babies on their backs. The babies were swaddled tightly, and slung nonchalantly in shawls knotted on the mother's breast. Sometimes a little round head peeped out, in one of the ubiquitous woollen caps with spaniel-ear flaps, and surveyed the world solemnly with huge black eyes. But the really small babies were more often completely covered—perhaps as a protection from flies or dust—with a layer of the shawl or swaddling, or perhaps a thick blanket. It never seemed to occur to them that this was dangerous—and I watched in horror one terrible occasion when a mother pulled her baby round on to her lap and unwrapped him to find him dead—he had obviously been smothered.

One day I had to go to the hospital to have my finger lanced to remove a septic thorn. It was all done very efficiently, even fussily, with local anaesthetics, in a neat little aseptic operating theatre. Afterwards, I lost my way, and wandered through the main body of the hospital, into a large ward where in two rows of high iron beds lay the tiny, shrunken inert bodies of some old men or women —it was impossible to tell which. They were quite silent, and stared vacantly, lost in pain perhaps, or numbed by their illness and the new, unfamiliar surroundings. A man in ragged blue overalls slouched on a box at the door failed to stop some stray dogs coming in from the streets, and these wandered about sniffing at everything, while a hunchback beggar in rags hobbled from bed to bed whining and rattling an old tin can. None of the patients moved, but a nurse gave him a small piece of bread.

I recounted this to the señora on my return to the *pensión*, and she crossed herself.

"I pray to my name saint that I may never have to go there," she said. "Everybody knows it is certain death."

I thought this a bit unfair in view of the battle the doctors were obviously waging against dirt, ignorance and superstition, but I saw her point.

Our Land-Rover arrived at the Customs station on the *altiplano* —but we still had to wait for it, because all the papers had to go to the Ministry of Foreign Affairs for a *liberación* and the signatures of several officials, and then on to another Ministry for the same treatment; and the Ministry of Foreign Affairs had got into a great muddle, all its papers had gone awry so it had suspended all business, and everyone's imported goods, cars, food, medicines, must wait while the Ministry's papers were tidied up.

But we got the Land-Rover at last, noted the theft of the tool kit and £25 worth of spare parts, and drove it home, on *Salida al Mar* Day, when Bolivia was celebrating her determination to win back her "exit to the sea", a strip of land down to the Pacific which she had lost in a war with Chile in 1879. Demands and discussions about this had gone on for a very long time, but unfortunately the Chileans were unsympathetic and the United Nations were impassive, and the cynics remarked that Bolivia had started the war anyway. But this did little to quench their hopes, and to celebrate them, parades of army cadets marched through the streets with banners, and bands both military and amateur tootled the national anthem and other stirring tunes. Cars and taxis wore stickers, and boys scratched slogans on walls, all declaring "*Bolivia demanda su derecha al Mar*" ("Bolivia demands her right to the sea"), and the air force staged a fly-past with all its little planes, which made up for being twenty-five years out of date by doing the most daring aerobatics, plunging at hair-raising angles towards the cliffs.

We were very proud and excited about the Land-Rover, which we had found at the Motor Show in London months before. It was a "long wheel base station-wagon" model which an enterprising firm had converted into a dormobile. So, as well as doing all the wonderful tricks that every Land-Rover can, such as bouncing across roadless wastes and through thick undergrowth undeterred, it had a roof that went up and bunks that let down, some large tin cupboards and a stove, and something the converters called the "conference table". (It had even, to our surprise, been exempt from purchase tax, as with all these additional luxuries, it was classed as a house.)

It also had locks on every window, and padlocks on the doors, the wheels, the spare wheel and the bonnet, and we thought it was impregnable. But we had not had it a week before it was stolen.

Tidily dressed for church one morning we went out to find it gone. We sat through communion filled with rage and uncharitable thoughts, and then rushed to the offices of the traffic police, the *Transito*, where some sleepy policemen refused to take out their motor-bicycles and start a search, because it was Sunday, and they declared they were off duty. Reckless in our anxiety, we bribed them, which was a dangerous departure from British diplomatic rules, and they found it down the mountain below Calacoto very quickly—almost too quickly, I thought. The thieves had tried the windows, then broken a hole in the roof large enough for a child to get through. They had unscrewed the dashboard and crossed the wires to make the engine go, and on abandoning it had made off with the cooker and water carriers. After this we took to disconnecting and removing the rotor-arm whenever the car was to be left out overnight, so that nothing except brute force would make the car move.

One week we went to Peru, for David to attend a conference in Lima, and were stunned by the thick air at sea-level, the swing of the big city, and the lush gardens full of bougainvillaea and poinsettia, roses and frangipani.

We went to all the museums to see the Inca and pre-Inca remains, the pillars and statues and pots and woven fabrics, and the reconstructions of villages. And we saw the palaces and furniture and silver of Colonial Spain. We stayed in a luxury hotel with three swimming-pools, and after swimming in one of them David returned to the marble-floored changing rooms to find his shoes had been stolen. Barefoot and enraged he marched in to see the Manager who had no apologies for this disgrace to his establishment, and simply shrugged, "In Lima it is always so."

But for this short interlude, we lived on for three and a half months in our little room in the *pensión*, and all this time I was house-hunting which was as time-consuming and depressing a business as it is in any country.

We advertised hopefully in the local paper—but the replies came in very slowly. Most of the houses surprised me because they were so dark and took no advantage of the view; often the windows they had looking out over the valley were filled in and "blinded" with stained glass. One address turned out to be a carpenter's shop: a man at a bench stopped sawing the leg off a chair and said, "Yes, the rooms upstairs are to let—they are too small for us now, but they are not quite finished. You see, the rain broke a wall down last week when there was a bad *derrumba* here."

Of thirty-five houses I saw, only a few seemed at all habitable. At one of these, a place with a stupendous view, I exclaimed in horror at the rent asked by the owner, a woman with luscious Spanish looks who lived in Paris and was very *chic*, clad in doeskin and crocodile skin, and heavy jangling gold bracelets. She looked me up and down and said:

"Yes, of course, it is too much for you." (She was asking double the rent allowance for the highest ranks in our Service.)

"But," she went on, "I am really looking for some nice American tenants, and I am sure I shall find them quickly enough. No, I cannot reduce the rent. For everyone life is expensive. For me—very expensive."

There was a place I always coveted on the road up from Obrajes. In one of the crooks of the pass up the mountain, with the river tumbling at one side, someone had made a little paradise of terraces, like a hanging garden, trailing with geraniums and bougainvillaea, and built three houses into the hillside.

By chance we met some Peruvian diplomats who lived in one of these houses, and they invited us to visit them. They were very gay and hospitable; they kept repeating our name and asking if they had got it right, and seemed to find us amusing, which made us feel flattered, as we were still diffident in Spanish. The house was quite small, but with one large living-room that was circular, with walls made entirely of glass to take advantage of the view.

Our new friends told us that one of the other two houses would soon be vacant, as Carlos, another glamorous Peruvian, was soon returning to Lima. So we were introduced to the landlord, who occupied the third house himself. He was a Hungarian *émigré*, heavily built with a magnificent leonine head. Beneath heavy white locks his eyes were brilliant and watchful; his effortless proficiency in

La Carnicera

The beggar in the market place

Family plate in procession

Oruro *Carnaval*—Devil Dancers

half a dozen languages inspired awe in me at once, while his languid manner suggested certain excesses in a long life of opportunism. He had with him his new young wife, a brittle blonde, and a son of about thirty-five, who professed to be a painter.

We sat on high bamboo stools at his "Bar", admiring the view and drinking vodka, while the three of them summed us up, switching bewilderingly from English to Spanish, French and Russian.

"You see," said the landlord, "we all know each other very well in this little colony. Yes, I call it a colony, it is so *intime*—like an artists' colony perhaps. We are such very good friends, and the houses are so close to each other, it is most important we should all have good relations. Now Carlos, dear Carlos, who is going. So sad. You know him, of course? And Lisa his dear friend, well I should say his *fiancée* perhaps. Beautiful Lisa. Ah, what wonderful parties we have had here, such parties, all day—all night. Ah!" and he sighed rapturously into his glass. I suddenly noticed a quick glance pass between the son and his young step-mother, and felt both staid and naïve, wondering whether we should be able to live up to this festive standard.

They took us to see the house, which had some good antique furniture and a certain wayward charm, but was very small and I noticed that under the wall coverings and all the clinging bougainvillaea it was constructed simply of asbestos sheets. It was hardly a setting for the accessories of babyhood and I could not believe that the landlord or his wife would take kindly to rows of washing festooned about the flowery slopes.

However, we were all rapturously polite to each other, and agreed that it was a lovely place, that the rent was justifiably high, that it was so important to be sure we would all get on well—and that of course it already seemed we would all become great friends. We agreed that we would all think about it, and the conclusion was quite obvious to all of us without any need to destroy the atmosphere by uttering it.

One day I went to an address high in the town, "the Soho of La Paz" its owner had described it in a sudden burst into English on the telephone. Climbing up the pavement of the cobbled main street,

D

past banks, and newspaper shops, street vendors and shoe-shine boys, I wondered what this could really mean.

The number I sought was nailed to the wall of an alleyway between a furniture store and a factory. It was dark and rather slippery, and as I climbed about four long flights of steps my heart began to pound with the effort, and wild pictures flashed across my mind of some compromise at gunpoint with no escape route.

I came abruptly out through an archway into bright sunlight and a courtyard entirely surrounded by the verandahs of an old house.

Jasmine grew down one trellis, "Golden Shower" over another; roses and marigolds blazed in small flower-beds, and several tubs held little formal trees. The place looked Spanish, but was too tidy; it had an odd air of French husbandry. It was empty and quiet. The noise of the street had receded into the far distance, and I could see the white tip of Illimani above the rooftops.

A gauze door creaked and slapped shut, and an enormously tall old man walked towards me, his bronzed, bony hand stretched to take mine.

"How do you do?" he said. "Yes, you are surprised. I speak English. I was not sure of your nationality when I telephoned. Your name does not indicate . . ."

We entered the house and sat in a dark, half-shuttered room in huge leather armchairs. There was brown linoleum on the floor, faded flowered wallpaper with a dado border, and faded colour photographs on an upright piano.

He had been at Oxford, the old man explained, at Exeter College. Did I know it? That I knew Oxford well delighted him. He poured out glasses of sherry, and we drank the health of his College, and to our fortunate meeting.

For about half-an-hour he reminisced—about youth and gaiety and the green summers, about his travels and the old days in his own country. I began to wonder whether he really meant to let his house at all.

"We were rich, yes, we lived well, but now—the government has taken everything. They took my lands and my factory. There is just one farm left where the Indians are loyal to me. We were good *padrones*, and they loved my family. So, we wish to go there, to save the place. We do not want to let this house, but we are old, times are hard."

Our discussion about the possible rent, and the possibility that he would leave his library of precious books for the use of such careful tenants—as he was sure we would be—was equally oblique.

A little woman came in, very fair-skinned and blue-eyed, with white hair swept high in the fashion of her youth. She wore black, her skirts almost to the floor, and a white lace fichu.

We were introduced in Spanish.

"I am afraid my wife does not speak English," said my host. "She was born in France."

I stayed longer, for coffee, and rough little almond biscuits, while Madame spoke in decorous, slow French of the days when people were civilised and cared about each other. She seemed so incongruous sitting there in her old-fashioned clothes, so delicate, it was impossible to imagine that she had belonged to the rough pioneering life in this country with such a blood-stained history.

Her husband watched her calmly, nodding assent, adding short remarks in English. It was growing late, and the sun slanted into the room catching his bronze features and white hair. I realised that his name must have some Indian connection. Yet his Indian blood had put only colour into some other stock, I thought. In this light his face had the withdrawn nobility of some Mediterranean god.

In the end, however, we found a house in the lowest suburb, Calacoto, where like the Americans, we too found it noticeably easier to breathe and walk upstairs; gardens here were less arid, and winds less harsh.

By La Paz standards, our house was quite luxurious. It had an enormous hall, two of whose walls were made of glass. A curved staircase led up to the second floor, where a balustraded platform round the sides of the hall led to the various bedrooms. This was supposed to be a distinguished architectural feature, but really only lent the place a jaunty, nautical air.

While the hall was light and airy, the study beside the front door was perpetually dark, as its two small windows were filled in with thick stained glass, depicting knights and ladies in poor *art nouveau* style. This room had its own door on to the front porch, and had, I discovered, been designed as the equivalent of a boudoir for the master of the house—the room where he could entertain his mistresses, and come and go quietly without the knowledge or interference of his wife.

The furniture in the house was sparse and shabby. The previous occupants had used the place hard: chairs and sofas were pocked with cigarette burns, the grey-green walls were stained by drink, and all the ceilings and light fixtures were encrusted with the droppings of flies. My first days were spent carrying buckets of disinfectant about the house, my skin prickling with disgust. But over the weeks we persuaded the Chancery to let us cover almost everything with white paint; and on a visit to Cochabamba in the lowlands I bought, from two old women squatting on the dusty streets, hundreds of metres of un-dyed wool, handwoven in Indian villages, to be made into chair-covers and curtains. After a few months the house began to look quite pretty.

There was a garden of no great dimension, surrounded by a high *macrocarpa* hedge, with big brown padlocked gates; and there was a swimming-pool, an unexpected luxury, but much too cold to swim in. We tried it one hot sunny day, and emerged blue and numb within seconds; after a short flirtation with a pair of ducks who in a brief half-hour of splashing made the bright water a duck-pond green, we simply fenced the pool off to protect the baby, and left it empty.

Our landlady, the owner of the house, was Señora Rosa, a capricious elderly widow. She would turn up unannounced always accompanied by an obnoxious grandson, who pinched the baby and broke his toys, while the grandmother picked the flowers I was carefully nurturing for the house, and ticked off the gardener whom I had employed to tend them. She sometimes asked me to tea in her other house up in the town, which was full of stained glass and faded *art nouveau* prints. There were lace table-cloths and napkins and enormous frilly paper doilies waving crisply over the edges of plates laden with sandwiches, buns, cream cakes, and ices, and I dreaded making the inevitable return invitation knowing that I could never somehow live up to this pastry cook's largesse.

The señora spent every winter in Miami. I pictured her walking slowly through hotel foyers in printed *crêpe de Chine* dresses that clung to her plump contours, ordering herself ices among the potted palms and aspidistras. She wrote to us from Florida. Her letters were predictably difficult to decipher, and almost impossible to follow. They were filled with long remarks about the warm weather in Florida, and good wishes for our baby, and other trivialities, but the last paragraph asked if we could send her a little money, say an advance of three months' rent (which came to a great deal), as she was finding life in Miami so expensive.

The valley in which Calacoto lay was strange and beautiful. It was wide enough for one not to feel hemmed in, yet it was totally enclosed. One had no view of the *altiplano*, none of Illimani. The cliffs were high, on one side dun-coloured, the other a rich brick-red. In the distance above the road's end the hills rose to a line of peaks.

The colours here changed with each hour of the day—from dun or blue of morning to gold or white at midday. In the dust-laden air of winter, the sun played tricks with light like the fantasy of a giant. In the short, blazing sunset, great spears of light would stab across the green shadows at the feet of these treeless cliffs, or startle puffs of red dust into purple clouds.

In the wet season, rain-clouds would swoop round from the gorge above and whirl about the valley like monstrous captured birds. When rain fell on us, it capped the hilltops with snow.

There was an excitement, in this high altitude, in being so much closer to the sun. The air was so clear, the light so pure, it seemed almost to have sparks in it, like fluorescence in sea water. On some dry days the blueness of the sky had a dazzling intensity; on others it was white, as though the colour had gone into a range of radiance beyond human sight.

The freshness of the early morning, before the sun had dried a heavy dew and the world blazoned into colour, was like shrill unearthly music. To turn into the valley at this hour was to enter the world of those dreams where the sleeper moves through shining landscapes, fields and forests without shadow, as though every tree were its own sun—to wake deliriously happy for no reason. It was like walking again through that radiance that bathes the memories of childhood, or like seeing the dream of Daedalus, or for sudden seconds being Icarus before his fall.

Nature was prodigal here, contemptuous, aloof. In the dry months the sun beat mercilessly. At midday, although it was winter, we ate outside in summer clothes and straw hats. Our skins became chapped, our hands horny, our lips cracked. Half-an-hour without a hat burnt the baby's cheeks to blisters. Children who sunbathed too long had to be treated in hospital for second degree burns. In good weather, the hardy skied at 17,000 feet, wearing layers of sun-proof oil, and polaroid spectacles. David climbed a peak to 21,000 feet in a blizzard and spent days in bed, shivering and chilled with the reaction to his burns. His companions spent a week in hospital with sun-blindness. Yet at night in the dry season we would huddle by the fire while frost fell outside.

Rains tore the landscape apart. In summer we shivered around the house in our winter clothes. Thunderstorms crashed above us, lightning struck houses or unwary travellers, cattle were drowned, and while we in the valley escaped the torrents lightly, and short work with mop and bucket restored order, those whose houses perched on the giddy slopes above, or in Villa Victoria, never knew when their moment of ill-fate would come, when they would feel the floor shift beneath their feet, see their mud walls forced open and their worldly goods washed away down the mountain.

Nights after a heavy storm throbbed with the noise of *derrumbas*, landslides, as the cliffs about us gave way, crashing like more thunder above the roar of the river.

Water for the city came from a glacial watershed high above among the peaks, but also from the brown river itself, which tossed down through the gorge like a frothing beast, sometimes in the open, sometimes tunnelling back underground. It was also a main sewer. The fields below Calacoto were a constant green, the stench like a seaport, and oblivious of it the women would wade about and slap their washing, spreading it on rocks or bushes to dry.

There was modern sewerage of a sort, but no one asked too many questions, and all tap-water was boiled and filtered before drinking. Our house had a borehole which we were assured was even more dangerous, but the water from it was fresh and clear. The altitude itself did something to reduce the danger of diseases which, though rife, did not take such toll as in the tropical lowlands. People always claimed that smells, however strong, would have been much worse at 2,000 feet, and that up in La Paz, alas, all flowers smelt less sweet. Germs and insects were supposed, like us, to suffer from the altitude. Nevertheless, we waged a never-ending battle against house flies, and from time to time found ourselves, our friends or acquaintances smitten with tropical parasites, jaundice or even typhoid. Groups of scavenging dogs roamed the streets at night howling and barking, and one month eight American children were badly bitten by rabid animals. We were perpetually being advised not to keep a dog or a cat, I took to ducks and geese instead. We felt compensated one day when a plague of caterpillars that had succeeded in killing off a large pine tree turned into clouds of scarlet butterflies.

On water, too, depended our supply of electricity. In winter, the streams dried up, electricity was cut three days a week and more if the power company (Canadian-owned and British-operated) was in difficulties. In summer, it snowed on the peaks and the glacial water-shed was temperamental. Storms, floods, winds, and revolutions all produced power cuts. Moreover, the power company which tried to run things on commercial lines, was frequently in financial difficulties. Rentals or rates were troublesome enough to collect from the well-to-do. A posse of men was employed for this, equipped with large step-ladders so that they could enter the property of the company's debtors willy-nilly and cut off their electricity. But in the crowded cliff-hanging areas, where rates were lower, consumption was if anything greater and more difficult to control. Often one house would supply electricity for all its neighbours within reasonable reach: every power-plug would have little Heath-Robinson adaptors strapped to it, and wires festooned ingeniously along the eaves from house to house outside. Of course culprits when caught were roundly punished and denounced, but a little judicious bribery, plus the fact that houses never really caught fire in the altitude, could keep detection well at bay.

Although there were large supplies of oil from the lowlands, there was no coal in the country, or gas, and so no other source for power. The voltage of the electricity when we had it was so low that most gadgets were unable to work without some aid. We bought a small Japanese regulator which with much humming and a constant smell of singeing would jolt a toaster, an iron, or a record-player into action. Cooking on paraffin soon became a habit, and often to read at night we would sit with all electric lights blazing, crouched beside the stronger light of a candle.

To heat the house in winter we bought logs of wood by the thousand kilos, inspecting each armful for damp. To make a fire at all in this half-bodied air was a problem solved only by large quantities of kerosene. Firelighting became a source of competition and argument, and a studied skill. Unrewarded by long efforts at boy scout stick-laying we had to learn the art of recklessly tossing on tinfuls of kerosene: terrifying puffs of flame would roar up out of the grate almost to the ceiling only to die down in seconds to a tiny glow, leaving us shaking but undeterred.

For us, with our borehole, a power cut also meant no water. Regularly throughout the winter, and at any sign of a crisis of weather or politics, we would go round the house filling baths, sinks and basins, saucepans and bowls, and the huge zinc bath in which our washerwoman, the *lavandera*, did the weekly wash.

Old and wrinkled with long grey pigtails and a black shawl, she slapped our sheets clean in cold water and hung them to dry in the sun. Hot water, she declared, gave her rheumatism; besides, it was bad for the sheets. She had great dignity and charm, and her weekly visit was something of an occasion. To us, she was always, formally, the *Señora Lavandera* while the cook, maid and gardener used for her the Spanish phrases reserved for the older and more distinguished, referring to her always as the *Doña* Josefa. None of us knew much about her life, and she was very reticent. Although I sometimes drove her up to the city in the evening, I never saw her home. That she lived alone and had no family I only learnt by chance one night during a revolution when I persuaded her to stay with us and not venture through the streets where there was still fighting. "No one will be worried," she said, "there is no one to tell."

IV

Juana and the Markets

HOUSEHOLDS OF THE more or less well-to-do Bolivians, and those of foreigners and diplomats in La Paz always had domestic staff of some kind. Our own quota of three was not exceptional.

Juana, our cook, was a *mestizo*, and *desvestida*, that is one who has discarded Indian dress for European. Whether she had ever really been married to her husband was not clear, but he had long since left her for another woman and as she had no protection under Bolivian law she had to fend alone for her two children. By the time she came to us, the daughter had produced an illegitimate child, whom Juana was also supporting.

They lived in two rooms of a small mud house across the river, at the mercy of a rapacious and negligent landlord. The rent was ridiculously high, the building decrepit, without electricity or water, and in the wet season it leaked and crumbled. But Juana, a woman of infinite courage, managed somehow on her small salary to bring her children up decently, well-fed and clothed, and given what education the local school could offer. She also tried to instil in her son a realistic sense of responsibility, a quality totally lacking, in her opinion, in all Bolivian men.

"They are rotten, señora, quite rotten, oh, no good, good for nothing. They never stick to their women, keep all the money for themselves and spend it all on drink."

The infiltration of her little family into ours was slow but sure, until we found them all in some way established in our house, and the child, little Roxana, learning to walk with our baby son Alexander.

Punctuality is in any case a very Protestant virtue. In Bolivia it

simply did not exist. Nothing and nobody could ever really be
relied on to arrive on time. After the European diplomatic scene,
where guests at a formal dinner can be found whiling away the time
outside their destination for as much as fifteen or twenty minutes in
order to be crossing the threshold as the appointed hour strikes,
dinners in Bolivia had a delightfully bizarre air. It was nothing for
the guests to arrive an hour late, for the soup to appear two hours
late and for midnight to strike before the appearance of the main
course.

In fact the whimsicality seemed to be general to Latin America.
La hora española made every allowance for temperamental vagaries.
At a dinner party in Lima, our hostess, an ambassadress of one of the
most precise countries of Europe, told us sadly how the evening's
guest of honour, a Peruvian cabinet minister, had that morning sent
her an enormous basket of flowers, with his apologies for being
unable to come.

We sat down, twenty strong, at a table elaborately laden with
silver, glass and yellow roses to mark the dignity of the occasion
that should have been, and by eleven o'clock had quite consumed a
large prawn soufflé, when a butler came rustling in in great concern
and our hostess rushed out of the room. We sat in hushed surprise,
all straining to make out the voices outside, and suddenly the
Swedish Ambassador, seated on the hostess's right, rose to his feet
muttering and shrugging, gathered up his knives and forks and the
remains of his soufflé, and sat down upon an empty chair beside me,
at the bottom of the table. Waiters swooped about restoring order
and pushing the yellow roses about to make room for new places,
and our hostess returned, with the cabinet minister, who must have
had to brush past his own bouquet of apology as it still stood in the
hall.

Juana was no exception to the whimsy. She was quite incapable
of producing a meal on time, but she had once worked in the French
Embassy, and her presentation was superb. Even a small, humble
stew destined to be eaten on our laps in the garden would appear
dressed as for a banquet.

But although she knew a good deal about French cuisine, she
still believed that the Bolivian national diet was the best, and

while she soaked fillet steaks in piquant sauces and grilled them over charcoal, she could not resist trying to persuade us to start with soup.

Soup in the highlands of Bolivia was the staple diet and eternal dish and in Juana's eye the cure for all ills, source of all important vitamins. Any slight ailment we might suffer from was put down to our refusal to eat soup once or better twice a day.

No kitchen was complete without its bubbling cauldron, receptacle for all nourishing titbits and leftovers. A haphazard mixture of any available meat (beef, lamb or llama), potatoes, maize, barley, rice, carrots, onion, chili, pimento, it was thick and piquant, and its pungent aroma as much a part of the air of a Bolivian town as the dry, tingling smell of dust, or the stench of human waste.

Each week Juana and I would pile baskets into the Land-Rover and drive up the mountain to do the household shopping.

The markets in La Paz followed the pattern of living—the higher up the cheaper and dirtier. I tried all in turn, including a wholesale market high up in Villa Victoria, where lorries arrived from the tropical valleys, piled high with vegetables or fruit, in large sacks, or tied in bundles with thongs and banana leaves. Here we came too, to buy charcoal for the brazier, or to try to find cheap potatoes, but I saw no other foreigners up here and after a few futile attempts at bargaining, returning home exhausted, bruised and ankle deep in mire, I gave up and went to a lower market and higher prices. At the Mercada Lanza we found a boy named Cruz, after a great Bolivian hero. In old patched jeans, biblical sandals, and grey knitted cap, he was always waiting for us, ready to carry the heavier baskets as they were piled higher with our purchases, and he must have been very strong, for marketing was a serious business and took the entire morning, as we bargained for everything but meat.

Whichever day we went, the markets were crowded, throbbing with noise. Outside we would jostle past stalls of jewellery and trinkets, and the silver sellers squatting on the pavement, their little spoons and baubles laid out on dark cloths, glinting in the sun. There were boys beside them selling home-made toys or fireworks, and fruit sellers with the season's delicacies from the lowlands, apricots or figs set out on little beds of leaves.

Food stalls were nearby, with doughnuts, little yellow cakes, bright mounds of sweets and cauldrons of soup. A crowd was irresistible, and a minute of pushing and peering would reveal a man with a cage of small rats on show as curiosities; or a monkey chained to a box, handing out little packets of some new medicament, its owner moving about exhorting the crowd to buy, shouting into a crackling microphone, and rounding on the inquisitive small boys who tripped in its wires.

Under rickety awnings in an alley leading up to the market hall stood stalls heavy with papaya lemons and bananas, kept by women from Cochabamba, distinctive in their high white board hats. Then the apple sellers had a corner where they laid out their boxes, polishing each bright fruit and putting the label on display "Manzanas de Chile".

And flanking the steps the potato sellers sat on the paving, their wares laid out in rows or mounds on old sacks or simply in the dust. Humble and scruffy they all looked, small Aymhara women from the *altiplano*, but they had one of the best positions in the market, a worthy vantage-point for the importance of their wares.

The potato was indigenous to South America, and many of its species were first found in the Andes. By the time the Spaniards arrived, many varieties had been long centuries in cultivation. They can be traced still in the art of early Peru. The coastal tribes, the Mochica, Nasca, and Chimu, made vast quantities of pottery, and buried it with their dead—pots in the form of humans, animals, birds, plants—these we had seen in the museums in Lima, walking from room to room past shelves of pots unearthed from old burial sites, and reconstructed pictures of the lives of these remote people. Every aspect of human activity was depicted, and there were strange, grotesque pots showing human diseases and deformities, or creations of gargoyle-like humour, and often a face would appear wretched and distorted from the form of a many-eyed potato tuber. Perhaps some were objects for magic ritual, others simply for use or decoration.

From a dealer in Lima I bought some Chimu pots, one of which was in the form of two potato-shaped jars, with chimney-funnels, joined by a bar. On top of one funnel sat a bird, and blowing down the other funnel, particularly if there was water in the jar, would make the bird whistle. What was its use, I wondered? Did some boy once take it into the fields to scare birds away from his potatoes while they were in flower, or to induce a god to bless the hidden crop? Or was it merely a vessel, or a toy?

Guaman Poma de Ayala, whose records are one of the few major sources of Inca history, described in detail and in crude pictures the intricacies of Indian potato culture in the Andes in the sixteenth century—the digging, planting and harvesting, the use of foot plough, and sacks carried on the back, secured with a cloth tied round the forehead—these are much the same still.

The *conquistadores*, and more so their immediate, more intelligent successors, were fascinated by this new food, so completely different from anything known in Europe. Specimens were taken to the Spanish court; barrels full, carefully preserved and tended, made their way across to Europe, and learned treatises were written about them.

"Of provisions besides maize, there are two other products which form the principal food of these Indians," wrote Cieza de Leon, another classic writer on the conquest and the Indians. "One is called potato, and is a kind of earth nut, which, after it has been boiled is as tender as a cooked chestnut but with no more skin than a truffle. . . . This root produces a plant exactly like a poppy. The other food is very good and is called quinoa."

Another description (Jose de Acosta) runs: "The Indians use a roote which they call papas . . . like to grounde nuttes. They gather this papas and dry it well in the sunne, then beating it they make Chunu, which keeps many dayes and serves for bread. In this realme there is great traffic in chunu which they carry to the mines of Potosi; they likewise eat these papas boyled or roasted."

Papa was the word in Quechua, the language which the Incas imposed on all the peoples they conquered. The word in Aymhara, the language of the Indians round Lake Titicaca whom the Incas conquered but never really assimilated, was *amka*, or *choke*. There are still many Aymhara Indians living around Lake Titicaca who speak no Quechua, but the word *papa* is now universal. However, when one learns that there are some 200 varieties of potato in

Bolivia alone, the picture becomes confused. I came across only a handful of these, the commonest, as they appeared with the seasons in the markets.

For Juana, buying potatoes alone was an art, a ritual. After the mass-produced, plastic-wrapped packages in Europe, this was a revelation.

We would move from one seller to another, feeling and bargaining, and she had her favourite seller for each kind. There were *papa dura, papa azul, papa amarilla, papa roja*; large potatoes with velvet, white flesh, brown ones with golden flesh, yellowish ones, also golden inside, others smaller, with white, juicy flesh that cut like apples, and our favourite of all, gnarled and knobbed with bumps and crevices and a dark purple skin, pink underneath if one peeled it thinly enough.

We bought *chuño* too, which was just as the old writers described it—small oval-shaped potatoes that had been soaked in water for a week or so and then left out on the open ground of the *altiplano*, scorched in the sun by day, and frozen during the night. The result was hardly recognisable, more like large pebbles that have been rolled in flour, until one picked them up and they felt light and dry, like nuts. At home we soaked these again before using them, and they were a favourite ingredient for soup, almost the size and shape of chestnuts, with a similar wrinkled look and an oddly similar, nutty taste.

Sweet potatoes, known as *batatas*, were looked down on as inferior food, more suitable for animals. The potato women also had *oca*, another tuber which I had never seen elsewhere, bright egg-yellow roots, shaped like knotted fingers. This had a delicate flavour, somewhere between carrot, potato and nut, and we ate it instead of potatoes, baked in butter until the skin wrinkled, and the flesh softened inside.

In season, too, there would be maize, known as *choclo*, immensely popular, but sold more as a delicacy than a staple food. I was surprised, as there were many things about this world which reminded me of Africa, and I had half-expected to find maize porridge. The nearest to ground maize was the *quinoa*, a type of millet ground to a yellow flour, and another, *cañahui*, also like maize flour, but a pinkish brown. Sure that these would be very nutritious I bought some and tried to make porridge like that of the Zulu or Basuto people, but the result was gritty and heavy. However, when we had ducks or geese at the house (poultry was bought live) they ate it with relish and grew fat.

Almost all the market women wore local dress—the brilliant skirts, up to a dozen, with petticoats, one on top of another, blouse, shawl and bowler hat, and their long shining black hair braided into pigtails. I was always surprised too, at how many of them in such an environment of poverty wore big gold pendant earrings and *vicuña* shawls, pinned with gold brooches in the popular shape of an articulated fish, or a fishing boat. Somewhere among the folds too, perhaps tucked in the bosom, there was always a spoon, at hand for the eternal plate of soup: and often as not a baby—in Bolivian Spanish and Quechua, the *wawa*—slung on the mother's back, at her breast, or lying swaddled and bundled, asleep in a corner. There would be other children, too, toddlers, tumbling about, learning to compete, perhaps to steal. Some, well-controlled, earnestly would mind the baby or, already in training for salesmanship and bargaining, sit like prim proprietors on tiny wood and raffia chairs perched on the cobbles. It was impossible to keep them clean, and obviously no one tried. Perhaps the markets were hosed each morning but by ten or eleven the gutters were running. Relieving oneself was almost as public a gesture as suckling a baby. (Mothers suckled their children till two years or more, as a protection, but infant mortality was still fifty per cent.) Inside the market too, dogs wandered about unhindered, fighting for scraps and adding to the filth.

The noise in the main market hall was deafening. We pushed and haggled our way from stall to stall, Juana pouncing like a hawk on anything below her standard, each carrot, each tomato, must be in prime condition, and she kept a wary eye on Cruz, too, just in case he disappeared into the crowd. Fruit and vegetables came up daily from the steep sub-tropical valleys near La Paz. *Papaya*, or paw-paw, with exquisitely succulent pink, scented flesh, was almost never out of season. We ate it every day. There were oranges, grapefruit, grapes, *guayavas*, *granadillas* (passion fruit), and the *chirimoya* or custard apple, which we would cut in half and eat with a spoon. It had an elusive flavour, delicate and unobtrusive like lychees, a thin rind, snow-white flesh and big shining black pips.

There were bananas, too, of several different kinds, golden, green, or small and speckled, and russet coloured ones of enormous size which were inferior and only for cooking, where they substituted for potatoes.

And in season we would find little heaps of prickly pears, carefully de-thorned, whose pink or green flesh added a strange piquancy to fruit salads.

Vegetables came often from the plains of Cochabamba (even fresh milk came from Cochabamba, bumping up the mountains each night in huge clattering lorries). There were small tender artichokes, beans, peas, red peppers and chilis, onions and garlic, sold singly or weighed out by the kilo in old hand-scales. Each seller had something different and we would move from one to another haggling and passing the time of day, pouncing on any new delicacy, a different fruit perhaps, or a bunch of fresh herbs.

There were fish women, with shrimps from Peru, always suspect I thought, and the huge trout from Lake Titicaca. For any fisherman, these were like mythical monsters from some taunting dream, so enormous were they, so bright in colour. There was a story that the trout were introduced by keen foreigners, who had no idea that they would reach such a size. In the glacier lakes high up in the *cordillera*, one could fish for trout of a normal size, and there were, it is true, other small river fish, but these Titicaca monsters exceeded any expectation. So prolific now, they were caught in huge draughts by Indian fishermen who went out at night in their reed-boats, with lights, nets and dynamite. They lay piled on the market stalls, great heaps of colour-streaked silver; round, vacant eyes that had once seen the secret depths of Titicaca, stupid, gaping mouths and pink, "salmonised" flesh. I once saw some more than a yard long, and we bought the flesh by the kilo. Dry and flaky like salmon, it had a rich, pungent flavour, and needed no more than a baking with onion, tomato and butter to make an incomparable dish.

Every corner and cranny, every girder of the corrugated roof of the market hall, was put to some purpose. Sellers without stalls squatted on the floor and one's movement down the aisles was a matter of picking a path over heaps of tomatoes and cabbages, past beggars, dogs and children, sacks of flour or tins of kerosene and lard. Even the rafters were strung with goods, little wooden chairs, baskets of every size and shape, bird-cages and baby's cradles.

We bought spices and eggs from a little wise woman who crouched on some boxes near one entrance with a pair of minute scales to weigh out her precious wares. She also sold round, sour cheeses, white and dry but passable. Juana would hold up each egg and squint at it against the light while I waited for tiny quantities of pepper, pimento, olives, rosemary or saffron to be wrapped into little paper twists. Sometimes Juana would lag behind here, to buy a package of some medicament, self-conscious about my curiosity and possible disapproval.

I kept a large medicine chest at home, and dispensed first-aid, antiseptics, cough-mixture and aspirins with generosity, but I could never persuade even Juana that it really was better to sterilise a wound from barbed wire or fishing-hooks with my medicaments than with old kitchen rags and a poultice made of stale eucalyptus leaves bought from the wise woman. Once, as I drove her to hospital with a septic leg, groaning with pain, and the terror, I think, that the doctor would simply cut off the offending limb, I thought that she had at last realised the truth about germs and sterilising. But unfortunately an injudicious penicillin injection nearly killed her, and we were back to the starting point.

The meat women were the bosses of the market, and their stalls flanked one whole side of the hall, beef at one end, mutton, pork and guinea-pig at the other. Pork was always suspect, and those who could afford to bought it only from a sausage factory high up in the town, owned by a tall, pink-faced German who dressed all his workers in white coifs, coats and boots, and strode about the slippery floor all day in similar dress himself, examining everything through thick, circular spectacles.

Mutton was usually scrawny and as high as venison, guinea-pigs I never quite had courage to try, but the beef came from Argentina. We bought ours from *la Carnicera* (the meat seller) Maria Chiquita, an ironic misnomer for this Amazon, who stood head and shoulders

E

above any Indian man, and must have weighed some twenty stone. Black bowler-hatted and swathed in a grubby white smock, she straddled her stall with a large axe, and a long, whippy knife which, when not in use, was stuck quivering in any chunk of meat at hand. On the counter in front of her lay a muddle of tongues, brains, livers, hearts and other, unrecognisable, pieces, while on the rafters behind her hung the mute carcases of Pampas oxen. Between these she would undulate, shouting prices to customers, and grumbling at her husband, a timid little man who sat on a stool almost hidden behind the swinging raw meat, slipping dirty bank-notes into a box and sipping endless cups of coffee brewed up on a kerosene stove at his feet. Maria had her prices chalked up on a blackboard—it was small use trying to beat her down.

There was no cut of meat comparable to any I had known before. We bought, by the kilo, a large chunk of meat called a *lomo*, which consisted of a long tail of *lomo* or fillet, broadening into a mass of humbler *churasco*, or stewing steak. The art lay in selecting the piece with the largest proportion of fillet to the rest, and persuading Maria not to include bits of gristle—or force us to buy more than a token quantity of the bones which were a compulsory part of any purchase. She would grouse as she weighed out the steak and tipped it into our basket, followed with the bones, slapped a piece of stained paper on top, and perhaps tossed a token of our discard to some waiting beggar or dog.

Juana weighed everything again on our return home, and if it was at all out would rail furiously on our next visit. We might even withdraw our custom for a week or two as a matter of *dignidad*.

"La Maria Chiquita is rich, señora," Juana complained. "How is it? She has two big houses, so big, and three lorries for fetching the meat. How does she get so rich? *Caramba!*" and she would scowl meaningfully.

Our main purchases over at last, we would take a back route out, through the alley of the *contrabandistas*, the smugglers, to have a quick look for any bargains among the stalls of smuggled or stolen goods brought in at night on lorries from Peru or Argentina: toothpaste, soap, sweets, plastic kitchenware, they could all be found in the local shops, but at a very different price.

We reached home exhausted, but usually triumphant, with enough general supplies to last the household for another week.

Coca, the plant from which cocaine is obtained, needs a separate explanation. On any spare piece of pavement outside the market, inside on the floor, and scattered anywhere in La Paz even on street corners in the richer suburbs one might find a coca-seller huddled on the ground. On one side she would have a pile of pale grey-green, flat dried leaves, very like bay leaves but smaller and more papery, and on the other a pile of peculiar "sweets" which looked as though long strands of black liquorice had been rolled in icing-sugar and then fashioned into little coils. In fact they were not sweets at all, and very nasty to taste, made from the ash of *quinoa*, dried, mashed and mixed—some said even masticated—into a sticky mass and then shaped thus for market. But their purpose was all-important, to extract the maximum effect from the coca. The "sweet" would be placed in one side of the mouth, and in the other a little pouch of folded coca leaves.

Coca is a fundamental necessity of Bolivian life, and has been cultivated from time immemorial with a seriousness not even devoted to the potato. For it provides not a mere means of life but a means to get above life, out of the struggle, away from care.

Grown in the warm valleys near La Paz, it was one of the chief reasons for the city's development: in the sixteenth century La Paz was simply a stopping point for the mule trains taking silver from the mines of Potosí to the sea. But coca went up to Potosí as silver came out, and La Paz flourished. Any attempts made by the Spaniards to stamp out the trade and the habit were fruitless, in fact any long sojourn in the country must then, as now, have made its uses obvious.

From childhood on, almost every Indian chewed coca. It was an indulgence far stronger than alcohol, far more efficacious. Chewing it with the "sweet" produced a state of freedom and rest, not a euphoria coloured by dreams of glory or grandiose hallucinations, but tranquillity, resignation. It brought unbelievable relief from hunger, cold and pain.

Gross excess, it is true, took terrible tolls. It was quite common to see coca sellers slumped in stupor, their eyes half-closed, mouths hanging open to show a few blackened bits of tooth, or beggars or wandering vagabonds in lonely places in a similar state, perhaps from cold as well as from coca. There were many people, medical or not, who claimed that all the apparent hopelessness and helplessness of the Indians, their indolence, their dullness, lack of will, their stupidity or fatalism, were all a result of coca. But no amount of such talk could reduce the prevalence of the habit, or lessen the truth of coca's extraordinary effects, even taken in mild quantities.

I was told of a recent British Ambassador who, travelling in remote heights of the *cordillera*, encountered two Indian men walking across the cloudy waste with a herd of llamas. His party stopped them, to ask where they had come from.

"Over there across the hills," said one with a vague gesture.

"How long have you been travelling?"

"Eleven days."

"But what have you eaten?"

"Coca."

One night, soon after our arrival in La Paz, I woke in the small hours sweating and shivering: my body throbbed with echoing thuds from my heart and I struggled to breathe. Convinced I was going to die, I roused everyone hysterically, and a doctor, young and glamorous and fresh from a high-powered training in the United States, appeared armed with stethoscope and pressure gauges. He was very thorough and calm and talked continuously with soothing encouragement; then pronounced that I was strong and healthy and had nothing to fear.

"You must just drink as much as possible of *maté de coca*." (The tisane from coca leaves.)

"But I don't want to become an addict," I said indignantly.

"Oh no," he laughed, "to do that you would have to eat two and a half kilos of coca leaves, and that is a pile *this* high," he indicated some three feet from the floor. "No, you do not need to worry. In Bolivia, we all drink *maté de coca*. It is excellent for many troubles."

And so we took to the leaf. Sleeping badly, digesting badly, we drank *maté de coca* after any meal, or at the onset of any of the "many troubles". Pale green and insipid, far from a pleasure to drink, and not aromatic like other herbal tisanes, we found it served in many Bolivian households, passed round as an alternative to coffee—and soon took to doing the same ourselves.

In mild quantities like this it bore no more resemblance to the dread cocaine than poppy-seed on bread loaves does to opium, and when one day the diplomatic arena was rocked by the dramatic arrest of the Mexican Ambassador to La Paz, caught by the American police in New Orleans, his diplomatic bag stuffed with ninety million dollars' worth of cocaine, we even found ourselves ludicrously surprised that he could have obtained it in Bolivia, and the innocent pathos of the coca-women became suddenly overladen with the sinister aura of international vice.

V

Responsibilities and Fiestas

MAGDALENA, THE HOUSEMAID, was no *mestizo* but a full-blooded Indian *chola* who spoke Aymhara, Quechua, and very tolerable Spanish. At the interview when I employed her, she wore a pretty green shawl, green skirt, green shoes and bowler hat; her hair was braided into two neat black pigtails, and she had gold earrings which shook and glittered as she moved her head. The tilt of her eyes was exactly right, and they shone, black and soft, in her lovely ochre face with an expression of such sweetness and sadness that I found myself making a long stammering speech about how I hoped I would make her feel happy with us.

In the house she wore a blue overall and tied her pigtails back out of the way with black wool. But when she went back to her home high up near Villa Victoria for a weekend, a fiesta or her day off, she dressed in the height of *chola* fashion—with the greatest attention to the colour of her skirts and shoes, and to the position of the gold brooch that pinned the folds of her shawl upon her breast. I discovered that she had no less than eight different-coloured bowler hats.

"*Para variar la moda, señora,*" she explained. ("To vary the fashion.")

Magdalena was forty and unmarried—sweet, demure and slow, in fact rather lazy. She liked to sit for long hours in the sun, gossiping *sotto voce* with the Señora Lavandera, or with her sister Teresa, who was even more attractive than she, and came frequently with her small son to pass the afternoon or evening, and partake of whatever meal was in progress. Teresa it seemed, did not work, for she had to look after her little boy—and their mother who was very old and never left the house. So I presumed that Magdalena was somehow

70

supporting all of them on her salary, though Juana, grumbling about her landlord, remarked that Magdalena's family were quite rich. "At least they own their own house, Señora. They have nothing to fear but the *derrumbas*."

Both Teresa and Magdalena were very proud of the small boy. His mother knew how to read and write a little and was teaching him herself as he was not yet of school age. He would bring his "work" to show me—small pink-covered notebooks, filled with wobbly letters in rows, page after page. I was very impressed, and tried to encourage him, and sometimes gave him new notebooks and pencils, and a drawing-book and some paints—but he became shy and would not show me any pictures.

All of us thought Magdalena a little prim. When I asked her what she did on her days off she said she went to Church, which she liked, and that they sang and had processions and sometimes *fiestas*. She was always very shocked at the local scandals, burglaries and riots, and the dramas of politics.

She seemed tranquil and contented, and I thought we must indeed have made her happy. She even began to put on weight—too much weight, I thought one day as I counted her putting twelve potatoes on to her lunch plate.

I began to tease her about it, saying she had better give up potatoes or life would become very expensive with all the new clothes she would have to buy. And Magdalena just giggled shyly saying, "Señora," in a chiding way as she always did when we teased her, and went on clumping about the room.

But one day Juana began to tease her as well. "You'd better watch your figure," she said, "or people will start thinking you are pregnant."

"But I *am* pregnant," declared Magdalena in high-voiced protest.

So her secret was out and we were all very astonished, and rather peeved that we had been so hoodwinked. And I discovered that Magdalena had for some months now been attending a pre-natal clinic at an expensive American hospital nearby. The doctors told her that she was dangerously over-age to bear a first child (well over forty, they said), and she must certainly have the baby in hospital.

I asked Magdalena whether she now intended to get married, but she said, "No, señora."

"Well, what has happened to the father?" I harried, feeling I had a right to know, if I was to pay for this confinement.

"*Ha viajado, señora,*" came the reply. He had "travelled"—and that was that.

Juana had no idea who the father was either.

"But it was the same with la Teresa too, señora, the men never stay. And it will be nice for Magdalena to have a little baby, and company for her old age."

And suddenly I understood. For in a place like this who would care for the aged except their children? Bearing a child was like taking out an insurance policy; it was a defence against the bleak treacheries of time.

So Magdalena went on attending the clinic, and grew larger and slower as the weeks drew on. I gave her clothes for the baby, and in the market I bought her a large basket cradle and lined it with white cotton.

Her hour came one day when she was up visiting her home and she had to be taken down to the hospital in an ambulance. The birth took a very long time and in the end the doctors had to operate to save both the mother and the child. But they weathered these trials, and Magdalena was thrilled with the baby whom she named Miguelito José.

When they were discharged, I collected Magdalena and Miguelito, and drove them in the Land-Rover up to her house. Higher and higher through the city we went, leaving the paved and cobbled roads far behind, and rattling up stony alleys until the road swung round a corner and I was stopped by a steel-helmeted soldier with a machine-gun.

"This is a military barracks," he said. "You may not pass."

He was very threatening, and it took a lot of persuasion to be allowed the last fifty yards to the bottom of Magdalena's street. The latter was hardly more than a gully between two rows of houses. The hill sloped steeply, and down the centre ran a stream of stinking refuse-laden water. There was only about a foot of earth on either side to walk on, and one crossed over on wobbling planks flung across the gap.

The old mother—bent, white-haired and toothless—was standing at the door of the house waiting with Teresa and the little boy.

We teetered across a plank bridge with the precious burden, and through the street door, bending and climbing up the steps that led into a tiny courtyard not more than about four feet square. The place was made entirely of mud, hard-baked, smooth and unpainted. A narrow staircase led up one wall to an upper floor, and two little doors led to rooms off the courtyard. Through one of them Teresa led us proudly to the room she had prepared. It was small and dark, but neat, and cleanly swept. Most of the room was taken up by an enormous wardrobe. There was a bed for Magdalena, covered with several beautiful fur rugs, a table with a paraffin cooker, some saucepans and plastic bowls filled with water, and on a chest in the corner lay my cradle, ready for the baby.

Magdalena seemed quite dazed.

"What shall I do, señora?" she said. "What shall I do?"

Teresa took the baby, shook him a bit, and plumped him into his basket cradle, where he began to scream loudly.

"Soo, soo, soo," she crooned at him, and turned to me. "What shall we do now, señora?"

Magdalena sat on the bed looking helpless. Through the door I could see the old mother and the little boy sitting on wooden boxes in a small patch of sunlight.

I turned the baby on his side and tucked him in, and began to explain how to care for him, feed him, wash him, lay him down, keep everything clean, and the importance of giving him extra vitamins—producing, as I said so, a bottle of English vitamin drops.

I went on about the importance of boiling and sterilising, but they still looked so blank, and the process suddenly seemed so complicated, I could not envisage them boiling napkins on a one-ringed paraffin cooker in this altitude, where it took twenty minutes to boil even a tiny kettle of water.

The baby continued to scream and writhe.

"He's hungry," I said, picking him up, his little ochre face puckered with frenzy, his mouth gaping in search of milk.

"Give him the breast now, and I'm sure he will sleep," I said, handing him back to Magdalena. He calmed down at once, and I left them there, all looking puzzled and awed.

I went back to the hospital to see the doctors. What with the operation and the anaesthetic and the oxygen, the confinement came to a great deal of money. But Magdalena soon brought Miguelito José down to visit us, and he seemed to put on weight and do well, and her place in the house was taken by Teresa, who was just as charming but less efficient. And at Christmas, Magdalena gave us a beautiful little silver tray and a set of teaspoons with Inca patterns on them, which I have used ever since.

Our landlady when we took the house, had uttered many threats about the garden, and after I had struggled vainly for a few weeks, and failed to make any impression on the desert—the legacy of the previous tenants, the wilted plants and parched, cracked earth, impregnable to my efforts with a spade—she produced a gardener named Pablo, an Aymhara Indian who had worked for her in the good old days when the garden was a sight to behold. Pablo knew a thing or two, she said, which was more than most Indians, of whom she had a low opinion.

So Pablo joined our household, swept the hall daily with a besom, and polished the floors. He also introduced, as his constant companion, his small orphaned nephew Nicacho, whose parents had been killed by a landslide, and whom Pablo, his own children having grown up, had adopted. Nicacho was seven, and should have been at school—and indeed sometimes turned up in the afternoons in a grimy white smock with a tattered book under his arm. But most of the time it was holidays, or *fiestas*, or the aftermath of *fiestas*, or the school was on strike, and Nicacho stayed at our place to be kept out of mischief. I said that if we were feeding the child he must do a little work, which Pablo took seriously, and I would see Nicacho struggling down the lane behind our house with enormous barrow-loads of rubbish to be tipped into the river (where everyone's rubbish was tipped). He was made to spend hours weeding or watering, and chastised for chasing butterflies or disappearing to play and throw stones at stray dogs with his friends in the streets.

Then perhaps, someone would discover him snivelling in a dark shed where he had been sent as punishment, and after a while Juana would take pity on him and slip him a sweet or a biscuit.

Nicacho smelt very unpleasant. He had never, I was sure, been bathed and seldom washed—nor had his clothes. When this became quite overpowering, and everyone was complaining, I spoke to Pablo, and to his wife who came to call on me. It was very difficult to get water where they lived, she said, and the Señora must know how it was with boys—but it was quite apparent that she was not over-fond of the habit herself.

So, feeling rather tyrannical, I made a rule that Nicacho should wash, or be washed, daily in our house, and to indicate my seriousness offered the only threat I could think would hold weight with the child, that if he were dirty I would not allow him to play with Alexander. I also took him, alone, up to the Indian town, where he walked open-mouthed through the street markets, as he had never before been higher up the mountain than Obrajes; and we bought him some new clothes which were the first of his own he had ever had, and a bag of sweets and a paper windmill on a stick, and I felt like a fairy godmother with a little pang of guilt that I had given him his first real dose of temptation and destroyed some sort of innocence.

On my birthday, Pablo's wife appeared again. She had come to *felicitar* me, and greeted me after the Bolivian custom with an *abrazo*: we shook hands with both hands in turn, at the same time brushing cheeks as it were, and patting each other on the back with whichever hand was free. It was always necessary to brush both cheeks or gaze over both shoulders—and the Spanish Bolivian men particularly had developed many variants of the process, with a great deal of squeezing or back-patting, whichever fitted the occasion, or the sex of the recipient.

Pablo's wife presented me with a pair of drakes, and I was very touched. We cherished them carefully and let them walk about the garden, where they marched up and down the terrace in front of the big windows, doing elaborate courtship dances to their own reflections. They fattened well, Pablo eventually slaughtered them, and Magdalena plucked the feathers for a pillow.

I also found myself equipping Pablo with clothing, as he persuaded me that he needed to look like *un vero jardinero*, a true gardener. We made a joint expedition to bargain in the street markets for overalls and shirts and jeans for him, and a pair of Wellington boots for the rainy season.

With a great deal of digging and fertilising, pruning and watering, the garden began slowly to show some return. We dug in a lorryload of peat from the mountains, and went frequently to a small farm up the valley to buy sack-loads of manure.

And we held long discussions about everything in Bolivian Spanish, which was distinguished from other Latin American accents by its gentleness and clarity and the ubiquitous application of diminutives, a habit Pablo had developed to lyrical proportions. Whether adjectives or nouns, he spilt the diminutives about with unheeding generosity. One day as we discussed a flowerbed, he announced:

"*Aqui podemos poner un pequeñito arbolito, y una poquitita de hierbecita alrededorcita con florecitas*," which, if translated exactly, meant, "Here we can put a very little little tree, and a tiny little of little grass, little-surrounded with little flowers."

I was surprised at how many little flowers flourished in the altitude under Pablo's care. On the pergolas and porches round the house grew bougainvillaea and climbing roses, jasmine and geraniums, and Golden Shower; and that wonderful creeper from the subtropical valleys, *Cobea Scandens*, which survived the winters as an evergreen perennial, quickly covered a sunny wall and was hung for months on end with profusions of its gigantic pale purple bells. In shady places we had irises, montbretias and arum lilies, delphiniums of enormous size, hydrangeas, pansies and violets, while pinks, antirrhinums, daisies and nasturtiums would grow almost everywhere. We covered the macrocarpa hedges with sweet peas, and I pruned a group of tatty standard roses so hard I thought they had died until suddenly they sprouted when the rains came, with long sprays of new growth three feet or more in length, covered with bloom, until they towered above us like young trees. We also had a little herb garden, which was not a great success, and inevitably a potato patch; and a cutting garden where Pablo grew beautiful dahlias and rather disapproved of my taste for cosmos. There were some fruit trees which bore a few gnarled apples and pears, tall clumps of hollyhocks, and a row of gladioli which I had always disliked, but tolerated as they were irresistible to humming-birds.

We saw very few birds up here, except sparrows, some noisy jackdaws, and a few hawks that wheeled lazily about above the river. But when the gladioli were in bloom, the humming-birds would appear from nowhere, flashing across the sunlit garden in a whirr of brilliance to hover before the garish flowers, sip from one or two, and dart away again. We could not see where they went, nor study their form, as they never perched on the flowers but only paused a brief instant before each, the whirring of their minute wings blurring a tiny circle about them like mist, or like a halo, so that they seemed magical, little pinpoints of light too bright to look at. The Bolivians called them *picaflores*, which was also the name for a fickle girl, or a flirt, and so teasing and capricious were they I could wait immobile for hours until the breathless moment when the dart of colour appeared; yet, at a blink of the eyes, it could vanish and leave me wondering if it had happened at all, or had I perhaps just been staring too hard into the sun. It became a tortuous game, and one lay in wait like a lover for this ecstasy of vision, and suffered the same sense of loss.

Pablo's true love of the soil struggled valiantly and often vainly with the other great love of his life which was *chicha*, the Indian maize beer. When the first flush of gardening excitement was over, he began to complain of dreadful *mal d'estómago*, stomach ache, which was so bad it kept him at home now and then. Deeply sympathetic, for had not I too suffered such pain in this terrible altitude, I offered remedies which he took obediently—but which had no effect. When I suggested a visit to the doctor he became wary and said coca was a better cure. It took some time for us to notice that the illness always struck on Monday. When it repeatedly lasted through Tuesday as well, David made a great show of anger and accused him of being a *tomador* (or habitual drunkard), an appellation with which Pablo meekly agreed, and we thereafter had to make a habit of bidding him a very fierce and threatening good-bye each weekend.

I had read somewhere that under the Incas the conquered peoples of the Andes had been given one week a month as holiday, for relaxing, feasting and drinking. Pablo gave no reason to doubt that he was the true inheritor of Inca colonial tolerance.

In fact the Spanish invaders, too, seemed to have taken with alacrity to this system, and Bolivia must have had at least twenty official public holidays, to say nothing of the unofficial ones such as the local saints' days and *fiestas*. Anyone trying to conduct business or any other sort of relations had to keep all of these constantly in mind, and be tactful about the two or three days following any major festivity, which were days of painful recovery and might even take as much as a whole week—all of which was very frustrating to some hard-working northern Europeans and North Americans accustomed to a more puritanical conscientiousness and prompt service.

At the time of *Carnaval*, for instance, everything closed for five days, people danced in the streets, and nothing could be had in the city at all except in the *Alecitas*. This was the big fair and street market up above the Plaza San Francisco, where among all the contraband, the blankets, clothes and pottery that were an accepted part of any market, were stalls selling miniatures of every conceivable object—clothes, food, domestic appliances, for this was the festival of the *Ekeko*, a gnome-like creature who was believed to trudge about like a pedlar with goods upon his back, bringing good luck to those who deserved it. So people bought little *Ekeko* dolls to bring luck to their houses, and miniature models of all the things they most desired, to hang upon the *Ekeko*'s back. Children danced everywhere, and boys threaded among the crowds playing pipes of Pan and reed flutes, and everyone who had a stall shouted at the crowds to buy, while the air hung heavy with smells of frying sausages and dough-nuts, *empanadas* (little envelopes of pastry filled with hot chili stew), and honey cakes and roasted nuts.

The feast of San Juan was another great holiday. For days before-hand people collected wood; it came up by the lorry-load to be sold in the city at ridiculous prices, and those who could not afford it chopped up old chairs, tables or boxes, anything to make up the bonfire which every householder built, to placate the saint and (for it was the dry season) to pray for rain. In the last red glow of sun-down, the fires were lit and gallons of kerosene thrown about to get a good blaze, and people danced round the fires or sat beside them keeping warm and watching the flames for some omen of their hopes or fears. So bright were the fires, and so many, in every boulevard or alley, that the street lights glimmered through the smoke like ships lost in a fog, and people coughed, sneezed and wept in the pinching fumes which clung in their clothes and their hair, and hung in a huge pall over the city. The next day was like a northern twilight with the sun a bleak, peering yellow blob, and it was three days before a wind came up to blow away the smoke.

The Bolivians were proud of their *fiestas*. Was not Oruro (they would say), that dull town of the tin-miners, famous throughout the continent for its *Carnaval*, second only to that of Rio?

The Oruro *Carnaval* and *Diablada*, or devil dance, had become almost a subject for pilgrimage. People streamed there from all over the country and endured any discomfort, sleeping on the floors of hotel foyers or in school halls, or in their cars in the perishing *altiplano* night to stand in the streets all day watching the dancers whirling by. They would gape at the anonymous figures dressed as bears or condors, priests or *conquistadores*, or wearing the famous devil masks; and they would watch the processions of floats and cars covered in pieces of silver plate, jugs, platters, bowls, which were all very old and had belonged to Indian families for generations and were kept, for the most part, hidden in nooks and crannies or under mattresses, only coming out once a year to be shown off at *Carnaval*.

Any festival or occasion—a wedding or a funeral—was an excuse for dancing, and it always surprised and disappointed me how badly the Indians danced. The bands, with their reed flutes and pipes, twanging banjoes and buzzers, tambourines and drums, never seemed quite able to get hold of the tune or the rhythm, and completely lacked the ability to improvise. And the dancers had neither passion nor grace, though only a little passion would have improved things, but hopped and shuffled, often too far gone to care anyway. And this all seemed odd, because the Spanish tradition was so different, and the Spanish-Bolivian dances were full of rhythm, charm and coquetry, and it was unthinkable among them not to know the national dances, as well as those of other neighbouring countries and all the great Latin American dances which were danced everywhere to the exclusion of whatever was fashionable in Europe.

Yet for all this the Indians were indefatigable dancers, and could keep up the hop-shuffle until they lost consciousness or no one else was left, whichever came first. And Pablo was as devoted as the best.

When Pablo's little village, which was in the hills above Obrajes, had its annual festival, one man was chosen to be host for the celebrations. While this was considered a great honour, it was also a great burden, as the host had then to organise the dance, hire a band, hire costumes for the chief dancers, and provide food and drink and general hospitality for everyone for as long as the festivities lasted, which was usually two or three days. It was all a very expensive business, in fact it could leave a man broke, or in debt for a long time, though the more prudent kept savings for the purpose.

Pablo was not thrifty, so when he was chosen for this honour he was a little panic-stricken. He borrowed several months' pay from us, and the only large tree in his village, which happened to be in his yard, was cut down to make room for the dancers and sold for fire-wood. For several days before the feast he failed to appear for work, being far too busy with the preparations.

I never knew how much Pablo paid for the costumes, but it must have been a very large sum. I heard from some missionaries how in a remote Indian village beyond Lake Titicaca, probably over the border in Peru, they had an annual festival for the "dance of the Condors", where the costumes, fantastic creations with capes and headdresses of enormous exotic feathers, were almost sacred, and handed down from generation to generation, and to hire only one costume for one day cost a man the equivalent of £30.

It was round about this time that Pablo took me to the street market of the *fiestas*. We left the Land-Rover somewhere in the Indian town on a forty-five-degree slope, and climbed slowly higher up little winding alleys, to reach at last a long, narrow lane, quite level, and crowded as though there were a permanent fun fair. It must have been every Indian child's dream of paradise. One little shop after another was filled with toys and musical instruments, *Ekeko* dolls and all their miniature pedlar-wares, baskets and bird-cages, spinning tops and go-carts, all in a bright, heaped jumble.

Woman in Tarija

Café group in Roboré

Sunset in Beni

There were whole shops devoted to nothing but fireworks, with catherine wheels and sparklets festooned across their entrance like the paper-chains of Christmas. Others sold sweets and honey-cakes, and candles decorated with pink and green flowers to burn for patron saints or the Blessed Virgin, and little holy pictures in piles between the caramel toffees, gazing blandly up at devil masks hanging in the rafters. And there were stalls of costumes, though the best costumes could never be bought, and wide counters spread with sequins and buttons and glittering twine, ribbons, beads and streamers and endless coloured baubles for sewing on coats or hats, for the Indians, while hopeless dancers, had an extraordinary eye for colour and decoration, and it became increasingly clear to me that the object of the dance was simply to move enough to show off the costumes, and jump about to make the baubles shake and shine.

Pablo's feast was a great success. The yard, even without the tree, soon became too small, and they jogged and jostled and tootled their way down the hill to the main street, where they shuffled down to Calacoto and then back up to Obrajes, and back to Calacoto, and so on for about two days—resting by turns in crumpled heaps in the gutter. Some wore small devil masks, with white tunics covered with glitter, and there were women with gaudy sequinned skirts, and hats covered with shaking streamers, and the condor with bird-head, the *conquistador* in tin breastplate and helmet, and several clowns with blackened faces. I suspected Pablo was the bear, who looked very stuffy and uncomfortable, tottering about, and falling down most of them all.

His recovery was gloomy and taciturn, with a suggestion of disillusion, but it was not long before he was himself again, and went out with an air of importance one afternoon, waving a large tin, saying we needed more kerosene. Later I heard piping and drumming in the distance, and walked up the valley, past the tin, now lying in a hedge, to find a little wedding procession winding along with Pablo in its wake.

I followed them at a distance to a walled field, where an arbour for the bridal pair had been made from canopies of calico. Some girls were walking about with jugs of *chicha*, and in a corner there were cakes and doughnuts on a trestle, with boxes to sit on. The bride and

F

bridegroom, she in white, with pink and green sequins bobbing and glittering, and he in tight yellow knee-breeches, with a white sequinned doublet, stood in the arbour, while there was a great deal of discussion and embracing. The company thinned out to eat in groups, the men on one side, women on the other; then the band struck up again, and the dancing began. The guests jogged about among the costumed dancers, and a small boy dressed as a clown or jester, hopped between them all, jostling and tumbling them over, and thumping the bridegroom who soon slumped in a corner, past caring. And near him I could see Pablo propped asleep against the wall.

After a while I walked away back down the valley, the thin music of the band growing fainter, and the cliffs moving darkly nearer as the sun set and the first stars came out.

VI

New Friends

WE FOUND OURSELVES moving between various distinct social groups in La Paz. The Diplomatic Corps, the Americans, the British community, the various *émigré* groups, and Bolivian society itself—all had their own identities and particular pursuits, and it was only large, official functions that brought all kinds together.

The Diplomatic Corps could be seen *en masse* at big embassy occasions, such as national days. We would stand in the long queues of guests, waiting to be received by the celebrating ambassador, and shuffling slowly past the rows of congratulatory bouquets which invariably flanked the driveway and steps—small squat vases stuffed with enormous sprays of gladioli, stiff and garish, their leaves always painted a festive silver. Once inside it was impossible to move against the crowd as it swept in waves towards the refreshment table.

At one such party I found myself in the corner of a marquee, wedged firmly between the table and the Cuban cultural attaché.

"What on earth am I going to say to him?" I thought. "What do I know about Cuba? How terrible, I know nothing about Cuban literature. Who are the Cuban writers? I can't ask him about the Leyland buses, I can't really tell him that I admire Castro. I wonder if the Cubans have a dossier on us, because we have lived behind the Iron Curtain? Shall I start talking about Hemingway? No, he must be sick of Hemingway." I felt stifled.

"*Señora buenos dias*," he bowed slightly, looking me straight in the eye, his handsome, tanned face only inches from mine; and I realised that throughout these panicky thoughts I had been smiling at him.

"You are hot?" he went on, "I will find you a drink. *Mozo!*

Aqui, aqui!" he called to some unseen waiter. A tray with two glasses of champagne suddenly appeared over the heads of the crowd.

"How clever, you must know the waiters," I said.

"Oh, he is my friend! *Salud!*" We drank, eyeing one another, and then each took a cheese sandwich. The cheese was like fondue, thick and stringy; it stuck one's teeth together. Suddenly our shared discomfort was hilarious; we chuckled until we choked, coughed until we wept, and then had more champagne to recover, until the crowd burst abruptly between us, and we were swept to opposite sides of the garden.

From time to time David and I would come away from these occasions thinking how absurd they had been, and that surely the English version must be better managed. But retribution came at the Queen's birthday party.

At first everything went smoothly enough, not very many of the bouquets were knocked over, not too many bricks dropped, nor waiters visibly drunk. Members of the Chancery and their wives darted about, giddy with all the introductions, and with the sun and champagne.

"The drink's all right, thank God," hissed the administration officer as he passed me.

"Yes," I said. "Why, were you worried?"

"Worried? Ha! Last year some crafty thief at the coast went through the whole consignment, cutting the bottoms off the bottles and sealing them again invisibly. Half the guests got sea-water to drink."

We were called to attention by the Ambassador at the microphone. In a long, eloquent torrent of Spanish he welcomed his guests, regretted that the President himself had been unable at the last minute to come, but rejoiced that the Foreign Minister had come instead, to join us on this great occasion when we celebrated the birthday of our Queen. Amid loud applause he edged the Minister gently towards the microphone.

In all formality the Minister should then, after the appropriate gracious words, have proposed a toast to the Queen; but perhaps he felt disinclined, for he clutched the microphone so that his voice growled horribly, and delivered a loud declamation on political ideals, in which he never quite reached the subject of *la reina Elisabeta* at all, and ended with a loud cry:

"Viva Bolivia!"

We all duly drank and murmured. A little ruffled, the Ambassador managed skilfully to bring the Queen into his answering speech, and to toast the President at the same time, and we all drank and murmured again. A band hidden somewhere inside the house struck up the Bolivian national anthem, which came blaring out into the garden, and lasted a very long time. It was followed by a trembling version of "God Save the Queen", and as the last bars creaked out everyone began to relax and chatter after these tense and stirring moments, only to jump to attention again as the melody was repeated.

"Perhaps the conductor is ashamed of having played so badly, and wants to make a better effort," I thought. But he must simply have decided that the tune was not long enough, for it began yet again with ruthless cacophony. The Minister looked at the sky, the Ambassador slowly turned purple, while his secretaries all tried at once to push through the crowd to the house. The tune started for the fifth time, "God save our . . .", and then came to an abrupt stop.

There is an unmistakable flavour about "the English way of life" abroad. It is characterised by a remarkable channelling of energy into providing local substitutes for both the housework and the social excitements of life in England. Sales in aid of local charities, sewing afternoons or cookery demonstrations, play-readings or even Scottish dancing provide a bulwark against the boredom, isolation and self-doubt of life in a foreign community. Members of the Railway Company in La Paz, and of the Cable and Wireless, and other companies, generally did longer tours of duty in Bolivia than diplomats; and many of their wives devoted themselves to these functions with great enthusiasm. One enterprising girl wrote and produced a revue, in which she persuaded several members of the embassy to take part, and the few diplomats who attended were surprised to see Drake, the commercial attaché, dressed as a turbanned Indian fakir, and David doing a cross between the twist and a Cossack knee-dance in a kilt of the Anderson tartan.

There was a timeless air about the old railway houses, with their wooden verandahs and dark, high-ceilinged rooms smelling of furniture polish. One had morning tea on the lawn, with English tea in silver teapots, and hot scones in chafing dishes. The sun shone as bright as a childhood dream; a garden hose, that emblem of established wealth, snaked away across the grass, and from round a corner came the low, almost metallic splatter of water falling on to the leaves of nasturtiums.

"I can't think what this place is coming to," Nell would complain as we sat munching and pouring, and crumpling little embroidered napkins between our fingers. "The government never stops talking about controlling contraband, and keeping the prices down. But I had to pay 12,000 bolivianos a kilo for meat this morning—and I never had to count the change in the old days. It's all these Americans —they simply don't care how much they spend. Look how the Bolivians fleece them!"

"Of course, the government thinks it can get everything for nothing," remarked one of her guests. "Do you know, only last week some men came from the World Bank to arrange a loan, and I have this on authority, the Ministry of Finance were delighted until they found they would have to pay the money back. Well, they didn't get the loan, at least the World Bank's got its head screwed on."

"They just get worse and worse," Nell went on, "all these good solid working peasants they put into government posts—why, most of them can hardly read or write! I ask you, how can you run a country like that?"

And the guest sighed and regretted the departure of the good old families.

"Mind you, even they were bad at times," Nell allowed, "but still, surely it was stupid just to banish all the tin tycoons instead of keeping them here and forcing them to pay to develop the country."

"That's a very dashing hairdo, Betty," someone interrupted, "don't tell me you still go to that dreadful virago at the Crillon?"

And Betty patted her hair and giggled, for Rita, who presided over the beauty saloon at one of the luxury hotels, was an incomparable source of gossip. Her devoted clientele turned a blind eye to the shortcomings of her establishment, although they might arrive to find Rita and her girls at *siesta*, lying massively in their grubby overalls on the floor of the salón among the unswept hair snippings.

Betty Solares was among those who accepted and relished Bolivian life, and had no illusions that things could possibly be better if she were in England. She had married a gay, handsome Bolivian businessman whom she had met at Sheffield University, and they now had four attractive daughters. Occasionally she went back to visit her mother somewhere in Cumberland, and returned to her adopted home with no regrets.

"My dear, I couldn't bear to live there," she confided to me one day over the bridge table, flicking the cards about with exquisitely manicured fingers. "I mean, it's such dreadfully hard work. Do you know how old I am? Forty, my dear, not a day less, and all my friends there, the girls I grew up with, look so old, like grannies—I couldn't bear it. And what's it all for? They never see each other, just sit in their little houses, slaving at the sink. And of course there's nothing like the family life you have here. You should see the clan I've married into—the quarrels, the dramas! I love it. Four clubs? Do you really mean it? Well, doubled, my dear . . ." and her hands fluttered across the table to collect one trick after another.

Bridge in La Paz was a major female occupation. It was quite usual to arrive at a tea-party to find oneself summarily placed in an intense foursome, with tea served at the card-table, and play continuing until seven or eight in the evening. The only comparable equivalent for men was golf. The course lay about five miles beyond Calacoto, reached along a precarious dirt road through a desert fantasy of eroded cliffs. It was like an oasis on the moon, the green sward surrounded on all sides by grey-brown, echoing cliffs. Playing was sensational, as a smart blow, however amateur, met so little air resistance that it could send the ball whirling off towards the distant peaks, perhaps never to be seen again: it made the game expensive, but most satisfying.

I sometimes took a picnic out to the golf course, and would invariably see Morris striding past, either alone, or with some other enthusiast. Morris managed to play golf almost every afternoon, and also to be a very successful businessman. He owned several small but productive mines, and had somehow or other managed to survive the nationalisations of the last revolution. Morris admitted that he found life very pleasant. He had a comfortable house in La Paz, and kept a yacht on Lake Titicaca. He sent his two children to school in England, and travelled to and fro several times a year. He had always planned to retire in Bolivia, until the government's socialist reforms really began to alarm him.

"If things get much worse I suppose I'll have to pull out," he admitted. "But I don't exactly relish the thought of an English retirement. How can I go back to green-belt golf courses after this?"

There was another Englishman in La Paz, a delightful old gentleman who had come to South America in his youth in search of adventure. This he had found in such measure that a return to England was unthinkable, particularly after the irrevocable step of acquiring a South American wife. The rumours about him, stories of intrigue in high politics, twisting the arms of presidents, slipping unnoticed across borders, disappearing when things became too hot, all reached romantic heights from which it was quite impossible to descend to the truth. One story most often repeated was that he had spent several years in prison somewhere after being caught gun-running; and another recalled how in the old days he used to have a standing order with a jeweller in Buenos Aires, who sent large consignments of gold cigarette-cases up to La Paz in the train "because they made such useful presents".

One might have expected him, as the years crept on, to become frustrated by the waning of his powers, and want to escape from it all to a gentler and more tranquil life, but he was in love with the place. La Paz, it seemed, was littered with beautiful houses that he had built for himself, selling one in a move to escape, only to return and build another. He lived now in the last of these, perched on a cliff at the top of a small pass. It was filled with his collections of porcelain and silver, and had a view of the whole city, the lower valleys, the cliffs and the *cordillera*.

We met him once at the airport, bound for Lima on some business, immaculate in a black homburg and *vicuña* coat.

"Take a last look at the mountains," he said as we walked out on to the runway. "Incredible place, isn't it? Do you know—you won't believe it, but I've actually packed up and left La Paz for good seven

times. Off we went, to Argentina, Peru, Spain, and each time I had
to come back. It's like a magnet, a drug. I dream about it. I really
cannot live without that view."

I said, "You've found the ideal place for a house this time though."

"Yes," he climbed heavily up the steps to the aircraft, and looked
again at the peaks. "Yes. I'm getting old now, and things are not
what they were. Life is often sad. But I can look out every day and
see that whole world before me. It's like being a bird—or a god.
I suppose that's the whole illusion." And groaning a little, he bent
into the doorway, as if grudgingly resigning himself to his week's
exile by the sea.

Bolivia at this time stood fourth on Britain's priority list of "aid
to underdeveloped countries outside the Commonwealth". But
dignity dictated that this could not be straightforward financial aid:
in the shadow of the dollar, anything Britain could afford to send
would appear pitiably small. So Whitehall had had to think of more
ingenious and practical means of distributing largesse. These took
the form of peripheral groups attached to the Embassy: nothing as
doctrinaire as "missions", they were teams of experts, and of Youth.

The youth team was part of the Voluntary Service Overseas and
consisted mostly of teenagers between school and university, some
of whom were earnest and thorough, others feckless adventurers.
They taught English, and occasionally football or carpentry, in
schools and colleges, and were in theory employed and paid for by
the Bolivian government. It was often uphill work for them: their
quarters were uncomfortable, their pupils not interested, or their
pay so erratic that they quickly fell into debt. Almost all of them
landed at one time or another in scrapes which they thought it the
duty of the Embassy to sort out. Some would turn up suddenly from
distant towns, and indignation at their greedy and graceless acceptance of hospitality in the form of comfortable beds and large meals
echoed in their wake as they departed, with rugs, vacuum flasks
and even money "borrowed" for the journey back.

Even Fitzwarren, who was loyally optimistic about them, became
disillusioned when two girls gave a rowdy party in a borrowed
house and telephoned him at five in the morning, sobbing with
terror, as some drunken Bolivians whom they had turned out

of the house had returned and were smashing the windows with bricks.

"One of them's got a gun," they cried, "we can see he has, and we don't know how to get the police." And Fitzwarren swore, and composed himself in his knight-errant garb of heavy tweed suit with wide flapping trouser-legs and Brigade of Guards tie, and charged in his Land-Rover the six miles up the dawn-dark mountain to make a furious rescue in his best Guards-officer Spanish.

McEwen led a team of experts on tropical agriculture. He was a cynical survivor of the Colonial era, who had gained his expertise in Africa. Erudite and fascinating on his pet subject of tropical fauna and flora, McEwen was ever ready for long discussions about the wild life of the Bolivian lowland forests, the scarcity of animals compared with Africa, but the inestimably greater wealth of plant life. He would spend days climbing about cliffs in search of orchids or new plants which had not yet been classified, and bring them back to La Paz to wilt and be examined beside large botanical encyclopaedias.

Most of his team lived in remote villages teaching the villagers tropical agriculture, and rarely appeared in La Paz. Sometimes when pay-day came round, the Embassy accountant had to go down to the forests in search of them, and they were very elusive, which frightened him as he was only accustomed to urban life, and found even La Paz quite alarming. He would set off bravely in a Land-Rover, from Santa Cruz for instance, drive thirty-five miles along a narrow track through increasingly impenetrable forest, then stop, sound the horn long and loudly, three times, and wait, crouching tense and watchful at the wheel as the noises of the wild drummed ever louder in his ears. And at last, after half-an-hour or more, there would be a great crashing and thumping among the trees and some blond giant with thick boots and a long beard, and a doctorate in botany or agricultural economics, would appear, peeling his way through the undergrowth.

Meanwhile, Allenby and his team of customs experts found themselves in another jungle. On the assumption that British customs officials were the most efficient in the world, they had been sent out to teach the Bolivians a thing or two, and found themselves at once amidst the violence and corruption that lay at the core of Bolivian life.

We ourselves had felt bitter when, after months, our heavy luggage, so carefully filled with all the stores the post report had recommended, arrived, and we found it had been broken into. Every suitcase had its top slashed open and the contents rifled, while cases of drink, still sealed with steel bands but suspiciously light, turned out to contain perhaps half a bottle of liqueur and one chipped cup left by some celebrating thief.

But Allenby's experience had been even more unpleasant. Coming for a tour of four years with his wife and three children, he had shipped his entire household. He found a passable house and at last his luggage was delivered. The two enormous crates had to be opened by a carpenter, but were completely empty; and as a final irony, Allenby had to pay for the crates to be taken away.

In a country where more than half of the population was illiterate and outside the money economy, any conventional form of taxation was bound to be neither successful nor productive, and as Bolivia's land-locked state and lack of industry made a great many imports essential, a custom duty on every object that entered the country, from machinery to toothpaste, should have been the government's logical and major source of income.

But unfortunately, human nature being what it is, the machinery of imposition and collection became a major source of income to many of the country's citizens as well, and the evasion of the whole process provided the daily bread of a great many more. Everyone in La Paz knew where and how to buy contraband goods, and most people knew how to get them into the country. The vast borders were impossible to man properly, the roads dangerous and slow to cover; landslides were frequent, lorries easy to hire, officials easy to bribe, and so many people were in the pay or under the threat of someone else, that it was hardly a wonder only a pitiful trickle of income made its way via unnumbered pockets into the nation's coffers.

When they discovered that on top of all this a certain Cabinet minister ran the biggest smuggling business in the country, the customs team bit their stiff upper lips and wondered how on earth to begin. But they had not become experts at London Airport, or the docks of Liverpool, Tilbury or Southampton, for nothing, or without acquiring a certain dogged courage. So they began somewhere, which was by trying to train a small nucleus of officials in honesty and the methods of detecting dishonesty, and supplying them with enough emblems of status like uniforms, arms and Land-Rovers, to enable them to pursue their duties and avoid temptation. By the end of two years they had trained about 200, which was thought to be a considerable achievement, even if they were still unable to know whether the taxes were really reaching the nation's coffers, because they could not keep track of all the other pockets along the line.

Being the director of the whole ambitious operation, Allenby had to travel about the country a good deal to see how things were progressing in the out-back where the borders were. At Guayaram-erin in the Beni, the frontier was formed by the river Mamoré, a main tributary of the Amazon. On the opposite bank lay Guajará Mirim, a twin town, but in Brazil. Here Allenby found himself in a very uncomfortable dilemma. He had flown down on one of his usual tours of inspection, and was sitting one evening at a pavement café in the main square of Guayaramerin. The heat was a welcome contrast to the frosts of the capital, and he sipped with relish at his beer, which was an expensive indulgence here, as it had been flown down from La Paz.

Suddenly he noticed several priests walking across the square. They caught his eye, perhaps, because they were so many, four altogether, and they moved, marched almost, with such an air of purpose, quite out of keeping with the climate. They came straight across the square to his table. Allenby was a Catholic, so naturally he greeted them politely and asked them to join him in a drink. They asked for beer, and Allenby ordered some bottles of the La Paz brew.

"Oh, please do not worry," urged one of the priests, "the beer from Guajará Mirim is so much cheaper."

"Yes, but it is not as good," said Allenby pointedly, firmly repeating his order. So they drank each other's health, and the noises of the town and the river, the trees and the insects, swirled softly about them.

Allenby could feel them summing him up, and at last the eldest-looking of the group leaned forward.

"I understand you are a Catholic, Señor Allenby," he began casually.

"Yes, Padre," Allenby wondered how they had found out so soon.

"That is very good to hear. I hope we shall see you at Mass tomorrow. It is the day of the *patrona* of Guajará Mirim, over the water there. You are surprised? Oh, yes, it is in Brazil of course. But what is that to the blessed Lord, or the *santa patrona*? The river is simply a fact of geography, a convenience of politics."

The padre's voice was light, measured and civilised. The night noises engulfed them again, and a warm, scented breeze eddied through the square.

"I understand, Señor Allenby, that you are an expert for the British government in—ah—*aduanas*, in finding the *contrabandistas*, no?"

"Yes, Padre."

"Yes. That is very good, there are a great many very bad *contrabandistas*, very corrupt. They exploit the people. They need to be caught, to be exposed, to be stopped. You are making a tour—ah—of inspection, no?"

"Yes, Padre."

"Yes. Well, I must tell you—we have all come to tell you—that here—*aqui*—is not the place to make this inspection. You must leave it out of your plans. What effect in any case does it have on the rest of the country, what the people do here? Guayaramerin is very small, Señor Allenby, and Laz Paz is very far away. But Guajará Mirim—Brazil—is very near, and half the people are related. Contraband is their life. Without it they would starve, the people here would die. The good Lord knows that we would never willingly transgress the law, Señor, but food is more important than taxes. We have our duty to our flock."

"I understand, Padre."

"Good. I am sure you are a good Catholic, Señor Allenby, and I am sorry to have to speak of this, but if you do try to stop contraband here, I am afraid we shall have to excommunicate you."

And as there was no more to say, the padres rose, murmuring

their thanks and blessings, and strode away into the soft tropical darkness.

With all the other good Catholics in the town, Allenby went to Mass the next morning, and lit a candle to the patron saint of the town across the river. And he prayed to her for enlightenment and patience.

Allenby and his wife came to lunch sometimes, and we would discuss his latest adventures. He was always trying to puzzle out the motives behind the corruption he came across, and to relate them to all the paradoxes of Bolivian nature.

"I suppose we'll understand it one day," he mused as we sat drinking coffee in the sun. "One day perhaps we'll be able to look back and see a pattern, and perhaps then we'll have answers to why they are so sentimental and clannish and yet do each other down at every turn, why they are filled with grandiose ideas of patriotism and humanity and will die for a slogan, and yet are incapable of the self-discipline needed to make the country work; or why they so adore children and are yet so incomparably ruthless and cruel.

"Of course, so much of it is simply economics," he went on. "Look at the post office. We all know quite well that everyone who is not privileged to use a diplomatic bag has to slip at least 10,000 bolivianos (about 7s.) across the counter to get a parcel out. And why are there no deliveries of letters? No one would ever receive them, and with most of the Indians earning per week what it costs to buy a couple of stamps for an airmail letter, what can you expect?"

And we went on to discuss *machismo* and *caudillo* and the concepts of dignity and insult, or the latest examples of cold blood and cruelty.

The story was well known of how Bolivia had been struck off all the maps printed in late nineteenth-century England. Angered by rumours of amusement and derision in society at his marriage to a *chola*, a certain Bolivian President arranged a ceremony of homage where everybody who was anybody was commanded to come and salute his wife. When the English Minister Plenipotentiary, arriving in all his regalia, discovered that these salutations were to be made to the bare behind of the woman in question, he refused to comply. The President, declaring himself and his country insulted, had the

Minister stripped and whipped and hounded out of the country seated naked on the back of an ass.

When Queen Victoria heard of these disgraceful goings-on she is reputed to have commanded that a gunboat be sent to punish Bolivia.

But someone pointed out that since the recent war with Chile, Bolivia no longer had any coastline which a gunboat could threaten. Whereupon the monarch simply had Bolivia's name and territory "erased" from all maps, and Englishmen were left with no obligation to know that such a country even existed.

Less well known perhaps were the tales of the blood-letting after one recent revolution, when the deposed president and his cohorts had been hanged upon lamp-posts in the main square of La Paz. People had come from miles around to symbolise some personal need for revenge by sticking pins into the corpses and then sucking the pins in their mouths.

A week did not go by in La Paz without some tale of violence. Two peasant leaders had a fight at the entrance of the Ministry of Agriculture, and each shot the other dead on the steps. A lawyer of the political party in power lost his temper on the way home one night, and killed a taxi-driver. On the day of the funeral, all taxi-drivers went on strike, and all bus-drivers struck in sympathy, paralysing the city, and the taxi-drivers made a solemn declaration that after the funeral they would all go and blow up the lawyer's house. Whether they did or not was never related. Some new scandal arose, and this one was forgotten.

David was intrigued by Allenby's work, and accepted with enthusiasm when Allenby one day invited him to join an inspection-tour to Roboré and Puerto Suarez in the distant province of Santa Cruz. They were to fly to the town of Santa Cruz, and then journey by train.

The Santa Cruz–Roboré railway was almost a legend, a pioneering enterprise that had been built long ago. A single track ran dead straight for 400 miles, ending at Corumbá, just across the border in Brazil. The engine of the train ran on wood; instead of coal-trucks there were large loads of logs, and if by some ill chance the supply ran out, the train would simply stop until crew and passengers, armed with axes, had collected enough fuel from the forest to continue. It took the train a full week to do the journey there and back, and I hardly expected to see David within a fortnight.

But he, Allenby, and an army colonel who had somehow joined them, travelled in comfort in a small, noisy motor car, with its wheels adapted to run on the rails. The driver revealed after an hour or so that the vehicle's brakes did not work. He slowed the pace by changing gear only, hoping that the loud explosion the engine made as he did so would frighten any animal that might be sitting on the track ahead, enough to avoid a collision. They clattered along without much mishap, slowing to a stop at small sidings to visit Allenby's customs recruits, most of whom complained that they were finding it very difficult to combat the *contrabandistas*, and that they needed more arms, more men and more uniforms (one of them wore only bathing trunks, declaring he had no uniform at all).

The *contrabandistas* had a polished technique: it was worth their while here, for Corumbá was full of cheap and desirable goods brought in from São Paulo, and the railway was the only reliable means of transport, there being no roads through the thick, swampy forest. But the big *contrabandistas* did nothing on the railway itself. They kept behind the scenes. They employed little men to do their work, and organise the goods, and they conned the engine-drivers into submission. News of any planned inspection would be bound to leak out at once. An engine-driver would stop the train a mile or so before the inspection point, and all contraband goods would be neatly removed and carried on foot along tracks through the undergrowth to be loaded on a few miles further down the track, where the train, its innocence proved, would stop again. There were even look-out men employed to guard against random inspections, and they travelled on the roof, so that they could warn the engine-driver of any hazard ahead.

At Roboré the customs officer was anxious to display his zeal. He arranged a special inspection, and Allenby and David were taken at three o'clock in the morning to the station, to meet the train from the border. But it was late. For three hours they stood peering into the darkness, and at last the train appeared, snorting and smoking through the dawn. Most of the passengers

Strange eroded valleys

The great court at Tiahuanā

Figure of the Weeping Go

seemed to be on the roof, determined to get a good view of the occasion.

Of course there was no contraband to be found. Few people had any luggage at all. The party inspected the whole train, moving from carriage to carriage down the line, the crowds jostling, the officials shouting.

The carriages were little more than cattle-trucks. Passengers slept in hammocks, or on planks, the floors had holes large enough to fall through, and often people and animals travelled in the same truck.

The official was disconcerted. He needed to make some display for the sake of his position. He picked on a small boy of about ten to vent his wrath, and with a shout of *"Contrabando!"* snatched a large melon the child was carrying.

"Contrabando, Señor, mire!" he shouted, and cuffing his victim he threw the melon on to the line, where it burst into pieces.

Allenby already had a clear picture in his mind's eye of the procession making its way through the forest outside the town. In the ensuing hubbub he slipped a 10,000 boliviano note to the child, who stopped weeping at once and ran off delighted with a present enough to buy a whole barrow of melons.

As our Spanish became more fluent, we found our circle of friends and acquaintances widening. The Peruvians were very gay and friendly, and we saw a great deal of Isabella, the daughter of a Peruvian politician. She had married an Englishman whose work had brought him to La Paz and was soon to take him back to England, where Isabella did not at all look forward to what she saw as a life of drudgery.

"It is bad enough here," she said. "Do you know, last week when my maid walked out was the first time in my life I had peeled a potato? I am quite frightened by kitchens."

Isabella had classic Spanish looks. Her face, so pale, and framed in thick black curls, was a perfect oval, and her enormous grey eyes gazed upon the world with that strange mixture of old wisdom and blank innocence which characterizes centuries of madonnas. She had a frail and saintly look, and a fund of the most scandalous stories.

G

Her gossip about any national group, but particularly about Peruvian or Bolivian society, was constantly fresh, and there was no one, it seemed, who did not have a very murky past, fraught with plots and bribes, alliances and amours, even stabbings or poisonings.

It was Isabella who revealed why Peruvians always repeated our name and seemed to find us so amusing.

"One day," she said, as we sat eating almond biscuits and watching our children tumble about on the floor, "when I know you really well, I'll tell you what your name means in Peru."

"What do you mean?" I was surprised. "Oh, come on, tell me now, surely you know me well enough?"

"Well," her beautiful eyes widened, as she searched for a way to express herself. "It means,—ah—the act of love—how you say it in English? . . ." and she said the word so delicately, with just such a tinge of distaste and so slowly that it sounded quite different from the usual expletive, which made me all the more astonished.

After this we thought it might be prudent to change the pronunciation of our name in this part of the world, but the Peruvians always continued to relish the joke.

As time went on, we met professors and politicians, writers, and priests. Carmen Victoria was a poet of considerable renown. She gave *salóns* in her big, dark old house in the city, where she dressed in long black crêpe garments and gave recitals of her poems, which were about love and death, and very sad. The events always ended with everyone in tears.

Joaquín became a great friend. His grandfather had been a president of the country long ago, but although he was an intelligent and educated man, Joaquín had been unable to find any satisfying employment since the last revolution. From Isabella I discovered that his great-uncle had crossed swords with the party now in power, and even imprisoned some of them, so they were now taking vengeance upon the family.

"You see how it is," she said, "people here never forget. They will harbour a grudge for thirty years or more, waiting for the moment they can have revenge."

All this had embittered Joaquín, yet he found in it also a sort of poetic justice, and he saw his resignation to his lot as a typically

Bolivian gesture. He had a passionate love for his country. We would
talk about the mountains, the snow, the stars, poetry, love, and again
about the mountains.

"They are so incredibly beautiful, so enormous, I love and fear
them," he said, "it is a constant reminder of death."

I said, "How morbid you are."

"I can't help it. There's a great gloom that sometimes engulfs me
completely. You know my grandmother was a *chola*? Well, here am I,
of mostly Spanish stock. I think in Spanish, I am baptised Christian,
but something in me worships the sun and the stars and the mountains, is totally subjected to them, and is drowned in fear and sorrow.
It is my Indian soul."

By far our most appreciative guest was Padre Montegut, a benign
and sophisticated Dominican from Catalonia. The padre made no
secret of his penchant for good living, and good conversation. He
was tall, a little gaunt, and well-groomed, his cassock smooth and
creaseless, his hair neatly brushed. He would sit down at the table
with an air of happy expectancy, undo his napkin with a flourish,
take in at a glance the table-setting, the flowers, the silver, perhaps
turn his own plate over discreetly to note the mark.

"Oh, what a pleasure it is, señora, to see such pretty things," he
would say, and if by chance we had made a strenuous effort in the
kitchen and some ambitious soufflé appeared, his delight was
irresistible.

"But señora, in this altitude, how ingenious, what an achievement!" and he beamed upon the party, more ready than ever to discuss any topic from Latin American politics to old Spanish romances.

Padre Montegut ran one of the city's numerous radio stations.
It could hardly have been called highbrow, but certainly tried to
encourage culture in general, and to temper the musical scene with
judiciously chosen classical works. It was with the padre that we
first met Miguel, whose piano recitals were a mainstay of these music
programmes.

Miguel had an old-fashioned, fastidious manner—decorous,
detached. His approach to music was serious and scholarly. He saw
his broadcasting, I thought, almost as a mission. When we had
known each other for some time he invited us to a recital at the

university. The audience was large, and very mixed, ranging from foreign diplomats and university staff to passing Indians who had wandered in from the street. He handled the evening with great skill, playing Scarlatti, Monteverdi, Fauré, Falla, and charming compositions of his own on Bolivian themes, each introduced by an eloquent little lecture.

A devoted patron of the arts, Miguel had the dearth of culture in his country deeply at heart, and had for some time been pressing the Embassy to help him promote good music in Bolivia.

One day when he arrived to lunch with us, I could see that he was unusually excited. He was as flushed and radiant as his formal ways would allow.

"I have had wonderful news from your Ambassador," he announced. "We have, at last, a conductor on the way to us, a true, professional conductor, who will make the Bolivian national orchestra!"

"But who will play in this orchestra?" I asked.

"Ah, that is the question. It is very difficult, a matter of negotiation. You see, there already is an orchestra. But it is terrible, terrible. They can play nothing. But of course they cannot simply be dismissed, and the conductor has had his position for six years."

"So what will happen? Won't he feel terribly insulted?"

Miguel smiled. "I hope not. We have a plan. You see I have been making a few enquiries—very discreet. I find that the conductor has never been truly interested. What he really wants is to conduct a brass band. *Bueno!* We must create a brass band for him!"

Miguel succeeded, the conductor retired content, and Thompson, a young English volunteer fresh from the Royal College of Music, arrived to find a skeleton orchestra awaiting him. Moreover, Miguel had been working tirelessly upon the Americans as well, and soon the ranks of enthusiastic but inexpert Bolivians were joined by a team of young American professionals brought in at great expense to give backbone to the strings and woodwind.

Thompson set to work with a vengeance, and within a remarkably short stretch of months they gave a concert in the Teatro Municipal. The Diplomatic Corps and the Cabinet braved the cold and the sordid surroundings to attend. It was a noble effort. Thompson had carefully chosen a programme which gave plenty of scope for emotive kinetics, while making not too much demand on technique. Miguel was delighted. He began to see the realisation of his dreams, and even to talk of playing concertos with "these brave young people".

We had first met Ramón in London, when he was completing a course at the London School of Economics. His father was in the Bolivian cabinet. Ramón came to a party in Kensington where most of the guests had no idea where Bolivia was, and had not even heard of La Paz. We never expected our acquaintance to survive the insult of all this ignorance, but he hailed us one day in La Paz, in the Prado, down which he was cruising, tanned and glamorous in a red sports car with a French film-star by his side. And so, once the film-star had returned to France or Brazil, or somewhere out of reach, we began to see him quite frequently, although his life was very busy as he now had an interesting and lucrative job in economic affairs, which his ability deserved, but his youth and inexperience did not.

One day, together with Drake, the commercial attaché, and his wife, we received an invitation to dine at the *palacio de gobierno*, (the palace of government), an enormous building in the main square, heavily built in the French style, and very heavily guarded. We all felt excited, privileged and a little nervous. Over several days we discussed at length what we ought to wear for the occasion, and Drake's wife quite lost her head and bought a *vicuña* stole.

On the appointed evening we donned all our finery and drove in our Land-Rovers up through the town to the *palacio*. Half a dozen guards with machine-guns stood about the entrance, and it took some explanation to be allowed even to knock at the door. After a while, a tiny slot of a peephole opened suddenly in the studded wood, and a pair of slanted eyes peered out at us. We had to give our names, and there was a lot of shuffling and discussion within, until the huge doors ground open and a guard appeared to conduct us inside. Through a large quadrangle we went, past guard-posts and defences, up staircases and through long, dark corridors until we had no idea how far we had climbed or how we should ever find our way out. Eventually, the bare, flagged passages gave on to carpeted ones, with rows of chairs along papered walls, and we were ushered into a *salón* at least 100 feet long, with golden damask curtains and a dais at one end.

Isolated in the middle stood a little circle of gold chairs, and upon these we sat and waited, under the glowering gaze of a uniformed officer with many medals and ribbons, and a revolver in a white leather holster at his hip.

Then Ramón came in, full of charm and zest, and introduced the officer, whom he addressed as *capitán*, and who was clearly a bodyguard. Soon the other guests arrived, most of them Ramón's cousins. The girls were very pretty, the men were very confident and all in important government posts. We had drinks, making polite conversation with a little nervous laughter. I realised that while Ramón spoke impeccable and witty English, none of his cousins did, and I feared that they would soon find our Spanish inadequate and boring.

Dinner was in another hall. We sat on either side of a long table, facing each other across the white damask set with crested plates and glasses, and enormous vases of gladioli, bright and official-looking with silver-painted ferns. The *capitán* dined with us but spoke not a word, and refused all drink. We discussed Bolivian economics and culture and education, and South American literature, and only Ramón dared to say anything really frivolous. When I thought of the evening afterwards I could never recall what it was we had to eat.

After dinner we sat again in the little circle of chairs, under the eye of the *capitán*, and the discussion moved to poetry. We talked about Shakespeare, and the English poetic tradition. Ramón asked if we knew any ballads or romances, and suddenly one of the cousins sprang to his feet and announced he would recite a poem for us.

He thundered, sobbed, whispered, sang, and it was an epic about a gaucho in Argentina long ago. We had to strain to understand the old Spanish, to follow the story of the gaucho's wandering and fighting and loving and moonlit serenading, and of his beloved horse. The room grew cold: it was winter, and someone must have turned off the heating. Midnight came, but the cantos went on, and we all began to shiver, except Drake's wife, who sat there looking serene and beautiful, wrapped warmly in her honey-coloured fur stole.

At last the story drew to a tremulous close, the gaucho grew old and his horse died, but love and glory would go on for ever. We all applauded. The cousin stood exhausted and triumphant, with tears in his eyes. I felt somehow ashamed that none of us could have given a similar performance; with all our education, and the great wealth of English, not one of our little group could have contributed to this moment. I could not think of one saga in English nor even a passage of Shakespeare which I could recite naturally and fluently.

"Why not a ballad?" I thought. "Oh, why can't I remember all those ballads I learnt as a child? Sir Patrick Spens—even there I can only think of the first verse." And instantly, the moment when we could have responded passed.

So we shook hands and said good-bye, and I left with a peculiar sense of loss.

VII

Different Worlds in the Cordillera

Having a Land-Rover was like an extra dimension to
our lives. The roads were so rough that for most cars it was
impossible to go far beyond La Paz itself, but our intrepid
vehicle was almost like an animal, and could bump along the
altiplano, weave down passes blasted out of the mountain, or be
coaxed up stony hillsides with equal facility. We could reach with
ease the *altiplano*, the glacier lakes high in the *cordillera*, or the
yungas, the deep sub-tropical valleys below, each a place so different
it was like a new country.

Even the separate valleys beyond Calacoto itself were small worlds
on their own, cut off and surrounded by cliffs and peaks. The route
to the golf course led on through the moon-landscape into wide
valleys with plantations of eucalyptus trees, and open ground
massed over with daisies and wild lupins. In the other direction, past
our house, the road wound up through farmland into the hills.
There was a vantage point here where we would go sometimes at
night to look back at La Paz, and to watch the stars. These were so
bright that the lights of the city sparkled dully in comparison, as
though glimmering up through deep water. We would trace out
Orion, and Andromeda, and the Southern Cross with its pointers,
and stare up at the Milky Way, shivering in the cold night air. I
found myself straining my ears too, tense and wondering, for the
stars blazed so fiercely that we listened beyond the distant night-
noises of animals and the wind in the grass, as though like primitive
people we could hear the stars shouting up there in the vast darkness.

The road led on from this place into the hills, past a few villages and, at the top of a pass, a lonely graveyard beside a small, reed-fringed lake. After this it became increasingly rough, dropping down into a series of strange gorges, whose steep sides had been worn into fantastic shapes by wind and water.

Where the river bank was wide enough, there might be a farmer, in the dry season, toiling with his oxen to plough the inhospitable shale in the hope of reaping some crop before the rains raged down in destruction. People said that if you went far enough along these gorges you came to a village right at the base of Illimani, but we never did. The road lost itself among the gullies of the river-bed, and we walked about, collecting peculiar pebbles and the dry, brittle remains of plants along the banks. We called to test the echo, and traced the colours in the rock that towered up above us. Some parts had been eroded into long columns like church pillars, others wrought like knotted tree-trunks. Others were like gargoyle-faces, or elusive, watchful animals which sprang to sudden life as the setting sun flung them into view, etched black and menacing against the dust-red sky.

During the rainy season, when the mountains and passes were dangerous, we would drive up at weekends to explore the *altiplano*. The high plateau both drew and awed me. Although said to harbour more than half the country's population, it always seemed empty, the plain splaying out to the peak-strung horizon, vacant, dun-coloured and silent. This silence was odd, too, for we might stop and climb a rock to sit in the sun, and if there was no wind I would sense after a while that there was nothing to hear at all, no birds, no tiny scufflings or scratchings of insects, no cricket-shrill, only deep in my ears the throb of my own blood.

We drove miles across open country; it was impossible to feel lonely in the Land-Rover, which clattered and roared, churning pebbles up against its metal framework, drowning all conversation yet making us feel almost cosy in its enclosure.

The emptiness of the plain was an illusion: after a while the horizon would unfold or crinkle to show a little cluster of thatched mud houses, mothered by the bulk of an adobe church, and round them all a patchwork of fields scratched laboriously into life. We would rumble past small allotments of potatoes or *quinoa*, where the soil had been tilled soft by centuries of handwork, and the stones removed to make neat dividing walls. We would stop in the square and walk about, and visit the church, where the high walls of the nave were hung with giant pictures of saints dressed in the elaborate doublets and puffed trousers of sixteenth-century Spain, and madonnas in stiff embroidered dresses like the *meninas* of Velasquez. Outside again, there might be a procession, or a market, or some festival, and we saw a wedding once in a small mud yard, where the women, wearing red skirts and little flat mortar-board hats hung with bright tassels, were all dancing to a band, while the men stood about drinking and occasionally came out into the street to thump each other.

Tilcomayo, Challapata, Calamarca . . . they all had old Indian names. At Calamarca there was a little shrine on a hillock housing a "black virgin" who was in fact a rock worshipped in some old religion long before the *conquistadores*. Here on feast days there would be *diabladas*, the devil-dances for which the *altiplano* was renowned, and afterwards everyone went to mass at the shrine, and the priest, with the adaptability which has been such a strength of the Roman church, blessed the masks and costumes of the pagan dance.

Despite my impressions on the plain itself, there were birds in plenty round Lake Titicaca. I saw coot and grebe, and various ducks and gulls one day as we picnicked on the shore, and thought I heard a lark although I could not distinguish it, even with the field-glasses. The lake was far too cold to bathe in, but the water had a magical depth of colour, and fishermen poled about in their boats made of rushes with high curved prows like gondolas, slicing across the reflections of reeds, clouds and peaks. The water mirrored and enhanced the changing colours of the distant landscape with such brilliance, and the air itself had such crystal clarity, that the whole world seemed extraordinary, and very moving. I felt I could easily understand why the lake had always had a mysterious hold on the peoples of the high plateau.

Lake Titicaca had been of almost sacred importance to the Incas. Manco Capac, the first Inca, was said to have been born there, on the Island of the Sun. On this little island, and the neighbouring Island of the Moon, there were still the remains of Inca terraces, and steps and stairways cut into the cliffs. At Copacabana nearby, there was a Spanish church, with a famous miracle-working virgin, whom pilgrims would come enormous distances to see and pray to. Perhaps the whole of this end of the lake had a tradition of pilgrimage reaching back long before the Christian priests, for the mysterious, ruined city of Tiahuanaco, most important in the Indian world before the Spanish Conquest, was also in the same area.

The history of Tiahuanaco is full of romance, muddle and paradox. For centuries the city has haunted the Indians, and tantalised travellers, historians and later archaeologists. It was built by a people who inhabited the shores of the lake before the Incas. They held wide influence, and built up a powerful and restrained culture, whose style in stonework and pottery was germinal to the work of many later tribes throughout the Andes and coastal Peru. But who these people were no one can fully explain. They disappeared long ago.

The city was a marvel to the Incas; they thought it holy, and when the Inca himself held a baptism ceremony, which was one of his customs, he performed the rite with water brought from Tiahuanaco. Mayta Capac, the Inca in 1126, conquered Tiahuanaco after crossing the lake in canoes made of rushes; perhaps this itself was a gesture of some spiritual significance.

I had discovered more about Tiahuanaco during the months we lived in the *pensión*. I read early records describing the place, referring to "a great hill made by the hands of man, resting on blocks of stone; huge walls and doorways made from stones of enormous size, and a hall covered with a roof of stone carved to look like thatch". These also described the waters of the lake as "washing the floors of the courtyards".

There was an Inca legend about the flood, which recounted how everything died except one man and one woman, who were carried to Tiahuanaco and told by the Creator to stay there as colonists or settlers, and another reference to the Creator "making the nations" at Tiahuanaco, fashioning people in clay, painting them in their various dress, and then telling them to go to their various places.

One early chronicler was told that the city had been built by a mysterious race of white, bearded giants who disappeared to another land. I re-read Thor Heyerdahl's *Kon Tiki Expedition*, and was fascinated by his theory about Tiahuanaco as the origin of the Polynesians, by his tracing of their strange pattern of migration and his discovery of carvings very like those of Tiahuanaco on isolated islands in the Pacific.

There was another tale that interested me. It was about a wandering preacher named Tonapa, who had passed by Tiahuanaco one day. The citizens, not perceiving that Tonapa was a holy man, stoned him to death. In vengeance the Creator turned them all to stone, catching them just as they were, standing, sitting, walking in the water, women suckling their children—a dreadful memorial and warning.

I was intrigued by these stories. I knew that the remains of the city were scant, and fewer than they had been once, before the scavengings of surrounding Indians, of the *conquistadores*, and of the builders of La Paz itself. It was strange how many people had been drawn to the place.

I also found a description of Tiahuanaco by a Victorian Englishman, a meteorologist who spent a couple of years, in about 1866, on the heights above La Paz, studying the stars from a small makeshift observatory and weather station. He became fascinated by the ruined city and wrote a book about it, lavishly illustrated with sketches of the remains then to be found on the site. One of these showed in detail a great gateway with cracked pediments, on which was depicted the Weeping God, whose face was one of the predominant motifs of the culture. Other sketches showed monoliths and carvings from Memphis and Greece, which the author, Mr. Inwards, thought similar to those of Tiahuanaco, and there was one grand reconstruction of the "great court" and the pyramid hillock, with wide staircases down to the water's edge, and barges sailing in and out from the lake.

The main statue of the Weeping God had, I knew, been removed to La Paz. It stood in a square in front of the football stadium. We went there once to see a series of matches. The visiting teams were struggling against the altitude, but play was very fierce, the referee was constantly attacked, and eventually a riot broke out. We left when the police swarmed on to the field and spectators turned upon each other, throwing hats, papers, and bottles. When we reached the Tiahuanaco statue I looked back. Police cars were moving in on the building; high above the grandstand an enormous orange balloon, advertising some mineral drink, lurched in the air; and the Weeping God gazed across in sad benediction towards the impassive peaks.

This Weeping God was geometric, and therefore impersonal in design, and all the figurings still appeared in the folk-art of the Bolivian Indians. He had a sceptre and a throne, worked with the heads of birds, snakes and fishes. His crown was decorated with pumas' heads, and his face surrounded with rays like the sun. His belt was carved into shapes of human heads, perhaps to show that he was a ruler of men, and his sceptre had the heads of a condor and a parrot, to show perhaps that he was ruler of both mountain heights and jungles. He was dressed, therefore, like a warrior, but large round tears rained down his cheeks.

The god was sometimes depicted waited upon by rows of kneeling figures in two designs, one with the head of a condor, the other human-headed, but winged and crowned, and wreathed about with motifs of fishes and serpents. The *conquistadores* found that an Indian was not looked upon as honourable unless he claimed his descent from a river, a lake or even the sea, or from a puma or condor, forest cave or mountain, "for the better praise and glory of his name".

The condor, the great, terrible eagle of the mountains, was held sacred by the Incas. We saw one sometimes when crossing high passes in the *cordillera*, and once tried to stalk a pair close enough for a photograph. Moving with infinite caution, downwind of them, we got quite near to where they sat on some small rocks in the sun. They were enormous, about the height I was as I crouched below them. We peered up through the spiky bushes and tall dry grass, unable to get a clear enough focus, and just had time to see their eyes and cruel curled beaks before they suddenly saw or sensed us and flew off. Their wings had easily a span of six feet or more; they swooped over, close above us, then swerved silently away, their giant shadows crinkling over the bushes as they wheeled down the valley out of sight.

Early writers also had tales of the anaconda, the sacred, giant snake of the lowland forests, as thick as a man's arm or even his waist—tales of horror we ourselves heard from the Indians.

It could not have been chance, or the search for something to attract tourists, which made these emblems central to any plastic expression in the country, from the silver knick-knacks in the markets to the scratchings on a village mud wall. Children learning needlework in schools embroidered the Weeping God and his condor figures, women weaving with llama and alpaca wool would work the motifs in somehow, and they even appeared on the knitted caps with flapping earpieces which men and children wore in cold weather.

We knew several villages on the *altiplano* where almost every house had what looked like a weather-vane fastened to its thatched roof. These were extraordinary, intricate things made out of tin, sometimes just old tin cans, cut with infinite care into decorative shapes. They were of endless variety but always in the same tradition, repeating condors and parrots, anacondas and crowned heads, and the old geometric pattern.

I traced the theme, too, in the dances where costumes were worn, worked in with fantastic or grotesque detail and brilliant colours, in all the materials and gew-gaws that the markets could provide. Of course other figures had joined the tradition—the *conquistador*, the buffoon, the bear, things derived from the European mystery plays, but there would always be the condors and the serpent-staffs. I even thought that the central figure of the *diabladas*, the devil-mask with its contorted twirling rays and crouching cat-figures, owed some lost debt to the forgotten god. It was a little far-fetched, perhaps, to see the Weeping God in a devil-mask, but I often wondered about this, and it helped to explain the strange relationship between the devil-dancers and the priests of conquering Spain.

I was curious to see what remained of the ancient, haunting city. It was an easy journey to Tiahuanaco across the *altiplano* from La Paz, along a patchy dirt road from the airport, and we went there one day at the end of summer, when the rains were ending and dust already hanging like ochre mist in the air. The road ambled across the great plain, winding to avoid small water courses, crossing a low ridge of hills and a shallow ford.

But for a group of cars left haphazardly in the scrub, we might have missed the place. All that could be seen from the road was a peculiar mound covered with grassy clumps, which merged, dun-coloured, into the brown hillocks beyond. About the mound, a medley of large grey stones jutted up above the grasses. Only when we got out of the car and started across towards it could we see plainly that the mound was too isolated, too precise in shape to be natural, and that there was in fact some order in the placing of the stones before it.

There was a gateway, made of three large stones, some seven feet high, referred to now as the gateway of the sun; and a pillar, rudely carved and much weathered, but recognisable as a face, perhaps of another sad god. It was difficult to discern any layout, or remains of streets or houses. We picked our way down an alley or aisle below ground level, flanked on one side by a wall with stone pillars jutting above it. Stumbling over stones and clumps of grass we clambered across a row of gaping "graves" which must have been left open by recent excavators, and there, uncovered for us as it was not for the travellers of a century ago, lay what must have been the great court of the legends.

Between large pillars were steps leading down into it—hewn steps of enormous size, which must surely, as all the legends noted, have been brought there by water, and from a great distance, for there was no such stone in these parts. The sides of the court were quite smooth and regular, stone matching stone, and at various different levels carved heads jutted out from these walls. Some were weath-ered beyond recognition, others simply grotesque or primitive out-lines, but many more were moulded and varied like true portraits. The faces stared down towards a group of stones in the centre of the court which could have been an altar, or simply a meeting place. I walked up and down looking at them. They seemed to glower with a common intensity. The court was well below ground level, the wind hissed through the grasses above and swished little eddies of dust about the floor. Sound was magnified, and our voices echoed if we spoke.

I felt disconcerted, almost frightened beneath the stare of these faces.

"Who were they anyway?" I thought, "and what business have they to glare at me like this across the centuries?"

"They're terribly realistic, aren't they?" said an American friend who had come with us.

"Yes," I said, wishing he had not spoken.

"Yes-s-s-s," hissed the echo on the wind.

I wondered whether they could indeed be the stoners of Tonapa the preacher, who had come to this terrible end, like childhood fears of the clock striking thirteen.

But there was something else about the faces too. As I studied them, and tried to explain away my uneasiness, I recognised that staring expression: I would see it again in any *altiplano* village.

It was the Indian face, the Indian personality, and a scrutiny that never failed to make me feel uneasy. It was something quite different from the surprise and mistrust with which backward people regard the more civilised, sophisticated and privileged. This face held also a blank indifference, something remote, beyond feeling, and incomprehensible, like the mountain world itself. Whether there was a mask, or simply a total withdrawal, was impossible to gauge. I felt in the present, as here before the faces of the past, always a distant onlooker, and an alien intruder.

We turned and climbed up the steps out of the court. At the top, someone had pushed a few of the big stone slabs about to make a table and benches, and we sat here to eat our lunch, watching other visitors clambering about, a large family of Spanish Bolivians, and two German youths in *lederhosen* who kept lying down in twisted positions to take photographs of stones against the sky.

Later we went back to see the gateway of the sun, and looked up at the outlines of the Weeping God and his attendants carved in the pediment.

"Do you believe the theories that he was Viracocha?" our American friend asked.

"I don't know. Maybe," I said. "I am finding it difficult to imagine any people holding this bleak ruin sacred, as the seat of the Creator."

"Well, belief and fact don't usually have much in common anyway," he remarked.

I felt that the uncanny atmosphere was affecting our tempers.

Despite my comment, I was interested in Viracocha, the god whom the Incas had worshipped as the Creator, and whose first "home" had been Tiahuanaco. I had discovered somewhere in my reading a prayer to him whose imagery and universality made the Incas seem less hostile and remote:

"O Creator and Sun and Thunder, be forever young. Do not grow old. Let all things be at peace. Let the people multiply and their food, and let all things continue to increase. O Viracocha, Soul of the World, Teacher of the Universe, Incomprehensible God."

We climbed to the top of the pyramid mound and looked down across the site of the city. The lake lay far away, a shining streak near the *cordillera*. The wind had grown sharper, and heavy clouds had appeared, trailing dark shadows over the plain.

There was a museum nearby, with more pieces taken from the Tiahuanaco site, pottery and carvings, and a haphazard collection of pictures of Inca customs, including trepanning. The building was a disused railway house, and the attendant, an Indian in a ragged uniform, sat outside on the steps, staring glumly at the narrow railway track which stretched out on either side of him, straight over to the horizon.

The present village of Tiahuanaco was not far away. It was small and poor, and we bumped self-consciously through its narrow, rutted streets in the wake of a lorry. There were a lot of people about, and in the main square we saw everyone moving towards the church, a large, handsome building with mud walls only partly whitewashed, and a tall Spanish tower open at the top, showing the bells. These began to ring with a slow, sad clanging which went on and on. I remembered that it was Good Friday. Some of the crowd went into the church, while the rest hung about in the square, as if waiting for something to happen.

We went in at the west door. Up at the altar the priest was chanting, surrounded by kneeling figures. They seemed very far away: the nave was enormous, dark and empty. In one place the wall had collapsed, and a heap of crumbled mud and birdmess lay on

H

the floor. The arched windows, high up near the roof, had no glass, and the sunlight came in in thick shafts looking almost solid in the dusty air.

The priest moved out through a side door, and we followed the congregation, to join the ends of a procession: in front the priest chanting from a missal, beside him two little incense bearers, and then a crowd of the faithful, carrying relics and tattered banners. In the middle was an enormous, ornately painted coffin borne by a group of pallbearers: it was the funeral procession for the dead Christ. A straggling crowd of black-suited men and black-shawled and bowlered women, barefoot children, and boys on bicycles brought up the rear.

Black cloth had been pinned shoulder high along the walls of the houses the dead Lord would pass. It was like the key to a labyrinth, for the route wound about and doubled back, up and down the narrow streets so tortuously that the priest once or twice found himself meeting up with the tail end of the procession. At various cross-roads there were "stations" where the crowd would stop its snail's pace and tuneless chanting, and kneel in the dirt, while the priest delivered a reading, a long dissertation and a prayer.

Each of these "stations" was marked by a peculiar, rickety canopy. Four "palm trees" stood at the corners, made of long poles covered in black cotton, with tufted tops of black crêpe paper; and slung heavily between them, swinging on strings attached to the top of each pole, was a large black mattress. They were such curious objects it was hardly surprising that children could not resist leaning on the "trees" until the canopy lurched dangerously, and adults shouted in warning disapproval as little bits of the mattress-stuffing fell down into the street.

The children soon got bored, and either were reprimanded or simply scampered away. The homage took some two hours to complete. At the end of it all the coffin was placed on a shrouded table in the square beside which, like rewards for hard work, were other tables set with enormous cauldrons of soup, and trays of little cakes.

As we left, the sunset blazed out through thick storm-clouds. Passing the ruined city was a herdswoman trying to beat order and speed into her flock of llamas and reach home before the rain. The storm broke as we crossed the last ridge of hills before La Paz. Over Lake Titicaca lightning flashed in enormous hissing spikes, and the village and the ruin were lost behind a grey veil of rain.

The other side of the *cordillera* that towered above La Paz, the Andes showed their peculiar, violent origin in full measure. The fringe of peaks that enclosed the *altiplano* was magnificent and awesome enough: their eastern rim was like a fortress-wall on the edge of the world, looking out across vast, blue-green space towards other planets. It was a place where perception of the real physical world became blurred with images of the mind and long memories of myth; as though the only way to accept it were to imagine oneself in some way a god.

The mountain walls were terrifyingly sheer. In an almost perpendicular drop, the snow and shale of the high peaks and wild precipices fell and divided into long ridges like huge fingers with deep, shadowy gorges between them. Far down, they twined and spread into narrow valleys, fertile and thickly forested. These were the Yungas.

Within twenty-five miles the land fell about 20,000 feet. It was quite feasible to go there for a day, or a weekend, from La Paz. But the shock of such a trip was overwhelming. We looked forward to the dry season when driving was safer, and longed for the thick air, the rushing streams and lush green forests of the lowland valleys. The change from the high plateau, the snows and glaciers, to the warm tropics was like a renewal of life for us. But on our return into the high altitude, we seemed always to need about two days to recover, stunned by the sudden, enormous changes, and by the vast beauty of it all.

To reach the Yungas, we left La Paz from the top of the city, and drove upwards through a few farms and villages into stony, grey-green hills. As the road wound up the slopes, we had occasional glimpses of Chacaltaya, the end peak of the *cordillera* behind La Paz, where the observatory lay, and also a few ski-slopes, only used by those who were tough enough to endure the sport at 17,000 feet, with no lifts. We moved on through rolling moorland, where herds of llama and alpaca grazed, and streams tumbled down into small pools. Then grey peaks rose around us, and tracks led off towards them, to the glacier lakes where the fishing enthusiasts went in search of young trout. Some people kept rowing-boats on these lakes, but they had to be used with great caution, as a fall into the icy water could be fatal.

The top of the pass lay in a silent, desolate world of rock—grey and brown shale, jagged toothed ridges, and huge, black walls of granite. Clouds often shrouded the higher peaks and snows from view; trails of mist floated through gullies between the rocks, eagles wheeled in the air, and a sudden gust of wind brought whirls of snow or driving sleet. At one point here the rock rose like a platform, jutting out over a vast drop where the cliffs and brown slopes disappeared in mist. Three large crosses stood sentinel on the edge, marking the place where some political leaders had been thrown to their death not long ago. Far, infinitely far below, when the mists parted, could be seen the road, snaking and twining down out of sight. The rocky platform was at an altitude of about 16,000 feet, but the visible drop, from the peaks like Illampu behind us, must have been well over 10,000 feet. The place was cold and hostile, and breathing was difficult; my heart pounded with effort, and with sheer terror. I began the descent always in a state of breathless anxiety and prayer.

We had to drive cautiously in the cloud, lest we meet one of the huge lorries loaded with fruit, vegetables, and passengers, grinding its way up to La Paz. Twisting and turning from one hairpin bend to the next, we moved down into new worlds. The landscape changed within minutes from cliffs and shale to grassy slopes with lonely little stone huts and walled enclosures for animals, and far up on the cliff the remains of an old Inca road following the contours. The grasses soon grew more lush, with streams and scrubby mountain bushes, and then the first trees appeared, and a village astride a stream, where arum lilies grew by the water.

Quite soon the slopes were thickly wooded, and the road more precipitous, winding out on to a promontory poised above a drop into deep gullies, and then back into another higher gorge, where the water-course made a natural turning. After this came larger valleys, their steep sides strung with white cascades, and the more accessible slopes planted with coca bushes. The road often reached the river at the bottom of such a valley before moving on into another, lower down. Here were farms on the hillside, with fields of vegetables as well as coca, and hydrangeas and agapanthus lilies, growing for the markets in La Paz. We could picnic by the river bank, watching the farmers climbing the steep terraces and fields to tend their crops, and we fished here sometimes, or I would study the cliffs through binoculars to find orchids hidden in the wet, leaf-hung shadows.

The road was tortuous and frightening. Simply a platform blasted out of the mountain, it was only the width of one vehicle, with wider passing places at intervals where the contours of the hill allowed. Often, after excessive rain or a sudden fall of rock, the road gave way, and portions of it disappeared down into the valley below; but maintenance was quite good in that a bulldozer could soon be commandeered to gouge a new surface further into the mountainside. The outer rim of the road itself was only marked by a fringe of trees or flowers, and by the innumerable crosses where unfortunate travellers had gone over the edge. In one place, a bus with thirty passengers had fallen down a drop so deep that no one could even go and look for it—3,000 feet of tree-clad cliffs made any search impossible.

The way to Coroico was the most terrifying of all, for the valleys were unbelievably steep. They were so deep too, and narrow that even in broad sunlight only the first few hundred feet below the road level were visible, and the rest lost in a blue mist. The sun set here before three o'clock, leaving a mysterious shrouded half-light until darkness fell. Huge grey-trunked trees festooned with moss hung out over the blue, the paw-paw trees were tufted black silhouettes, and long curves of bamboo leaned into the mist, their thin stalks strung with little spurts of leaf like necklaces of stars.

At the end of the journey the road curved through villages to Coroico itself, which lay on a hump of the mountainside, looking out across more, lower valleys. The gardens all seemed burgeoning and overgrown, with their paw-paw trees and banana palms, amaryllis lilies, and the strange, scented creepers which festooned the walls and slopes. The buildings were nondescript, but the town was enchanting, poised on this little vantage-point. All around it were blue-green, misty valleys, and beyond them, back towards La Paz one looked up into the sky as if for some new galaxy—to see the great snowy peaks. The people here were different: there were more *mestizos*, and negroes and mulattoes, and the Indian faces were softer. Children ran about everywhere, half-naked and laughing.

There was one hotel in Coroico. When night fell, we would sit indoors drinking beer or *pisco* (the half-matured brandy of Peru and Bolivia, very fiery and strong), and eating the standard meal, which was a bad lamb stew. Moths fluttered up against the lamps, and the cicadas dinned outside. We felt relaxed and happy. The brooding spirit of the mountains which so dominated the *altiplano* seemed to have no place here at all. It was too hot, perhaps, and life was so much easier. But it was also, I thought, that the whole mountain world was so very far away; one could not feel dominated by the peaks, they seemed so infinitely high they might just as well have been the moon or some other planet.

One weekend we went down to the Yungas on a camping expedition taking with us Wyner, a tall, talkative American who specialised, he told us, in discovering "exotic places". He claimed that he knew a secret valley where we could camp in an orchard, and although I was sceptical, he found it, somehow recognising a track leading off one of the hairpin bends far down on the Coroico road. We bounced along a rough path beside a river, and came to a citrus grove. Enormous piles of oranges and lemons lay everywhere among the trees, and Indians moved about with loaded mules. They were bringing oranges down from a village we could see high on the slopes above us, perhaps 4,000 feet or more up the mountain. They looked suspicious at first, particularly when we set about our evening meal, but we gave them some of our bread, and mugs of soup, and they asked us to guard their oranges for them through the night.

We lay on the bunks in the Land-Rover, and Wyner talked about a French Duchess, to whom he said he was related.

"And there's this fantastic chateau . . ." It rained a great deal, and we all slept rather badly.

In the morning we got out our fishing tackle. Wyner told us that he was an expert with spinners, and showed us how to use them. He lent David one, and marched off purposefully downstream. We both found the spinner impossible and kept getting our lines tangled. After a while David changed to a fly, a march brown on which he caught several small trout. I was frying them for breakfast when Wyner returned empty-handed. He was so taken aback that he suddenly felt ill, and spent the rest of the morning lying under a tree complaining of terrible pains. I handed him the first-aid kit and went back to the river.

The water was full of cascades and whirling currents, and very difficult to fish, even in waders. I had no luck, and was terribly stung by midges. Later David and I walked upstream, following a path along the bank through groves of bamboo and flowering trees, past waterfalls and overhanging cliffs, and little bridges just wide enough to take a mule. Sometimes the cascades flattened out, the banks broadened and the water burbled over round pebbles into pools, overhung with trees and dappled with sun and shadow, almost like Wales or Ireland. Then the steep cliff-sides closed in again. When the sunlight was thinning we turned back, picking flowers and ferns from the dripping rocks as we walked beneath them. We found Wyner back at the citrus grove. He had recovered his temper, and packed everything ready for the journey home, and as we drove up towards the misty peaks, he was very gay and appreciative, and full of his usual fund of risqué stories.

VIII

Shakespeare on the Altiplano

IT WAS SHAKESPEARE who was responsible for our first extensive tour of the interior. That year was his 400th anniversary, and someone in Whitehall decided it would be a good thing to promote him on the international scene. So large Shakespeare posters were sent all over the world, to places like Addis Ababa and Bogota and Cambodia, and a Shakespeare Company toured South America like strolling players, only in aeroplanes, doing *A Midsummer Night's Dream*, *The Merry Wives of Windsor*, and some of the bloodier tragedies, a repertory carefully chosen to appeal to romantic and blood-thirsty temperament. La Paz, however, was left out of their itinerary, and the Chancery, muttering that at least the Duke of Edinburgh had thought them worth a visit, had to be content with a copy of Olivier's film *Hamlet*, undubbed and without Spanish sub-titles.

David was Press and Information Officer, and so in charge of putting across the British way of life. His department was full of informative pamphlets, large posters of Beefeaters and Beautiful Wales, and Commonwealth Development, such as steelworks on the Ganges. But there were also projectors and tape recorders, and it was obviously his duty to take Shakespeare to the Bolivians.

This took a great deal of organising in advance, the Bolivian post and temperament being what they were, but at last it seemed that most of the "contacts" in the places we proposed to visit would probably be ready to receive us (or at least we knew how to find them if they were not), and so we set off one fine dry winter's morning. The Land-Rover was packed to bursting with coats and rugs, binoculars, cameras and pamphlets, film, screen, tape-recorder, and the enormous projector which, in addition to its sound-box and about 300 yards of flex, had its own little dynamo to convert and strengthen the electric current that was bound to be low and unreliable wherever we went.

I was to share the driving. (I had arranged to leave Alexander behind in the care of some friends.) We took with us Forgues, a small Bolivian from the Chancery, who knew the way, and knew how to make the projector and all its extra machines work together. And we also took an Irish-born German baroness, who was the B.B.C.'s "stringer" in Argentina, and had come up to Bolivia to "see what was going on" and to make contacts with the country's many radio stations.

She found Bolivia "thrilling", and "exotic", and "marvellous"— "so wild and different", and compared her rapture now, at the scenery and the colours, with her city-life in Argentina, where she commuted daily to her office along twenty-five miles of super-highway.

"The snows, the light—look at those gorgeous colours!" she exclaimed as we ground up the hill towards the airport and started to bump and rumble across the *altiplano*.

"Oh look at that dear little boy, and his hat. How quaint! And the llamas! And what strange hills, and the sky—so gloriously blue," and she peered at it through her dark glasses which were strapped firmly to her head with a tight tartan scarf.

But after a while with the bumping and the heat, and the noise of the Land-Rover thundering along the gravel, we all sat in silence. The dust began to pour in from all sorts of little unseen holes, and we coughed and spluttered.

The Baroness tied another large scarf over her nose and mouth so that she looked a bit like a bespectacled Moslem, and she lifted it only to cough, or insert a sweet, or shout something to Forgues in her Argentine Spanish which was thick and slurred and very difficult for even Forgues to understand.

"Do you speak Quechua or Aymhara?" she shouted.

"Say again, señora?" he called back in his shrill Bolivian falsetto.

"I said do you speak Quechua and Aymhara—so that you can talk to these people?"

"I don't know, señora," shouted Forgues, uncomprehending,

and she lapsed into puzzled silence, while the dust puffed in in thick jets, and settled on our clothes, and caked into little lines on our hands and eyelids.

Our first stop was Oruro, the tin-mining town where Patiño had first stumbled upon the vast deposits of metal that made him rich. In the last revolution the tin-miners had beaten the army. Since then, they had become waywardly powerful and held the government in a stranglehold which no amount of American dollars seemed able to dislodge. At the slightest encouragement such as the sacking of a union member for idleness or rioting, they would down tools and march on the town with blunderbusses and dynamite, of which they had a constant plentiful supply. Indeed they were threatening to do so at this moment, because of some dispute with the Mayor.

"And I don't blame them, poor things," said the Baroness. "Look at the life they lead—all the terrible cold and phthisis, certain death within a few years, and such low pay. No wonder they want revenge on whoever's keeping them down!"

I said, "Well, they're keeping themselves down partly. Everyone knows that they keep all the best tin for their own pockets. They mine all day for the government and put the best bits into little ledges in the rock, and then when they go back for the one hour of the day in which they mine for themselves, they just walk in and pick up all the titbits they have hidden. And where does the money for *that* go?"

"Chicha," sang Forgues, who understood enough to get the general meaning, and the Baroness said "poor things" again, and started to talk about Peron and the poor in Argentina, how they had loved Eva, who rode through the country in a train, throwing presents and money to them through the window, but how terribly wicked it had all been, and everyone had danced in the streets and laughed and wept when the régime fell . . .

We checked in at the Hotel Central which was old and brown, with wicker chairs in the hall, and fly-papers hanging from the ceiling. David and Forgues went off to find the university, and the Baroness to make her contacts in broadcasting. I decided to explore the town.

It was a dry, bleak little place, with a neglected look as though the miners were still prospecting and not yet established. The few trees were spindly and wind-battered, and the houses, with corrugated-iron roofs and brown verandahs, had no gardens to speak of, though here and there someone had scratched a patch of zinnias into bloom in the dusty yard, and a dejected pepper-tree lent some shade.

But the market was in full swing, and I found it easily, by following boys bumping along the ruts on bicycles with squawking chickens and ducks tied by their feet to the handlebars, and old men tottering under enormous baskets of oranges and limes, pineapples and papaya.

Outside the market there were rows of barrows with bright mirrors, satin ribbons, hair curlers, plastic combs, and home-made knives and sickles. I bought some six-inch long safety-pins, sure that they would come in useful. Men and women walking past wore blankets slung round them for warmth, clasped at the shoulder with these pins. It was cold despite the bright sun.

I ducked into the market hall beneath a festooned chain of enamel chamber-pots, and in the sudden shadow bumped into a child of about four carrying a baby in his arms. I caught them before they fell and apologised. They were called sharply by a woman sitting on a bundle of llama skins, who snatched the baby and began to suckle it. She spat out a pad of coca and ladled some soup from a pot beside her. Another child came shuffling through the dust with two plates of stew, and they all sat close on the skins, eating in silence.

I moved slowly about the stalls, fingering things.

"Que cosita quiere caserita? Comprame, comprame pues caserita," ("What little thing do you want, little housekeeper? Buy me, buy me then, little housekeeper!") came the high, soft voices, and numberless transistor radios thumped out rumbas and sambas in endless buzzing rhythm.

A beggar pulled at my sleeve, bent, leaning and cringing.

"Una limosnita señorita, mamita." ("A little alms little miss, little mother.")

I turned towards him. His eyes were filmed and running, and he had open sores on his hands.

"Is he a leper?" I wondered. In a wave of revulsion and panic I gave him some money, and watched him hobble away, pushing a stray dog out of his path with a stick.

I passed the meat market, a railed enclosure where the aproned duennas swung huge axes about to splinter the carcasses. Nearby was a well, and a woman crossed to it every now and then to draw a bucket of water which she dashed on the floor to swish the offal and dirt into some open drains. It had little effect and people slipped about on the paving.

I stopped at a hat stall and bought myself a bowler, in a rich brown colour, and not quite liking to put it on, went and sat at a café. Children and dogs were scuffling about between the tables. At the counter a woman was boiling soup, and grilling llamas' feet which she laid out in rows beside piles of fritters dipped in honey. But I was not hungry, and drank some beer, while boys walked up and down shouting lottery tickets for sale. I watched a youth with a bird-cage on a stand—there were budgerigars inside, and attached to the cage by two chains, he had two "Viewmasters" with circles of pictures, and was calling passers-by to look at the "*historias fantasticas de los Estados Unidos*" ("fantastic tales of the United States") for about 3d. I took a turn and pushed round a rather worn peepshow of the Grand Canyon.

Back in the hotel, the Baroness was reading the La Paz papers. She had established her contacts quite well, she said, though it was a little difficult at times. "People are always out, aren't they—and one can never be sure of their hours."

There was no sign of the others, so we decided to have showers. The one in the Baroness's room did not work at all, but mine did. A naked electric wire came out to the shower jets, which shot out strong spurts of water, warm and vibrant with electricity. We expected shocks, but the current was quite mild, and one felt a tingling that was alarming but just tolerable.

"What does it feel like now?" I called to the Baroness as she splashed and scrubbed. "Warm soda-water," she shouted back. When we had both finished and dressed in warmer clothes, and wondered several times what was happening to David and Forgues, whether they were having an amusing time or a disaster, or had met a riot of miners, we decided to have dinner.

The dining-room was ill-lit, and empty, but someone had tried to enliven it with posters of Spanish bullfights, and Bolivian *diabladas*, and a large print of Picasso's "Maternidad". A lone waiter hovered about, slapping at the flies with a napkin, and nothing on the menu was available, but after half-an-hour some soup appeared. When we had waited another half-hour for a lamb stew, the Baroness went to her room and brought down a bottle of whisky. We drank it neat, as we were cold, and it somehow killed the taste of the mutton, which was high.

We thought gloomily of sitting through another meal with David and Forgues, but when they appeared they had already eaten, as guests of some professor at the university, who had taken them to an Arab restaurant, of which there were several in this town. The *specialité* had been sheep's head. One peeled off the flesh with one's fingers in the Arab manner, and ate the eyes with toothpicks.

We walked to the university. Inside, in the ill-lit brown corridors, students were queuing for our film performance. They looked very young, and stared at us vacantly. Forgues had set up the apparatus in a lecture hall, with the screen against some dark-blue curtains, and a great many wires criss-crossing the floor from one machine to another.

The audience filed in. David was introduced in a warm, flowery and flattering speech by the *direktor*, and made a return speech expressing himself honoured to visit the university, "centre of so much cultural ferment". And Forgues turned the lights off and the machines on.

In an attempt to make up for the lack of Spanish dialogue or sub-titles, David had prepared a résumé of the story of *Hamlet* in Spanish, and made a tape-recording of Joaquín reading it in his impeccable Bolivian voice. The plan was to play parts of the tape to introduce each reel of the film, but either the voltage was too low, despite our dynamo, or someone was sitting on one of the wires, for Joaquín's voice, usually so light, almost feathery a tenor, came across as a deep, slow incomprehensible growl. Amid the inevitable tittering, David persuaded the *direktor* to read the résumé aloud, and the film began again.

The audience coughed, shuffled and whispered. I wondered how much they would understand, and what the ghost would mean to them, or the king, or a mediaeval castle in the Scandinavian mists.

"But look, the morn, in russet mantle clad,
    Walks o'er the dew of yon high eastern hill,"

said Horatio. I tried to think myself Bolivian and born in this high plateau where the dawn filtered late over the white peaks, and to feel myself a stranger to Chaucer and Shakespeare and the Elizabethan world-picture, and heir instead to the Cid and Cervantes, the *duende* of Spanish poetry and all the distant residue of the *conquistadores*. I thought of Lorca's dawn:

"*Puedo ver el duelo de la noche herida*
    Luchando enroscada con el mediodia."
("I can see the duel of the wounded night,
    Struggling entwined with midday . . .")

Beside me sat a girl chewing gum and picking her nose in the dark, as light and shadow peopled the screen, and the inimitable words shook me as always into a new consciousness.

Hamlet appeared on the battlements of Elsinore, looking out over the sea.

"To be, or not to be . . ." he began, and I thought I felt a tiny tremor of recognition in the audience. Then suddenly the sound track crackled as if struck by lightning, and burst into Spanish. Hamlet sat on the battlements still, but spouting a torrent of inflammatory, anti-government propaganda.

"*El realismo,*" he seemed to shout, "*el fatalismo, el communismo, el cubanismo . . . el organismo . . . la justicia . . . la futura . . .*" and dropped his dagger into the white waves to a loud fanfare of rock 'n roll.

The *direktor* leapt up and stumbled out of the hall. He came back very apologetic. The university radio had been broadcasting in another room, and by some electrical whimsy, our sound track had picked up their wavelength. They had now been stopped, he declared fiercely, and we all settled down to Shakespeare again. I wondered whether this radio was among the Baroness's contacts.

There was a second showing of the film, which drew a gratify-
ingly large audience. But it was late, and the Baroness and I did not
stay. As we walked back to the hotel the town was empty and quiet,
and moonlight shredded through the leaves of the pepper-trees,
falling in pale, tattered patches on the pebbled streets.

The road to Potosí snaked away across the plain, past a salt pan,
through river beds and isolated villages. It was easy to get lost.
There were no signposts, and we had only our map, and Forgues to
guide us.

Forgues was not very confident of his memory; so many of the
roads looked the same, he said, and with no landmarks, how could
he be sure? Once, we stopped a van to ask the way. The occupants, a
man and woman, said they were on their way from Canada to
Chile. They unfolded an enormous map of the whole continent and
pored over it, and after a sharp dialogue in Polish, told us we were
going on the right road, but in the wrong direction.

In villages we would stop for further assurance. Forgues would
emerge from his handkerchief-mask, open his window and lean out
to hail the nearest person.

"*Caballero?*" he would pipe, and a shepherd, shopkeeper or
beggar would come forward, surprised at being addressed with this
old-fashioned courtesy.

Just past a village called Huancame, as we bowled along a straight
stretch of road, Forgues again unveiled himself and leant forward
urgently to shake David's shoulder.

"Señor!" he shouted, "*Militares*," (soldiers) and he pointed ahead,
where we could see now a small grey hut and, as we drew nearer, a
chain across the road.

"*Guardia Civil?*" the Baroness boomed through her scarf. "No!
Militares," he was very agitated, and "Señor"—like a plea for safety.

"*Caramba!*" said the Baroness and hastily undid her veil and put
on some lipstick.

Throwing barriers across the road was common practice at this
time; it was often done by civilians, who held up convoys of
Americans and surrounded them, shouting angrily and waving
sticks until they paid their way out of the situation. Talk of revolution was never far from anyone's lips, and it was regulation for us

to carry the British Embassy Emergency Kit. This consisted of several small Union Jacks, with sticky backs one could lick like a stamp and affix to vulnerable parts of the car like the bonnet and windscreen; and a long white label with *"Embajada Britanica"* printed on it.

But as the people likely to hold us up would almost surely be illiterate, and might well confuse the red, white and blue of the Union Jack with the red, white and blue of the Stars and Stripes, it seemed clear that Whitehall really expected her sons to do their duty with whatever language and objects came to hand in such uncomfortable moments. So we had packed the Emergency Kit thinking of the bagpipe-playing diplomats in Indonesia, and by this time it must have been well-buried under all the projectors and pamphlets in the back.

There were about six soldiers standing on the grass verge by the hut, unslinging their machine-guns.

"O Madre mia!" pleaded Forgues, and we crunched to a halt as two of them came forward across our path, with bayonets pointed. The dust hissed and sifted down round us, and David got out.

"Buenos dias, tenientes." It was careful tact to address them all as lieutenants, so that even if they were not, they could be sure of one's respect. *"Diplomates . . . britanicos . . . ingleses . . ."* we heard, as they moved him towards the hut and demanded his passport.

We sat in tense silence. The soldiers did not put up their guns, and stood watching us sullenly, their ochre faces shining in the sun.

David called Forgues, who invoked the Virgin again as he climbed out of the car.

"They want the morning newspapers," said David grimly.

We had left Oruro that morning long before the paper-sellers appeared on the streets.

"Good Lord!" said the Baroness, "I suppose that means we all get marched into the hut."

But Forgues said, *"Bueno, señor,"* and dived into the back of the Land-Rover. After some noisy ferreting he emerged with an armful of *Hamlet* pamphlets, from the British Council, printed in Spanish, with little pictures of Elsinore, and the ghost, and Gertrude in her

Boats on Lake Titicaca

Herdswoman near the shores of Lake Titicaca

On the road to Coroico

draped bed. These he began to distribute, several to each soldier—darting about like a little old lady with a bag of sweets. "Some for you, and some for you . . ."

The soldiers were interested. Two of them put down their guns on the grass and began to peruse the pamphlets upside down. The leader shouted curtly to the bayoneted guards, who undid the chain and let it flop chinking into the dust, and came across to get their copies. I suddenly noticed that none of them were wearing shoes.

David and Forgues leapt into the car and we set off before they could lose interest. Forgues and the Baroness crossed themselves. Through the back window, framed by their ashen faces, and blurred by the dust, the soldiers became a distant picture, the figures bent in concentration upon the story of "*el fantasmo del Rey de Dinamarca*".

At Challapata, the next village, we stopped to buy bread from a woman in a tall white hat. I followed her into her house, which was very dark but clean-swept, and smelt of smoke and baking. In the corner was a bed covered with bright blankets and she kept the loaves of bread in a large earthenware pot.

After this the road climbed into the *cordillera*, and there were no more villages. We lunched by a stream like a Scottish burn, with grey rocks and spiky grass and moss, and drove on deeper into the mountains, toiling up one pass after another, the road hanging over vast gorges and cliffs, canyon after empty canyon of red rock. Large and sturdy in La Paz, the Land-Rover here appeared puny and insignificant, and we felt lost in this landscape, so harsh and dead-looking, with no bird or animal to reassure us. Like travellers in myth we called out with excitement at seeing the tiny cluster of some village far below, a distant shepherd with llamas, alpacas and a few sheep, or even the minute square of a field scraped upon the bare hulk of a mountainside. We sat in silence, alone with our thoughts, each afraid of the huge emptiness of it all. We only stopped once, to watch a little colony of rabbits sunning themselves on some rocks, and we got out to follow them as they scampered away, as though we needed some new conviction about life.

The sun set early, and it was dark by the time we reached the last gorges before Potosí. We wound through them, crossing the Devil's Bridge, and other arched Spanish bridges, and could just make out at times the old, narrow track cut into the cliff sides which for centuries had carried the mule and llama trains that picked their way through the *cordillera* and down to the Pacific.

IX

The Imperial City

POTOSÍ IS THE highest city in the world, and also one of the most remote and strange, with its passion-torn history of sudden glory, and swift decay. It is remote in distance from the sea and rivers and trade routes, from fertile valleys and from other cities. Even in its heyday, in the seventeenth century, it was incredibly distant from its greatest sphere of influence, which was Europe. Cold, uncomfortable, hostile, it was reached only by weeks of journeying through terrible mountains or jungles.

But it is also strange in another sense, for it was once indeed a great city, yet its greatness was based on one thing only—the exploitation of its mountain of silver. There was no other reason to be there; the sole preoccupation of its once enormous population was the pursuit of riches.

Potosí never managed to overcome or outlive the miner's mentality, the atmosphere created by people who thought, spoke and dreamt of nothing but great wealth, for whom any other occupation was insipid and meaningless, and who lived always in the hope of sudden luck and vast fortune. This atmosphere implied also that the fortune, once made, would be as quickly spent, and with little care. The treasure spelt its own doom, and the city from the start carried the seeds of its own decay.

The intense and ruthless pursuit of riches left their legacy in the whole continent, as did the phenomenal racial mixing that seventeenth-century Potosí set in motion. Both the glory and the decay fascinated me.

There is a tale about the discovery and origin of Potosí. One cold night a poor Indian named Gualpa was tending his llamas on the slopes of a mountain. He built a small fire of dried dung, and sat beside it, trying to get warm—and from under the fire a bright stream emerged and began to flow downhill, shining in the moonlight. The stream was not water but silver.

Whatever the truth of the story, the date of it is certain—1545. The discovery was astounding: the 16,000 foot mountain, a peculiar volcanic cone-shape, seemed to be solid silver.

It is quite true that for centuries, since before the Incas, mining had been carried on in this area. The Andes here are very rich in minerals: gold, silver, lead, copper, zinc, antimony, bismuth, wolfram; and the Andean Indians from early days developed ingenious methods of mining and working metal. By alloying tin with copper, they made bronze for tools, knives, weapons and ornaments. Silver and gold they used for luxuries only, and mined less extensively; there was no place in their society for the pursuit of riches for their own sake.

The mining and smelting processes were laborious: the Indians had no picks or drills; they scraped the ore out with hard wood, or the horns of deer; their anvils were stones, and for bellows they had long bronze tubes. Silver ores were pounded in stone mortars, and mixed with lead sulphide; they were then melted over a wood or charcoal fire, in a furnace pierced with holes to provide ventilation. The furnaces, or *huairas*, were fired at night on the hilltops, where the winds blew constantly through them, keeping the fire going at the proper heat. Early descriptions of the Inca world just after Pisarro's conquest refer to as many as 15,000 of these furnaces burning at nights on the peaks near Potosí, so that they looked like some vast festal illumination.

None of this labour was undertaken by individuals for their own personal profit. The Indians used the mines, they did not live for them, and the metals were valued according to their actual use; thus copper was valued more highly than gold or silver. So the attitude of the *conquistadores* was something so alien that the Indians failed to understand it, and were soon relentlessly exploited and, in a sense, robbed. Almost all the metal deposits known to the Incas were also known to Colonial Spain, but she never developed any except the mines for the two precious metals.

News of the discovery of silver at Potosí spread like fire. The

Spaniards named the silver mountain the *Cerro Rico*. They flocked there from throughout the continent, and soon from Europe. Every treasure-seeker's dream seemed about to come true.

A huge mining town grew up at the base of the *Cerro Rico*, at an altitude of over 14,000 feet. The discomforts of life at this height, the cold and exposure, and the dangers of the mining itself, were extreme, but there was nothing men would not endure for the sake of riches. Within only a few years Potosí became a wonder of the world.

Charles V, Holy Roman Emperor and King of Spain, moved swiftly to assert his authority over this windfall. Administrative positions were created, viceroys moved to and fro, and grandees arrived from Europe. An enormous mint was built to coin the Crown's share of the silver, for the king claimed by right one-fifth of any such treasure.

Potosí was made an Imperial City. The first coat of arms, granted by Charles V in 1553, contained a proud, defiant declaration:

"I am rich Potosí, the Treasure of the World, The King of the Mountains and Envy of Kings."

By 1570, when Viceroy Toledo made the first census, Potosí had 120,000 inhabitants. In 1650 there were 160,000, and it was by far the largest city in the continent. Lima in 1600 had only 15,000 inhabitants, Mexico City 40,000. Seville itself, one of the great trading towns of Europe, had a population of some 90,000 in 1594. London experienced a phenomenal growth during the sixteenth century, and by 1605 there were about 75,000 inhabitants in the city itself, and another 150,000 in the environs. Yet in 1530 the population was about one-third of this, and it is probable that at the time of the Armada Potosí had more inhabitants than London.

So Potosí became a legend. Its name hung on the lips of men the world over whenever they talked of money; and it became a word in common usage to express riches beyond measure and worth beyond price.

"*Vale un Potosí*," wrote Cervantes in *Don Quixote*—"It is worth a Potosí."

Early maps of South America show the Imperial City straddling the continent. Even in China it was depicted, by a monk-cartographer, as Mount Pei tu Hsi.

The violence and extravagance of life there was all that could be imagined of a city whose riches had attracted such an enormous and polyglot community of treasure-seekers; miners, administrators, traders, vagabonds, and women. The entire population was said to dress extravagantly and eat and drink to excess. In 1556, to celebrate the accession of Philip II, there was a *fiesta* lasting twenty-four days, which cost eight million pesos. In 1663 the governor, Don Luis de Andrade y Sotomayor, gave a *grandiosa fiesta* to celebrate the festival of the Blessed Sacrament. In one plaza of the city there was a circus, with "as many animals as in Noah's ark" and fountains simultaneously spouting wine, water and chicha.

By the turn of the century there were fourteen dance halls, thirty-six gambling houses and one theatre, at which the admission prices were forty to fifty pesos. There were some 800 professional gamblers and 120 prostitutes, most famous of whom was a courtesan named Doña Clara, who filled her house with luxuries from Europe and the Orient, and held salons where the richest miners competed for her favours.

The city was full of turbulence, treachery and assassinations. Gambling, intrigues, antagonism between pure-bred Spaniards and *mestizos*, and rivalries over women, all frequently led to riots tantamount to civil war. Everyone went armed: even the town councillors met wearing swords, pistols and coats of mail.

Vast fortunes were made and lost. Successful miners became tremendously rich, so did successful traders, administrators, smugglers, and even some Indians.

No one has managed to make accurate estimates of the effects of the silver of Potosí on the world, or how much there really was. Even the known amounts are enormous. One eighteenth-century treasurer of Potosí estimated that between 1556 and 1783, the Spanish received 151,722,647 pesos. This was the customary Royal Fifth. (The Royal Fifth of Atahualpa's ransom, which Pisarro sent to Charles V, was 155,300 pesos of gold and 5,400 marcos of silver.) The miners during this period, he estimated, received 820,513,893 pesos.

These calculations can take no account of the amounts of smuggled silver, which must have been vast. The miners had already developed the custom of *capchas*, the general free-for-all between Saturday night and Monday morning, when anyone could go underground and dig ore for himself, and sell it to the masters of the mine. Successive viceroys, to say nothing of the mine-owners, tried to stop this custom, but in vain.

However, everyone spent the silver, so the whole world was soon in a sense a great deal richer. All over Europe metal money became easier to get. This, of course, affected price-levels and upset trade to a large extent, and the whole process of economic disturbance gave a strong fillip to capitalism. Merchants prospered, and landlords and peasants found it harder to make ends meet. And the King of Spain, suddenly very rich indeed and determined to stay so, had his responsibilities, and his sphere of influence, greatly increased.

The miners of Potosí spent their wealth in two ways: first, on possessions and parties. The market of Potosí must have been an extraordinary sight. There is an early description of the goods at the "great fair" which make the city seem like one of the great ports of Europe, even Venice.

"Silks from Granada were there, stockings and swords from Toledo ... iron from Viscaya, linen and knitted goods from Portugal, embroideries of silk, gold and silver, and felt hats from France; tapestries from Flanders, cloth from Holland, swords and steel from Germany, paper from Genoa, satins from Florence, sacred paintings from Rome; crystal from Venice, hats and wool from England; wax from Cyprus, ivory and precious stones from India, diamonds from Ceylon, perfume from Arabia; rugs from Persia, Cairo and Turkey; spices from Goa; porcelain from China, negro slaves from Cape Verde and Angola, pearls from Panama, food from Tucuman, Cochabamba and Santa Cruz, horses from Chile."

All these had to come up the trail through the *cordillera*. Probably the route was far less lonely than it is now, for the llama and mule trains must have been ceaseless. Through Potosí, Lima prospered.

And so, illegally, did Buenos Aires, then in the Province of La Plata, which was a port for smugglers who dared the suicidal routes across the jungles between Potosí and the Atlantic coast.

A new class grew up, that of the *peruleros*, the merchant-adventurers. Commerce became something which Spaniards who had hitherto been too proud would now deign to indulge in. The *peruleros* had no limit to their field. They moved about the continent undeterred by peaks, rivers or jungles, in fearless pursuit of bargains and buyers. (It was a *perulero* travelling through Brazil who named the now famous Copacabana beach in Rio de Janeiro, after the shrine of that name on the shores of Lake Titicaca.)

The miners also, however, disposed of their wealth in other fields. They spent huge sums of money on public works, and on influencing the king. Much of the construction of the city was done at their expense. They built lakes in the hills above, to collect rain-water and thus provide hydraulic power for the ore-grinding mills; they built themselves splendid houses, and they endowed churches. The Spanish Crown, by arrangement with the Pope, held supreme authority in ecclesiastical matters throughout the New World. The king was responsible for the well-being of the Church, and bishops were responsible to him. So for the miners one way to gain the good-will of the king as well as the blessing of God was to endow the church.

As by the mid-seventeenth century there were eighty churches in Potosí, there was much chance for the miners to spend their money conspicuously. But they did so also further afield, in Sucre, on the *altiplano* and in Lima, providing for the flowering of Colonial Baroque art. And further than this, they also endowed the Church in Spain.

Moreover, rich *Potosinos* made "gifts" or "loans" to the king, for which they expected some return. In time, regular representations went to the court of Spain to make known the wishes of the Villa Imperial. The miners' councils in the seventeenth century were well-organised and could afford the best lawyers in Spain to plead for them. They made requests for steady labour, for cheaper mercury, and freedom from bureaucracy, for exemption from military service and from sales tax. They wanted imports to be properly organised and they wanted the Royal Fifth to be halved. The king had to watch his step with the miners; unlike modern governments subjected to pressures from big business, he had no electorate to appeal to; he was constantly decorating them with new titles to keep them quiet.

Despite this show of efficiency, the mining was never conducted on a really progressive basis. Methods of extraction and refining were not kept up-to-date. The mint and the miners employed forced labour, with the utmost cruelty: a term in Potosí became like a sentence of death, particularly for the unfortunate negroes imported from tropical homelands. As for any really civilised or intellectual life in the city, a little scientific research was done in the monasteries, but there is no record of much learning or scholarship, or even of a printing press.

By the eighteenth century, the city was in decline, but it was still important enough in reputation for Bolívar, the hero-Liberator after whom Bolivia was named, to go there in 1825, for flamboyant liberation ceremonies. He processed through the town in a throng of dancing hysterical admirers, and two children dressed as angels were let down from a triumphal arch to make a speech to him. There were seven weeks of festivities, bull fights, dinners, balls, fireworks and illuminations. In one day Bolívar made seventeen speeches in reply to laudatory orations. He also made a symbolic ascent of the Cerro Rico upon whose summit he made an oration declaring that all the wealth that had come out of the mountain was as nothing compared with the liberty of the peoples he was freeing, a striking comparison even if the image was inept.

But Bolívar's companions thought Potosí a mere shadow of its former self, and nothing could stop the inexorable decline, for the great deposits of silver had now vanished. The ore being mined now was of an increasingly low grade, much of it not worth the expense of extracting. In many places the mines had reached water which there was as yet no method of pumping out. In 1804 there had been a terrible drought, followed by famine and disease. The population of the city numbered now only some 8,000. The Cerro Rico still reared its strange brown cone-head above the city, but inside it was a warren of empty passages and abandoned workings. Like the treasure, the great population of miners and traders had dispersed.

Over the years, after this, with the advance of mining methods, sporadic attempts were made to revive Potosí, as though it were impossible that the legend could die. But the silver ore that remained and was accessible was of such low grade as to make it hardly worth extracting.

Then, in this century, when tin became a commodity so much sought after, and the big mining families such as Patiño, Hochschild and Aramayo, developed Bolivia into a leading producer in the world, Potosí had a brief resurgence into activity. A number of mines were started round about, and even the Cerro Rico itself was worked again. But the deposits were not rich, and the mines remained small, and did nothing to alter the city's decrepitude. There was something pathetic and undignified about the whole attempt: as if a great actress were trying to make a come-back in vaudeville.

Today Bolivia has no metal money at all, only paper.

X

Broken Baroque

WE SAW LITTLE of Potosí that night as we bumped up the cobbled slopes into the town. The streets were narrow and hardly lit at all, and we threaded our way down one and up another until we found our hotel. We were greeted by a tall and fat man in a grubby waiter's jacket. A thick mop of black hair fell in fronds across his forehead and his eyes rolled wildly. His face made me think of the robbers in Grimm's fairy-tales.

Potosí's fame in Bolivia now rested solely on its authentic period charm. Nothing, people told us, had changed since the seventeenth and eighteenth centuries. The Hotel Londres was like an old hostelry. It was built round a courtyard which had a well, and water troughs, and stalls for animals, while a staircase up one wall led to the upper floor, and rooms for the owners. As lorries and jeeps had replaced animals, most of the stalls were in disuse, though a couple had been boarded off to make small rooms. One was a primitive bathroom, and in another were two iron beds with bare mattresses. Forgues declared he would sleep down here as he had to guard the projectors and dynamos, and did not wish to carry them further in this altitude.

The rest of us went upstairs, to be shown the *Salón de Comer* (the dining-room), and the other rooms, which were little different from that Forgues had chosen, though they had wooden instead of mud floors, and the beds had blankets. Plaster was peeling off the walls, and mould growing in its place. The ceilings were stained and sagging, and the windows were patched with cardboard, but we stripped the beds and found no insects, and the waiter made up for any material shortcomings with the effusiveness of his welcome. He toiled up and down with our luggage, tripping and panting. He

139

disappeared for long intervals to fetch lukewarm water for us to wash in and then leant against the washstand to ask us about La Paz, and about England.

"England," he declared, "ah, in England, señora, all the people are very happy! They are very rich, no?"

"No," I said, "the Americans are rich, much richer than the English."

"But señora—the English money is worth much more than American money."

"No indeed," I said, "the American money is worth more. Everyone wants dollars."

"But no, permit me, señora. How many dollars are there in one pound *esterlín*?"

"Well, two and a half—more or less."

"There you are—you see exactly as I said—the English money is much more valuable. Don't give me dollars."

And he stumped out.

When we reached the dining-room for dinner, he led us, his face beaming, to a table in one corner. Already waiting for us were four plates of grey soup with thick lumps of rice floating in them. The Baroness looked pained. Forgues said: "What have we here?" and tasted it noisily.

David said, "It looks like porridge that has been thrown in the sea and fished out again," and spoilt what appetite any of us had. The next course was small bits of meat half-raw, sinewy and with yellow streaks. It was followed by a plate of cold mounds that must have been potato-cakes. None of us ate anything.

It was terribly cold. The Baroness complained that the altitude must have upset the boiling point of water. She had ordered tea, she said, and it was luke-warm. She went into the kitchen herself to supervise the filling of her hot water bottle.

David and I went back, shivering, to our bleak room, with its iron bedsteads, and washstand, enamel jug, basin and bucket. There were candles for light and little jars of drinking-water. Over my nightclothes I put on two sweaters, wearing one as trousers with my feet in the sleeves. I climbed into my sleeping-bag and then into the bed, but under eight blankets it still took a great deal of neat whisky to get warm enough to sleep. In the morning we all had splitting headaches, from the altitude and the alcohol; and breakfast, of scrambled eggs with garlic, only added to our discomfort.

We were in Potosí several days, meeting people, and showing *Hamlet* in the university, where the students were very left-wing and the foyer held a large exhibition of photographs from East Germany.

One morning David and Forgues went down a mine, right into the heart of the *Cerro Rico*. (The Baroness and I were not included in this adventure: no women were allowed underground, as they were thought to bring bad luck and make the minerals disappear.) Wearing tin helmets and white overalls they were taken by an engineer deep down to see the working surface. On their return to the main shaft they found that the lift had been broken by an explosion. So they spent many hours sitting down there in the dark, with Forgues praying and the engineer muttering *"Que barbaridad, que raro."* When at last they came out into the chill sun, the annual ceremony of sacrificing to the God of the Mountain was in progress. Some 200 llamas, spitting with fear, were being driven, dragged and pushed uphill to be slaughtered. The entrails were blasted with dynamite against the entrance of the mine, and later the meat cooked and eaten at a feast.

Left to my own devices, as the Baroness was making her contacts with the six radio stations in the town, I wandered about, taking photographs, with my new technique of sideways shots to allay superstition. I would stand facing in one direction, pretending to be taking something straight ahead but pointing the lens at something else beside me. With a little practise at focusing the lop-sided picture, I could photograph people like the market women who were camera shy to the point of throwing vegetables. This I found exhilarating, partly because of the pretence and the chase, but also because I realised that in their eyes it was wicked, and I was trying to steal their souls. Afterwards I felt ashamed at my lack of respect for them.

Even at midday Potosí was cold; the air was noticeably thinner than in La Paz, and the streets painfully steep, so that I panted for breath, and too much speed set the blood dinning in my ears. There was a pretty square, with some cypress trees. Old people sat on benches, and the cathedral was white and shining in the sun. But there was no peace. Loud-speakers hung upon the walls of buildings all about, hooting out the programmes of the six radio stations, so that the talk of the passing citizens, the shouts of children, the grind and splutter of lorries, jeeps and old broken-down taxis were all drowned in a ceaseless metallic cacophony.

Narrow streets led off the square, and whichever way one looked there were mountains beyond, the far peaks of the *cordillera*, or the Cerro Rico itself, that lifeless red-gold cone of riches and doom.

It seemed very true that the town had changed little since the seventeenth or eighteenth centuries. I walked down narrow, dark alleys where the wooden balconies leant out overhead, almost touching each other. I had to flatten myself against the wall to let a loaded mule or llama by. There were houses with big stone porticos where I looked in, beneath carved coats of arms, to paved courtyards with fountains and statues. Dominating it all were the white churches, with their high Spanish towers blinding against the blue sky, and the open arches at the top showing the bells in black silhouette.

I felt puzzled by the place. Walking about, I moved constantly from brilliant sunlight into deep shade, and the sudden contrasts played strange tricks with my sight. If I looked into a house from the sun, bright blobs of colour swam into my gaze, and merged with the darkness into blurred shapes, like people moving in the shadows.

In one lane I found myself at the Church of San Lorenzo, its great carved doorway guarded by two enormous stone angels, standing with their arms akimbo as if daring sinners to enter and confess.

"It has not changed," they seemed to say, "the grandees clattering about the street, building their big houses, running the mine, and the mint, quarrelling about the price of silver . . . Potosí is a jewel of the Empire; and the silver runs like a river down to the sea and the waiting ships . . ."

"And yet it has changed completely," I thought. "The silver has gone, and those Spanish grandees are dead, the mint is a museum now, and these big houses ramshackle and uncared for."

The wind wheeled about the rooftops, lifting and clashing the broken tiles; the belfries were cold and silent, for the monks and nuns had gone too, and only a few priests remained to rock the bells and call the faithful; and now only Indians from the high mountains roamed the streets with their llamas to gaze at the women of Potosí.

But the place was still Spanish. The rooftops and belfries, the courtyards and the carved angels held a distillation of Spain, its aloofness, dignity, passion, cruelty and fantasy. Ghosts of Castile, and Andalusia, watched me from the dark doorways as I blinked in the piercing sunlight. The tumult of Europe, the glory of Baroque, the horrors of poverty, gluttony for wealth, the ruthlessness of exploitation, the shame and the decay were all here. The wind whipping dust about the crumbled cornices, shuttered windows and cobbled streets seemed to sigh across centuries. And the comings and goings of today were like children playing hide-and-seek, peeping through the tattered curtains of the past.

In one house, under a wooden balcony, a hatter sat at his work. I peered through the window, and then went in. The Potosí hats were different from the bowlers of the *altiplano*. With tall crowns and wide flat brims they looked a little like Welsh hats, black, brown or green, and decorated with bright bands and rosettes of ribbon.

The hatter offered me a chair, and I watched him for a while. He was making a white hat, like the women wore in Cochabamba and the plains, and showed me how they brought him a crocheted bag, which he would wet and heat, and pull on the block—"So"—and then starch over and again until it was stiff and shining, and a hat—"very good, very strong, very fashionable."

"Like panama?" I said, showing my ignorance.

"No, not like panama. That is grass. This is cord. It is very intricate, made with the hands—one must know well how to do it."

He passed me some hats, which I tried on, and the crowns were all too small, but I chose a brown one, and he offered to put a broad pink ribbon round it, which he declared would look very fashionable.

"You have great skill," I said to him. "Do you have an apprentice —or an assistant—someone to teach about your work?"

He shook his head sadly.

"Ah, señora. It is a great sadness to me. My trade is a dying one.

It is a dying art. The girls are not wearing hats any more. Today, you see, all the *cholitas* want to become *señoritas*."

"Oh, what a pity," I said. "If only they knew how pretty they look just as they are."

"But you know, señora, I think it's the same all over the world now—in England and America, and Spain and Africa, yes in all parts, it seems to me, all the *cholitas* want to become *señoritas*, and to look the same as all the other *señoritas* everywhere. And why? They will no longer look *distinto*, which has always been their charm."

And he sighed as he ironed the brims flat with the steam hissing up in clouds, and then moved lovingly from one creation to another, dusting the white hats with starch and buffing them up to make them shine.

The first Casa de Monedas, the mint built by Viceroy Toledo, had stood on the site of the present Casa de Justicia. A second mint, built in the seventeenth–eighteenth centuries, lay below the main square, enormous, dark and forbidding, with thick stone walls like a fortress or a prison. It was now a museum.

I paid my entrance fee to a guard, and was taken round by the curator himself. We walked across a cobbled sunlit court into huge, vaulted halls where collections of the silver coins were displayed in cases beside the machinery that made them.

"Look at these great wooden wheels, and the chains here," the curator said. "Some machine, no? And here is the ring where the mules walked to push the wheel, and if you stand on this ramp here —so—we can look down, deep down into the cellars. You see the wheels down there? They were pushed by negro slaves." And we went on to see the big arched furnaces and ovens, also built by the slaves, and the stamps and moulds for the coins, with Spanish arms and figures.

In the basement, in cold, damp, stone-flagged halls, were collections of furniture from colonial times, many lovely old pieces, rotting, worm-eaten and in disrepair.

"What a pity," I exclaimed, as the curator pointed out as authentic a desk whose inlay had now split into fragments.

"Señora?"

The pass across the summit

Market—Cochabamba

Portal of the Casa de Moneda

Alley in Potosí

"How sad that no one has been caring for all this beautiful furniture. Would it not be possible, Señor, to move it upstairs, where it is light, and not so damp? And to polish it and dust it?"

He looked surprised.

"*Bueno*, señora, I shall have to tell that to the Director of Economics of the city."

Upstairs, above the mint, was a series of beautifully proportioned halls, galleries and living-rooms that had housed the Administration. But for their walls, which were covered with pictures, they were completely empty. Feeling indignant about the furniture rotting in the cellars, I followed the curator past pictures of saints and martyrs, flagellations and inquisitions, and Madonnas in plump skirts floating in skies full of stars. There were portraits, too, of the administrators who had run the mint for the King of Spain: younger sons of noble families who came out in good colonial tradition for a term of service in the Empire.

We gazed out from a balcony at the roof-tops of churches and houses, and the winding valleys below, where the last dusty paths of the mule-trail and the little arched bridges disappeared behind red cliffs.

"And so," said the curator, embracing it all in a gesture, "so the silver has gone. Away down those little paths it went to the sea, to Europe."

"It is ironic, is it not, señor, that Bolivia, which had the richest deposit of silver the world had ever known, now has not one silver coin in its money?"

"Yes—they took it all, they took it all."

"Well, what happened to it? No one could say Spain is rich now."

"Señora," he took my arm and pushed his face close to mine. "You know where all the Spanish silver is now? England!"

"No!"

"Yes, for sure. *El pirata Drake!*" he nodded with firm assurance.

"How can I deny that?" I thought. "Perhaps it's quite true anyway, and if not *el pirata Drake*, then some other pirate, equally brave and reckless, and what of the 'pirates' of industrial England, whose goods were so coveted by Spain and paid for in her silver?" And I thought of that silver being hoarded and circulated and withdrawn and

K

recirculated, and minted anew as English, with English arms and monarchs' heads stamped upon its face. Perhaps some of it was in circulation in England still, while here fate had changed the Imperial City, and the mint stood empty, a giant relic.

A wind rattled about the building, whipping scarves of dust across the roof-tops and I stared through its whirling shapes trying to see muleteers threading down into the gorges, and thinking about the marqueses in their doublets and plumes, and the black-eyed Andalusian women watching them through the shutters.

"Señora?" the curator was waiting to take me down.

One day the *jefe de cultura*, the town official in charge of cultural affairs, invited us all to lunch at his club. We sat in dingy brown leather armchairs, eating a collection of hors d'œuvres, mostly red peppers and tinned palm tree kernels. The *jefe* was a thin, weary man with bloodshot eyes and many gold teeth. His hobby was the history of Potosí, which he kept describing as "*bastante remarkable*", ("pretty extraordinary") and he told us, in a sepulchral voice, some of the grislier stories of the past.

"Did you know about the *caballero* in black? No? That is a very strange tale. He would ride about the streets always on a black horse, with a black cloak about him, his black hat pulled down over his face. He was like a rider of the night. And he rode always like this for five years, always holding something—so—under his cloak. It was a skull he carried.

"One day he died, and they found the skull wrapped in his cloak. Inside it was a note saying, 'Had you lived three thousand lives, three thousand times would I have killed you.' And the skull—was that of his best friend, whom he had discovered to be his wife's lover."

Behind us people passed to and fro, and the sun, filtering in through stained glass windows, cast stripes of pink and green across the *jefe*'s pallid face. He ordered some beer, and more bread.

"And there's another tale—very strange," he spat out an olive pip. "You have a jeep? Good. Along the road down the valley back to Oruro, you pass the old mining camp and turn along a track into the hills. Up there is a farm—very beautiful—where once lived a mayor of Potosí. He was married to a woman of Andalusia who had arrived lately from Spain. She was most elegant and proud—and like all Andalusian women her soul was fire. One day she went to church and found a *chola* woman sitting in her place, and the *chola* refused to move so she had to go to the back. She was in a terrible rage at this insult, and insisted that her husband must take revenge on the woman—bring her to Court—denounce her publicly—hire an assassin. She became very hysterical. And her husband calmed her down, saying he would see to it, but never got round to doing anything."

"Of course not," exclaimed the Baroness, who had a poor opinion of hysterical women, and obviously sympathised with the husband.

"So, things went on in this way until one day the Andalusa got her husband drunk or drugged or something, and took him up to the attic where she crucified him."

"*Que horror!*" we all exclaimed in chorus.

"Yes indeed, señores. She crucified him, and up she went each day to stick pins into him in revenge for his failure to redress her insult—until at last he died.

"You can see the place still. A later owner made it into a chapel to atone for the woman's sin."

And so we parted company. The *jefe* was most eager about our film, which was to be shown that evening, and said he looked forward to seeing "*el vero Shakespeare*". But when the time came, he sent a message to say that he could not attend, as it was his birthday.

In a fit of morbid compulsion we went to see the farm he had told us about, which lay in a lonely valley among small fields hedged with poplar trees. A family of geese wandered in and out of the chapel, and the owner sat us on cane chairs in his *salón* and gave us glasses of sherry from Chile. He complained about the sadness of the times, and how his farm, and the country itself, was in a state of decay.

Among the peaks above this valley lay Tarapaya, the crater of a volcano, with sulphur springs, and we went up there on the way back for the waters were famous as a cure for many ailments, and we thought a bathe might alleviate our altitude discomforts. The crater was quite round, and very large, filled with grey water which bubbled and belched, and gave off little hissing curls of steam. The air was sick with the smell of sulphur.

At one side a stream left the crater and flowed out of sight across the hill, and we followed it down to a rectangular pool cut into the mountainside. This was the Inca's pool, Forgues said, and he would come here on a litter, travelling for weeks across the *cordillera*, to cure his rheumatism.

Centuries old, it looked new and modern, the grey stones sliced as precisely as if they had been cut with some fine machine, and no cement or daub had been needed to join them, so exact and closely placed were they. At one corner, steps led down into the pool, and the bather could sit in comfort, lapped about by the warm grey water, enveloped in drifts of cloud at times, watching a lone condor, or simply gazing out across the valleys and cliffs.

We pictured the sun king coming here, in his flowing robes and gold armlets, pictured his hawk-faced courtiers, and wondered whether they had built shelters or had tents, for they must have needed some protection from the harsh winds. And I wondered if they had brought gold with them, the king's plates and cups, even gold sheeting perhaps, for his pool in Cuzco had been lined with gold.

We went back and bathed in the crater, although there was frost everywhere on the ground. David swam across it several times, which Forgues thought very rash, in view of the bubbles. The Baroness, in her haste to get out of the cold wind, dived in with her sunglasses on, and we all had to pluck up courage to duck down and grope for them in the dark slime near the bank. By the time we retrieved them, Forgues was looking very pale; I felt weak and giddy, and my heart thumped like a giant on the march.

When we returned to Potosí, we told the waiter at the Hotel Londres that we had been to Tarapaya.

"Ah yes," he nodded. "It is a very strange place. And some people go there to swim in that evil-smelling water. But only at the very edge. It is *peligrosissimo* to go out into the middle, for there is a whirlpool and you will be sucked down deep into the volcano, which is without bottom."

"Really, is that so?" the Baroness said.

"Yes, really and truly, señora, down into the darkness of hell. And the bodies return to the surface after two days, cooked—yes, cooked—like the meal of the devil."

XI

The Colonial Capital

WE LEFT POTOSÍ for Sucre early one morning when the sunlight was still milky and the air not yet cuttingly dry. There had been a heavy frost, and tiny splinters of ice glistened on the streets and rooftops as we bumped out of the city and turned off towards the *cordillera*.

We drove first down several valleys, past farms with crops and plantations along the river-beds, and then climbed up into mountains which were this time lower, less harsh and bleak than the other approach to Potosí, but still as empty and awesome. The road threaded endlessly in hairpin bends along the cliff edge, in and out, in and out, and we ground along in low gear, tense with the thought of going over the edge, the Baroness and Forgues crossing themselves at each crucifix we passed. At one stage David noticed we had been going an hour without changing out of the bottom two gears, and our average speed was seven m.p.h. Several times the lock of the Land-Rover was not wide enough for us to complete a corner in one swing, and we had to edge round, reversing and turning, within inches of the cliff drop.

As the sun drew higher, the air seemed to dry more, until it had a bite that seared one's skin like the iciness of a winter's morning. Dust hissed in at us, and though we drove hand-on-horn, we saw oncoming lorries before we heard them, as they puffed up dust-clouds on the bends in the cliff ahead. We would find a passing place and draw in to let them by, and long after they had gone, the dust would hang in the air, a motionless, timeless cloud, then, sift down, shaping and reshaping golden in the sun to settle on the road, or film brownly the dry plants on either side.

Later we reached kinder country, and stopped for lunch near a small bridge where a river ambled between peaceful fields, and men worked at the crops, or lay under the trees in noon-day sleep.

Near a farmhouse, a man leant on a wall, watching his pigs, while beside him two patient oxen yoked to a plough stood waiting among the brown sods, the dust still rising about them like steam. Past the fringes of high, dry grass behind him lay fields of golden wheat, and thin stooks standing sentinel over rows not yet gathered. Other fields were dark brown, already scored by the plough, and in the distance were bright patches of orange-gold where maize cobs lay drying in the sun.

We drove all afternoon through these golden valleys with ridges of dun and grey mountains between, and everywhere they were harvesting or ploughing. We saw threshing-parties, driving donkeys round and round to trample the grain until it lay in piles which the women would then toss across the smooth-stamped threshing floor so that the grain fell and the chaff blew away. On distant hillsides we could see them too, the rich yellow dust blowing across the tiny figures. The children were all in the fields with them, leaving the villages empty.

So struck were we by the rhythm and beauty of these scenes, and the sense of harmony and fulfilment, that when after about 100 miles we suddenly saw fences and a combine harvester, it was a jarring shock. We watched the machine come snorting through the grain beside some little mud huts, belching exhaust like a grotesque benediction from the Industrial Revolution, and saw it for an instant as though we were the primitive threshers, bent in the rhythm of centuries' dialogue with the soil. It seemed then a harsh, intruding giant, magical, sinister, gnawing the earth close, spewing the riches and dross, roaring across the hillsides like an alien god—or devil.

At sunset we found ourselves descending towards a wide valley. The road forked, and uncertain which path to take, we stopped an oncoming jeep to ask the way.

The driver was a friar in a dusty brown cassock. He gave a pessimistic grimace at our questions.

"*Bueno*. Both roads lead to the river Pilcomayo. With the lower one you can go down there," he pointed. "Somewhere there is a ford. A few lorry drivers know how to find it. But I can't recommend it. This afternoon a lorry got stuck in the middle and had to be abandoned."

"And this road, the top one, Padre?"

"Yes, I have just come this way, across the bridge. But your jeep is very big. And it's getting very late. I don't think they will let you cross. They don't like heavy things on the bridge. Last month, one of the cables snapped and a lorry tipped over into the river. You could stay the night at the village down there," and with that he drove off.

The village was a cluster of mud huts down below us, where several dogs were baying farewell to the daylight. It did not seem inviting, so we decided to risk the higher road. We soon reached a very large suspension bridge slung across the valley on steel cables with great stone towers at each end. It was barred with chains, but the curator saw us after a while, and allowed us to cross. "One man to drive," he rapped, "the others on foot." The Land-Rover crept across in a clatter of wooden slats, and we followed it, as the bridge creaked and swayed, the cables made weird twanging noises, and the dark waters where the lorry had fallen swished loudly, far below.

As we crossed, the valley was caught in the last blaze of sunset, and the towers became pink citadels in the black hillside. From far upstream the huge width of the river was a wild pattern in red and black, with fiery streaks of water, and long shining sandbanks like primeval animals lying stretched asleep.

We drove up into more mountains as the moon rose, gold at first in the dusty air, then its cold white self, moulding the bushes and escarpments, and showing deep black crevices in the road where the next rains would bring a landslide.

Then at last there was Sucre, a pattern of twinkling lights below us in a bowl-like valley, and we bumped through the streets asking the way, reaching our hotel with a long retinue of children who ran beside us, trying to hang on and peep into our strange vehicle.

At the Hotel Paris, we were shown to the "best rooms". David's and mine was large and dark with no windows, and an enormous evil-smelling tiled bathroom whose taps gurgled loudly and constantly, but produced no water. The doors opened on to a colonnaded courtyard, with a few dusty plants in pots.

Grimy and hungry, we went to the dining-room, where at one long table sat some twenty giggling girls under the chaperonage of an air force captain. At another table, neat and aloof, sat two Japanese: their suits were immaculate, and they ate in silence, staring. There was a hush at our entrance, and David, passing the girls, said what he meant to be "*buen provecho*" that is, "*bon apetit*", but it came out as "*a provecho*" which implied, "I am going to take advantage of you". This caused a sensation among the girls and an air of enraged propriety in the air force captain. We retired round a corner to eat our meal, a single sausage in a sea of wet mashed potato, followed by fried eggs in gravy, and then prunes.

Next day the Baroness flew home to Buenos Aires, in a very small aeroplane, with a party of schoolgirls going on a pilgrimage.

It was Gonzalo Pizarro, brother of the Conquistador, who first established the region of Charcas. Sucre, the capital, was founded in 1538 by Pedro de Anzures. Through the centuries it had four different names, first Charcas then La Plata (presumably after the silver of Potosí), later Chuquisaca, and then Sucre, after the great general of that name.

Potosí sprang suddenly to fame in 1545, and became a *Villa Imperial*, but Charcas always remained a steadier, more permanent and cultural centre. Moreover, at 10,000 feet with an equable climate, it was a haven for the rich miners of Potosí. Here they built themselves large, distinguished mansions; the colonnaded patios they filled with fig trees, vines and bougainvillaea, and within high white walls they enclosed orchards of peach and orange trees.

By 1549 Charcas had become a bishopric, and within another ten years it was granted an *Audiencia*, or seat of justice and administration, within the Viceroyalty of Lima. Up to the late eighteenth century the Audiencia of Charcas included most of what is now Bolivia, as well as Tucuman (now Argentina), and Paraguay. It was only in 1776, with the threat of the Portuguese colonial thrust in Brazil, that the King of Spain, Charles III, made a new Audiencia for

Rio de la Plata, in Buenos Aires, and Charcas became known as Alto Peru.

In the eighteenth century, the city had almost a golden age. A distinct regional character, and a steady economy were the tranquil base for a cultural flowering that made people speak of it as the 'Athens of South America'. There were big monasteries and churches and fine buildings. The University of San Xavier, and the law school, the Academia Carolina, were justly famous. It was from them that the first liberal ideas irradiated the continent, and in Chuquisaca that the first declarations for independence were later made against imperial Spain.

Much later, La Paz was made the capital of the country, leaving Sucre as legal capital only. So the city had lapsed into a minor role, and become a backwater.

Little changed now, it was a quiet, distinguished relic of better days. The city had been planned on a noble scale, with wide streets leading off the central square, and a logical demarcation of quarters for markets and trade, administrative buildings and big, sedate houses.

The square itself was like that in any Spanish town, with its statues of heroes, the benches where old people sat gossiping in the shade of tall pine trees, the little booths selling drinks and cigarettes, and the assiduous boot-blacks. On one side were modern municipal buildings, and the cathedral, on another the Legislative Hall, with its Baroque balcony from which Simón Bolívar made the declaration of independence.

Our guide and mentor in Sucre was Don Felipe, an elderly cynic, and himself a relic of the "better days," before the Revolution destroyed the class structure of the Republic, and Land Reform took the estates from the *padrónes* to "give the land back" to the Indians.

Tall and lean, hawk-faced and tanned a deep ochre-ish bronze, Don Felipe was the product of an old established class, and once, long ago, in the diplomatic service of his country, he had spent eight years in the Bolivian Embassy in London. This had left him with a complete mastery of the King's English, a large library of English books, a small wardrobe of English clothes, and an undying taste for, and loyalty to everything English, which was not simply a sentiment but a rock-like conviction. He spoke of the English as "we".

Don Felipe had inherited an estate in his country, and in the recent revolution he had, like the other old families, lost his lands, and been forbidden to go out to his country house. He lived now in a small house in the back streets of Sucre, with his wife, a plump, asthmatic woman, half-Scottish half-Spanish, and born in the Philippines, who, like Don Felipe, taught English in the university. They had four children.

The house had an air of musty, dilapidated scholarship; we dined with the family by the light of paraffin lamps, and then sat drinking their home-brewed *pisco*, discussing the university, the students and the hopeless state of the country.

Don Felipe, who had grown up among the Indians, and spoke fluent Quechua, seemed to loathe them and the "régime" equally, with all the passion of the mighty who are fallen, untempered by resignation.

He said, "Of course we should have left years ago. Fifty of the best families in Sucre are now living in the Argentine. It might not have been easy for us—but it would have been better for the children. Look at my son, Gonzalo.

"Here he is, with distinctions in every subject for his whole university career, and he can't get a scholarship to go to study in the States because we are the wrong sort of family. Socialism? Pah! It's just another layer of bribery and corruption worse than ever before. Worse than you English will ever be able to understand."

I pointed out that England, too, now had a socialist government, though admittedly more cautious and circumspect about the timing of its progress.

"Socialist? Maybe," he said, "but England is still a free country. I tell you, the worst thing that happened to Bolivia was the withdrawal of Spain. The Spanish were bad enough, but they were better than this Republic."

Waving us all to move back, he picked up a can of petrol, stood by the opposite wall, and flung a jet of it across the room into the fire. Flames shot out and roared up to the ceiling, and I knocked my *pisco* on to the floor, but within seconds the fire was back to a small blaze, leaving only a huge black smudge on the wall above.

With Don Felipe we toured Sucre, and whether walking the streets or colonnades, or relaxing in cafés, we seemed incessantly to be locked in exhaustive discussion of the country's history, the machinations of the university, and the wrongs of the revolution.

There were various formal calls to be made on legal dignitaries. We met a Señor Thomson, an aging Scottish engineer entrepreneur, who sat by an afternoon fire in his dressing-gown and slippers while his Bolivian wife sat in the next room with her friends, playing bridge for high stakes, gossiping and eating almond cakes.

And we called on a town official in the *Municipal*, a lumpish building, its halls and staircases painted with gory, tasteless murals depicting battles for liberty. The official, who had crew-cut hair, and a heavy jowl, greeted us affably enough, summing us up with small, shifty eyes. His hands were very soft and white. He expressed great interest in Shakespeare and promised to attend our film, and we soon felt the moment to depart.

"Well, that's that," said Don Felipe as we trotted downstairs. "Dreadful fellow—just one of a bunch of thugs. He's nothing but a jailer really. In the reprisals after the revolution he used to torture his political prisoners by putting pencils in their ears and then banging them together."

We crossed the square to the Legislative Hall, once a Jesuit chapel now a council chamber, but still intact, with the choir at one end covered in thick gold leaf. On gold-leaved panels along the walls hung portraits of Bolívar, Ballivian, Sucre, and heroes of the independence, the ubiquitous O'Higgins and other Irish liberators who had been dashing about the continent at the right moment in search of adventure.

The university building, originally a Jesuit college, had a majestic symmetry. The enormous colonnaded quadrangle, the council chamber with its huge table and carved chairs, the intricate ceilings everywhere, and the "paranympho" hall, all made a perfect and intact example of Colonial Baroque.

On the ceiling of the entrance hall were moulded and painted the blazon and double-headed eagle of the Holy Roman Emperors. This I noticed with a shock of surprise, forgetting for a moment where the link lay. For to me this eagle meant the Hapsburgs, and the Hapsburg aegis brought to mind Vienna and Prague, heavy splendid Central European urbanity, Mozart, Haydn, forests, fairy-tales.

Then I remembered the Schatzkammern in Vienna, and the robes and crown of Charlemagne preserved now behind glass, and the manœuvrings and marriages preserved in books. I tried to push my mind back and remember the marriages which had criss-crossed Europe, uniting it, and the wars which had disunited it. Charles V, Holy Roman Emperor, and a Hapsburg, had been born in the Netherlands, which always remained his first love. But he had kingdoms scattered all over Europe. And he was also King of Spain and the vast territories of the New World.

"How incongruous," I thought. "No wonder he abdicated in the end, and divided his kingdom, and retired to a monastery."

But it all seemed so remote from these white colonnades under the blazing sun, where the Indians were shepherding their llamas through the dusty streets. The eagle gazed out, one head towards the Baroque halls, the other towards the primitive world once conquered, an absurd emblem of unity, conquest, and long muddled history.

We called on the Rector of the University, an elderly oculist. His hobby was collecting legends of Sucre, of the heroes of the Revolution, and he told us about the Colonel's wife who rode into battle beside her husband with a baby on her hip. "Her husband was killed but she fought on, and was herself made a Colonel of the Regiment. *Que brava*, no?"

A lovely old house on the main square which had been the seat of the Inquisition, was now a museum of Colonial art. In the courtyards where the clerics once walked stood a collection of old carriages, and inside the house we were shown splendid pieces of furniture, tables, bureaux and travelling chests, with details in inlaid wood. One marquetry desk was a wonderful example of the fusion of European Baroque and Indian style. It was inlaid with a tree-of-life, where monkeys, humans, pumas and birds, dogs and llamas

were wrought into the pattern with flowers and fruit among the
twining branches, and beside it all stood strange birds in the stiff,
abstract geometric shapes of the Tiahuanaco style.

One room was devoted to pictures of the presidents of the
Republic, all in typical declamatory stance: Santa Cruz the great
leader, Belzú the demagogue, Linares the autocrat, and Córdoba,
handsomest of them all with his piercing blue eyes.

There were many rows of holy pictures, too, one of a Christ
which was carried regularly still, in religious processions, a wooden
panel painted both sides, the back shown pocked with bleeding
wounds.

But I was drawn and haunted by a painting of Potosí. It must
have been painted in the seventeenth or even the late sixteenth
century. The style was primitive, the detail intricate. It showed the
Imperial City lying in the lap of the Cerro Rico, its roofs, walls and
turrets caught in a rosy light. In the hills above were the lake-
reservoirs, with streams gushing down the slopes into the City.
Here were the fountains, the courtyards, the towers, the churches.
It was thronged with people, and laced about with pageants and
processions. Priests, choirs, monks, nuns moved in a tide through
those alleys below the balconies, the campaniles, and the citadel
walls of the *casa de monedas*, chanting or praying beside their banners
and relics.

Don Felipe also took us to the National Library and archives, to
show us documents from the old empire, and copies of the first
newspapers printed in Sucre. There were long shelves of leather
tomes, with silent students walking up and down. The curator led us
to a dank room at the back, and called a shy, shuffling Indian who
obviously could not read, to climb a ladder and fetch down some
copies of the Bible in English. He brought copies of Shakespeare too,
and a first edition of Dr. Johnson's dictionary, battered and rotten-
smelling.

The monastery church beside the Cathedral housed a famous
miracle-working Madonna, the *Virgin de Guadeloupe*.

A portly monk took us through panelled rooms with beautiful
carved, painted ceilings, to the Madonna's chapel.

On the altar, above the crucifix and candlesticks, was a large steel dome. The monk wound a noisy crank at the side of the altar, and the dome split into two doors, which creaked open like out-of-use wings to reveal her.

"Climb up, climb up," he urged, pointing at the altar, "you get a much better view up there."

Rather shocked, we climbed a rocking ladder and stood precariously on the marble among the pots of flowers.

I had half-expected a sculpture, but the Virgin was a painting. In a silver frame, she stood about four feet high, in embroidered bodice, a puffed skirt and little silver crown. From her neck to her feet she was covered with jewels: pearls, diamonds, topaz, emeralds, gifts over centuries from the rich miners of Potosí or the rich landowners of yesterday, hung gleaming upon her, worked into the pattern of the painted embroidery. Some were solitary stones, others set in gold or silver. Angels flanked the middle panel of the dress, with silver heads and tiny trumpets, each of their skirts made of enormous, irregular pearls. And I saw a dog also pinned at the side, its body a pearl, with head and feet of silver.

Her face was sweet and vacant, and she stared ahead, as she had stared, no doubt, at the givers of the jewels, at their confessions and supplications—in silence. Silence hid all the stories, treachery or slavery, love, illness, death or simple piety, behind those jewels that adorned her like the tokens of a thousand lovers. And clearly she was passionately loved still.

"The Virgin has many more jewels," said the monk. "But we cannot show them. They are locked away."

Don Felipe rasped: "Yes, several rooms, full of them. Thousands and thousands of dollars' worth. Enough to build hospitals, schools —but would the people allow it? Never. The Virgin must keep her jewels. And the people must go on sighing for love of her and following her through the streets in ecstasy when she comes out for processions. Do you know some Madonnas have even been made Generals and given a general's salary?"

But Forgues crossed himself and lit a candle to her—and I could see that he was picturing her sailing through the tides of the street like the processions in the picture of Potosí, like the Madonna of the Solitude in Lorca's poem:

Virgen con miriñaque,
virgen de la Soledad,
abierta como un immenso
tulipín.

En tu barco de luces
vas
por la alta marea
de la ciudad,
entre santas turbias
y estrellas de cristal.

Virgen con miriñaque,
tu vas
por el rio de la calle,
¡hasta el mar!★

We showed *Hamlet* on several evenings, in the paranympho of the University. Don Felipe had found a *locutor*—a young student with an "exceptional voice" who could read the synopsis between reels of the film. But he failed to arrive—"He is in love," volunteered another student. "He has lost his wits."

However, there were no other mishaps. Many of the town dignitaries came, and several old lawyers, sad, bent figures whom I imagined living in dark, high rooms in the legal quarter of the town. "There is no rule of law now," someone said, "politics is all and everything is done through the party."

The Indians in Sucre were of a quite different physique from those on the *altiplano*. They were wilder looking, and taller, with less flattened features. Some wore round, squashed pudding-basin hats,

★ This, I think, is one of Lorca's most beautiful short songs. The richness of the images cannot be conveyed in translation, and so I include some of the alternative meanings in brackets. A *saeta* is a short religious song, a ballad, sung during a religious procession; it is often spontaneous, as if to express an ebullience of fervour, faith and (here) love for the Virgin. "Virgin in a crinoline, Virgin of the Solitude (alone), open (spread, candid, innocent) like a vast tulip (an infinite flower); in your ship of lights you go through the high tide (surf) of the city, amid turbulent songs and crystal stars. Virgin in a crinoline, you go through the river of the street, down to the sea!"

others, the men, had helmets made of hard black ox-hide, moulded like Conquistador helmets, edged with bright beads and sequins that hung in a fringe round the face. And occasionally I would see a woman in the complement of this headgear, a wide tilted affair, like a boat or the Wife of Bath's finery, covered with a glittering sequin pattern.

The men wore ponchos woven in brilliant stripes; they had belts of heavy leather studded in silver, and sandals made of leather sewn to old car-tyres. They carried purses to match their ponchos, and often a small guitar made from an armadillo skin.

There were other Indians who came, Don Felipe said, from the "deep *campo*." "They are very wild," he remarked. These wore homespun clothes—flapping shirts, and wide trousers, cut short to show off their calves. Their hair was uncut, and fell in a tangled mass down their backs, below squashed hats. We met a group of such young men in the square once. They had come in, they told Don Felipe, to pay their taxes and get land-rights.

In the market streets, naked children lay about or toddled among live chickens, ducks and stray dogs. On one stall I saw a whole pig roasting. Beside it a woman was selling brightly coloured maps and almanacs, and illustrated charts on astrology. A stand with orange drinks also had large cans of *chicha* for sale, and tins of pure alcohol made from maize or sugar-cane. I saw a ragged, toothless old man carefully wrapping a handful of coca leaves and folding them into his poncho.

A long queue stood beside a man with a bird cage and Viewmasters, waiting to see "The Wonders of Milan", "Pinocchio" and "Disneyland," and there was another crowd where a gambling entrepreneur took up the whole width of the street with his game. He stood on a chair above rows of upturned enamel bowls waving tickets which would draw lucky numbers to win prizes of pencils and plastic spoons.

Sucre was renowned for its antiques, not for sale in shops, but available through agents who were in touch with old families in distress. It was soon noised about that we were interested, and I several times went to tea in old houses, sitting in the *salón* on French chairs while old pieces of silver were brought out for inspection. At

L

first an astronomical price was asked. I refused, offered another, and was refused in turn. I regretted, hesitated, suggested coming tomorrow, got up to go, and then, as though it were all a matter of decorum, the price was quite amicably settled. In this way I acquired some silver spoons, goblets and a tray. One old lady tried to persuade me to buy her Sèvres tea-set. Saying I might have friends who were interested, I asked to see it, and she produced with great care and reverence a large box of tissue-papers, out of which emerged some cheap little pink cups painted with pink and gold flowers. I turned them over and saw the stamp "Sèvres. Bavaria", but I had not the heart to disillusion her.

One evening we came back late from the cinema. (We had seen Audrey Hepburn in a dubbed version of *Breakfast at Tiffany's*. The screen was raw cement and mice scuttled in the aisles.) Two dark, cloaked figures came out of the shadows to accost us.

"Aha," said a female voice, in English, "Ah! Hah! You must be the American Ambassador!"

We hastened to correct her. They were a mother and daughter, diffident and ashamed, and desperately in need of money. They simply wanted a few dollars, they explained, to buy food, which was now so expensive. With tears in her eyes the mother showed me a small silver bowl.

"In this," she said, "I had my soup as a child."

And there was a heavy gold filigree ring, a family heirloom. I bought them both, feeling sad, and somehow guilty.

Don Felipe's *finca* lay some ten miles from the town, and he took us there one day for lunch. Tearing through bushes and thickets we bumped along a hill-track which had become rough and overgrown with years of neglect. Once a pig snorted out of the undergrowth and rushed across our path.

"Kill it, go on, kill it!" cried Don Felipe. "My father always killed the Indians' animals. He killed 352 llamas and fifty-nine pigs, and a great many donkeys. They're quite hopeless about their animals and most of them are half-starved anyway."

I stared after the vanished animal, thankful it had escaped.

The *finca* was in a deep valley, lower and hotter than Sucre, where the river, which was wide and turbulent, ran between steep banks and bush-covered hills. The house lay hidden among walnut trees, at the end of a shaded drive. It had white walls and a terracotta tiled roof, and a verandah stretching along the whole front façade to a parapet above the river. The verandah was built out on arches over cellars and store-rooms, and flights of stone steps led down into the orchards, where long rows of orange and lemon trees were inter-planted with chirimoyas and figs, and vegetable beds lay beneath them.

Gun-shots stung the air as we arrived, and Don Felipe's son Gonzalo appeared on the verandah, holding a gun, with a revolver stuck in the belt of his jeans.

"It's the rats," he explained as he greeted us. "We've been trying to get rid of them ever since we arrived. They seem to be living up in the loft. We had a *gato de monte* (mountain cat) here yesterday too. I shot at it, but it got away."

Don Felipe took us into the house.

"You see how it's all falling to bits," he said. "I can't repair it—it would cost too much money. For six years I wasn't allowed to come near this place—it's a wonder it's still standing. The Indians took all the estate, but they left the lands round the house, and no one came here at all. I suppose I should be thankful. Some of the other *padrónes* had their places robbed and broken or burnt. Still, six years is a long time to leave a place to rain and wind and all the birds and animals that find a way in. We just camp here now."

We walked about the rooms, which were high and dark, and must once have been beautiful. There was golden flocked velvet on the walls of the *salón*, and Chinese rugs lay on the floor—but every-thing was in a pitiably derelict state—the walls stained, the ceilings sagging, the carpets and chairs in tatters.

"Who built it?" I asked Don Felipe.

"My grandfather. He built the whole place from the estate: the bricks behind all this are mud, and they made the tiles for the roof from clay down the valley there. He left it to my mother but I quarrelled with her. She left me the house because she had to, but none of the money that should have gone with it, and so I never had enough to keep the place going properly."

We went to sitting-rooms, bedrooms and nurseries, all in the same state, and I felt sickened because it could have been so fine, and was now so uncared for.

Gonzalo and his friends were preparing lunch on a paraffin cooker in the kitchen. They wanted no feminine interference, they said, so I wandered through the inner courtyard where there was a fountain, fed by a spring from the hill above the house. An arched gateway led into a garden, with paved walks, arbours and benches. The walls were covered with plumbago, and long sprays of roses, and the borders were full of irises and amaryllis lilies, and other flowers I did not know. They were all overgrown with grasses and weeds and wild creepers, but the place must once have been much loved. I skirted the house, crossing the spring, and walked down into the orchard below the walnut trees, all the while feeling very puzzled, for it was like a sudden return into my own childhood: I had known a place in Africa uncannily like this—just such a house, with gardens of roses, and below, a long orchard, and a grove of walnuts by a river. (There had been a "cool-chest" down by the water, I remembered, where milk and meat were kept. It had walls of wire mesh filled with pebbles and was splashed by the water—snakes sometimes got in among the pebbles, and we children would play "dare" to go and tap the mesh with sticks.)

But here it was as though I had abruptly walked into a room in my own mind where my childhood lay, and found it musty and unkempt, and this distressed me because I wanted it to have remained as I remembered it, and indeed more beautiful than it would ever have been had it suddenly become a reality, in the present. This place, twenty years later, in another continent, was like seeing my own past in ruin and the recognition was a physical pain.

I walked between the orange trees, where the one-legged gardener and his wife were chipping at their potato plot with a little wooden pick, and my waking dream faded as we spoke in slow Spanish about the year's crop, and when the rains came in this valley.

Don Felipe called from the verandah, and I climbed the steps. He had made a large jug of *pisco* and orange, and we sat drinking, gazing out over the shiny-leaved citrus grove.

He said, "You see how the garden is? All I am allowed to employ is this one poor man, who at least is faithful to me but how much can he do? And his wife's a halfwit."

I agreed it was very sad, but what about the house? Even a coat of paint would improve things, I said.

"No, it's quite impossible—I could never find anyone to do it—and it would be far too expensive. I suppose really I should just get rid of the place. I wish I could find some rich American to buy it."

It was clearly not within consideration that he or his three able-bodied sons should turn to doing the repairs themselves. This would be too far from the Spanish *padrón* heritage. I felt resentful, as though somehow the place were mine, and I loved it—and wondered how he would find an American however rich who wanted a hacienda in the middle of the Bolivian backwoods.

He talked about the primitiveness of the Indians: "I have spoken Quechua all my life and know them as they really are . . ." Democracy in Don Felipe's opinion had been applied too soon and had only retrogressive consequences; all elections were rigged and the Indians were exploited far more by the Communist-run trade unions—the *sindicatos*—than they ever had been by the *padrónes*.

"And in any case they are not up to it. I tell you, since the arrival of the *conquistadores* the Indians have made almost **no** progress. There's more evidence to show they are hereditarily backward than able to advance." As for the Inca empire—all those Romantics had blown it up into something quite out of proportion to the primitive culture it really was. "Look at the Indians in the States—after hundreds of years of contact with white men they are still living the same tribal life in their reserves." The only real hope for progress was gradual cross-breeding with European or Oriental races.

"Well, couldn't you try to get the Indians here to co-operate with you—and teach them how to run the land properly yourself?" I ventured.

"Teach them? Don't think I haven't tried—I have—time after time. I tried to work out a scheme with these *campesinos*—I suggested that we do things on a fifty-fifty basis, but what happened? They took ninety per cent and then quit work. Why should they take trouble? Why improve the place? There's no impetus. They have one holiday a month that lasts three weeks and all they want is enough money to buy *chicha*.

"Look what they did to the land," he swept his arm to embrace all the surrounding hills.

"Where are the only big trees? Round this house. They cut all the others down—all of them—to sell for firewood by the donkey-load. Even though I taught them, they would never think of planting new ones. They are utterly wasteful—and the *sindicatos* want everything to go to rack and ruin and no money to come to the *padrónes*.

"But if anything ever goes wrong—it's still to the *padrónes* that they turn."

"And you want it that way," David teased him.

"Well—no one else is going to help them."

We had found out before that he went to great lengths for these people. It was not long since the night when an Indian woman had been brought to the house on a rough litter. She was in childbirth, the child half-born and already dead. There was a terrible storm raging. The family lorry had broken down, so, at three in the morning, Don Felipe, who must have been well over seventy, walked the ten rugged miles back to Sucre in the storm, to find a doctor. They had saved the woman's life. It was clear that somewhere behind all the bitterness, he loved them.

Don Felipe went on about the ignorant, over-sensitive and under-imaginative liberals, and the politicians who used liberal ideas only far enough to suit their own ambitions. Real progress in primitive countries, we agreed, as the last drops of the potent mixture were poured out, could only come gradually, and he lamented the passing of the British Empire before its work was properly done.

In the orchard below, the one-legged gardener leant on his crutch muttering.

Don Felipe called down to him, in Quechua, and the reply came back in an Indian wail.

"What does he say?"

"He says he has a dead man's bones. Let's go and eat."

The lunch was simply sausage and fried eggs, but very good as we were all hungry, and there were oranges picked from the orchard, still warm and fragrant from the sun. Later, to sober up before returning to Sucre, we walked downstream along the cliff and bathed in the river. The water was very violent, and as I struggled against the current, still in the haze of the *pisco*, I felt the day, and my memories, being pulled away from me, and I lay to dry on the rocks exhausted, yet refreshed with the relief.

XII

Election in Cochabamba

IT WAS ANOTHER day's drive to Cochabamba, where David was
to show *Hamlet*, make contacts, and observe a forthcoming
election.

We stopped for lunch *en route*, in a river-bed, a very pretty
place but the wrong choice as we were consumed by flies which
were so small as to be almost invisible, but left bites that soon
swelled into enormous torturing welts.

Forgues, who was less afflicted than I, was sympathetic, but said
there were far worse perils at lower altitudes—the beetle in the Beni,
for instance, whose one bite affected a man's nervous system so that,
although it might take years, you would gradually sicken and waste
away in a life of misery and pain. Scratching and slapping my legs,
which by now were bleeding, I asked Forgues if he had heard of
Darwin, whose illness might have been from this beetle, and he had
not, but had I heard about the Señorita at the American Embassy
who had been bitten in this way and was even now dying in
hospital in the States? This was a real tragedy, he said, for she was
very beautiful.

In a valley among blue hills, Cochabamba was at only 8,500 feet.
It seemed full of flowers, and friendly people, who rode their
bicycles down the long avenues of palm trees and jacarandas. The
colonnades of the main square had recently been painted pink in
honour of President Tito, who had paid a goodwill visit. Many
Germans had settled in Cochabamba, and sponsored such develop-
ments as delicatessens, a good book-shop, a yacht club on a lake up
the valley, and a really luxurious hotel, with immaculate, tiled
bathrooms. It all seemed more civilised and comfortable, and less
exotic, than the world we had just left.

Our first two days there were public holidays: Corpus Christi, and the day of the Heroines of Cochabamba who had been butchered during the Wars of Independence. (The men had gone off to the hills to look for the Spanish forces, which had seen their chance, and rushed down out of hiding to take the city, and also the women who had refused, resisted, and lost.)

This gave us a chance to get used to the thick air, and enjoy the luxury of good food. We ate constantly at an outdoor restaurant, sitting in a garden of dazzling flowers. Bees and butterflies flopped into our wine, but we hardly noticed as we discussed how La Paz was "above the kissing line". Up there, we observed, one never felt creative, or procreative, with all the heartache and flatulence, exhaustion and sleeplessness—while here, why, there seemed to be lovers everywhere. We felt excited and eloquent. How wonderful, we thought, Mexico City must be; its altitude was the same as this— perhaps that explained some of the vigour and élan of Mexican culture. . . . .

The University was on strike, and at the last minute we had to arrange to show *Hamlet* in the *Club Social*. The performance was only a partial success: everyone was far too excited about the election to be interested in Shakespeare.

We seemed to have left La Paz a very long time ago. Since then all of the ten main opposition parties had decided to abstain from the election and all its corruptions. An ex-President of the Republic, seeing that this ruse was not really going to work, had gone off to Oruro to stage a hunger-strike. The ex-Vice-President, "to save shedding the innocent blood of the Bolivian people," had challenged the President to a dual. But the President refused to take this up dismissing it as "the typical last resort of a bourgeois," and the hunger-striking ex-President was lampooned in the press as "Mahatma!"

Everywhere we went, conversations rang with the words *tensissimo, discontentissimo, abstensionismo.* The Party was rigging the election, people told David. All the ballot boxes would be filled with vote-papers before the polling began. The Indians would be given a week's wages, filled with *chicha*, and driven in lorry-loads to each polling station in turn, and back to the country. "*La violencia*" on the day of the election was certain, they said, and David should keep well under the bedclothes and see that I stayed there too.

Cochabamba had an Honorary British Consul named Geraldine, a plump middle-aged woman with a pretty face and a quick tongue. Born of English parents, she had grown up in the tropical Beni in the days when it was easier, cheaper and safer to get downriver to the Amazon and Brazil, and thus to Europe, than upstream by dugout canoe, and then overland and through the *cordillera* by mule-track to La Paz. So she had been to school in England, but had returned and married a Bolivian whose vast estates had been lost in the Land Reform. Geraldine was doyen of the Cochabamba Consular Corps, and a specialist in revolutions.

"I'll certainly take you round the town on polling day," she declared. "I love revolutions, and I always spend them driving about in my car. Of course my husband absolutely forbids it, but I disobey him—and it's just as safe as being in your house really. There was poor Mr. Ellis last time, standing at his window to watch the fighting—I saw him hit by a stray bullet and fall down dead."

Just before midnight on the night before election day, Geraldine had an anonymous telephone call from a man who said he must come and see her at once—about a matter of great secrecy and importance. Minutes later a band of what she described as "opposition thugs from good families" arrived in a jeep to tell her their sensational secret. They had "incontestible evidence" they said, that the American Consul had ordered the police to besiege and capture the university. It was against International Law for a consul to interfere in party politics, and she, as doyen of the Consular Corps, must at once put a stop to this, reprimand the American Consul, countermand his orders, put him in his place. They were very threatening and might well have been armed.

Geraldine was not a woman to browbeat. With a little shrewd questioning, she found out that they had no idea either what the Consul looked like, or who had overheard him giving these orders to the police. She produced a large tray of glasses and her husband's best whisky, picked up her telephone, and called all over the town to contact the American Consul, contending, meanwhile, that she didn't believe a word of this wild story. The Consul was located after a great deal of trouble. He had been up in the hills all day exercising his dogs. The "thugs" refused to believe this, argued, and refused to go. Two hours and many drinks later, they agreed to make an appointment to see the American, and staggered out. The news filtered back that their source of information had been a lift-boy in the hotel next to the American Consulate.

We expected to hear gunfire at dawn, but woke to bird-song. Things were so tranquil that Geraldine lost interest, and David had to do his "observing" alone. There were a few anti-government speeches but mostly peaceful little queues outside the polling stations, and every now and then a lorry-load of bewildered-looking Indians whirled past. There was a small riot at the university, where they had decided to stage a hunger-strike, and David called on the Rector who was very cross that he had been forced to fast for eight hours, and therefore missed his lunch.

Next day we listened to radio reports. One of these announced that at a polling station where forty voters were registered the ballot-box had been opened to reveal 400 votes for the Party, who had obviously been working very hard everywhere and won hands down as everyone had predicted. Oruro was in a state of siege, full of strikers, and fasters, and miners letting off dynamite.

We packed the car and drove up into the *cordillera*, and reached La Paz when the city was already engulfed in darkness, but the snowy peaks still rosy with the sun.

XIII

Return to Potosí

SOME TIME LATER David had to make another tour, on Embassy business. We took Forgues with us again, and also the film equipment, for it seemed a pity to waste the chance of showing some good documentaries. Far the most popular of these was a sensational study in colour of the Farnborough Air show. Huge crowds would collect to gasp at the jets, bombers and delta-wings, and vertical take-off.

Don Felipe had long promised to take us to see some "really authentic, primitive Indians", and at the weekend we went with him to Tarabuco, a village forty miles south of Sucre, where Indians from the deep *campo* came each Sunday for a market-fiesta. The village itself had no distinction: a dirty little square, with alleys of squalid houses and shops leading off it. But it was crowded with people such as sometimes came to the Sucre market, all in brilliant striped ponchos, and sequinned hats. They strolled about, talking, bargaining, buying, strumming their armadillo guitars, and staring at us, conspicuous as we were with our white skins and modern European dress. There were intricately-woven purses for sale, and blankets in brilliant colours, and we walked about the square, and down some of the streets, peering into shops.

Don Felipe pointed out a group squatting on the pavement with white lumps of rock-salt set out on sacking. They wore brown, rough-woven clothes, and small four-cornered hats like Tudor caps.

"They come down here to barter," he said. "They exchange their salt for corn."

We turned to look at another group, where an old woman was handing a twist of paper to a man with a bandaged head. He paid her and moved away.

"Witches," said Don Felipe, "from Potosí, I expect."

"What are their remedies?" I asked.

The old woman looked up at us. Her face was cracked and rutted like mud in the sun, but her eyes were bright, like an animal's. She picked up twisted roots and pieces of rock and wood, turned them about in her gnarled hands, and sifted strange powders through her fingers as she explained their powers to Don Felipe, and he translated from the Quechua:

"This one is for toothache; this one to bring a child; this—to take a child away. This root is a cure for cancer . . ."

"Where do you come from?"

"Potosí. It is famous for remedies."

"How long did it take you to come?"

"It is forty leagues. It took us ten days."

We forgot the time and did not notice the sunset, and the first stars were out when we left. On some level ground outside the village, a little family were unloading their llamas for the night.

Don Felipe peered out at them. "You see how self-sufficient they are? That Indian has his llamas—they carry his goods for him (only thirty kilos each so he has to have a good many), he eats their flesh, burns their dung, his wife weaves clothes and sacks out of the wool. They bring salt down from the mountains and go back with grain. They probably have no money at all. At night they stop and unload, the sacks shelter them from the wind, and the llamas keep them warm while they sleep under the stars. What do they need of civilisation? Why should we try to change them?"

I had admired the striped ponchos of Tarabuco, and wanted to buy one, but the people had been somehow too aloof and self-contained for me to ask them, and the ponchos were obviously precious possessions. However, one morning very early I went down to the market in Sucre. In a narrow street an Indian in a *conquistador* helmet was standing in a patch of sunlight. The chill of the night was still in the air, but all he wore over his shirt was a striped miniponcho of the kind which was worn sometimes, like a large collar, over the full-sized one, for extra warmth. He had draped his big poncho on a ledge of the sunlit wall, as if for sale.

He asked the equivalent of £4 for it—I began to bargain but then felt I could not—it was clear the man did not want to part with his poncho, and this distressed me. I thought I might simply give him some money and walk away, but that in turn might offend him. So I bought the poncho, and went home feeling that I had cheated him and not he me. I spread the garment out on the hotel bed to look at it more carefully. The main colour was a peculiar purplish-bronze—the other stripes were stingingly bright; they must have been dyes like those from the Amazon forests, which had been used by the Incas and by races before them. I thought the poncho very beautiful, and pictured it being woven in the man's mud house. It had obviously been worn, for there were some tiny darns at the neck, and he must have washed it for it felt damp still, and smelt heavily of sheep, with a tinge of wood-smoke.

Wise after the culinary disasters of our first tour (I had lost a stone in weight), we now bought food in the markets as we went along, and had our meals on hillsides or in the Land Rover, depending on the cold. In Sucre I took the paraffin cooker up to our room and we shuttered the doors firmly to escape detection. Forgues was very appreciative, and slipped out from time to time for bottles of burning Argentine wine. Quite soon all our clothes were heavily impregnated with smells of paraffin and fried sausages, but it warmed the room too, and as we wore our sleeping-bags in the hotel beds, this simply gave an added camp-fire atmosphere.

One evening I was preparing dinner when there was a tapping at the door. I expected to let in an irate proprietor, with complaints that the hotel would catch fire, but saw a small, bent old woman in a black shawl, clutching a bundle of crumpled newspaper.

"*Antiguedades* [antiques], señora?" I let her in, quickly shutting the door.

Her Señora had sent her, she said, a very noble Señora who had suffered much in recent times. From the layers of newspaper she produced an enormous pair of ear-rings in silver and diamonds, each dangling a gigantic pear-shaped pearl.

She grinned: "Are they not magnificent, señora?"

"Well, yes—they are magnificent."

"They are very old, very valuable—and you can have them for only 2,000 dollars."

"Two thousand dollars? *Caramba!*" I was genuinely horrified. "We can't possibly afford that."

"O come, señora," she whined a little, "it is not much for something so precious."

"No, no, no," I said, turning back to my frying-pans.

But she refused to believe that we could not afford them, and launched into an explanation of her salesmanship.

"But now you must *regatear* [bargain] a bit, señora. Give me a price."

"Nothing at all," I slipped an egg into the sizzling fat. "I have not that sort of money."

"No, no, no, not like that, señora. Now you should offer me say 1,700 dollars. And then I could offer 1,850, and then perhaps we might talk a little and I could let you have them for 1,800."

I tried to look impervious, but thinking she must still tempt me, she pushed off her shawl, undid her grey hair, which fell about her shoulders, and screwed the ear-rings into her own lobes.

"But are they not magnificent, señora?" She pushed her face close to mine, and shook it, fluttering her lashes. Her eyes were fine, enormous, black and sparkling, but she had almost no teeth and the impression in the light of the flames was grotesque.

Tired of repeated refusals, I offered her some sausages, which she ate with noisy appreciation.

"I have a niece in the United States," she announced chattily. "Is it possible you might have met her?"

"But we are not American," I explained, "we are English."

"Ah, yes," she was thoughtful. "And England is another country, is that not certain?"

At Potosí we stayed with Thornley and his wife at Arofilla, a disused mine recently started up again. Thornley, a mining engineer, was another of those Englishmen caught in a romance with the country that had deepened into love. While he was kicking his heels in England after leaving the Far East, his imagination had been fired by an article about little-developed Bolivia. He had become convinced that tin from the high mountains must be flowing out, down the rivers, and had come out on the slender chance of finding someone to back him in a search for this tin. He now ran Arofilla, and spent long weeks camping beside the Pilcomayo river, where he had recently found enough alluvial deposits to support his theory.

The mine compound lay in a wide treeless valley and was marked by a long line of poplars, which had constantly to be defended against the surrounding peasants, who had chopped down and burnt all their own trees, saying they only brought birds to ruin the crops. Thornley's wife, who had once been in the Royal Ballet, had tidied up the camp, struggling to make a garden. She limped, badly at the moment, as a car accident on the *altiplano* had broken her leg in seventeen places, and left her lame.

We found her household in a state of bewildered exhilaration. One bleak wash-day the clothes had mysteriously disappeared from the washing-line. Everyone in the nearby village blamed Esmeralda, the Thornleys' new cook. But Esmeralda had been fifteen years with her last employer and was known to be honest. Indignant at this insult, she marched off to Potosí and bought at great expense (thirty pesos or almost £1) an armadillo skin stuffed with potatoes and a few herbs. This she hung up on the front door. Next morning all the stolen clothing lay in a neat pile on the doorstep.

The camp foreman was so impressed by this magic that he wanted to borrow the skin to get back his stolen drilling tools. But Esmeralda insisted on the price she had paid the wise-woman in Potosí. A meeting was called and thirty miners agreed to put up one peso each. At dusk, they hung the skin up on the compound gate, and by the morning all the tools had been flung in, over the wall.

Esmeralda nodded sagely. "They knew—they knew what would happen. Thieves who ignore an armadillo skin stuffed with potatoes get great and terrible yellow spots, and if they do not give back the goods their skin shrivels up and they wither and die."

It was mid-winter, and we were thankful for the comparative warmth and shelter of Arofilla. In Potosí the *surazo*, a wind straight from the South Pole, had been blowing for three days. At night the air fell to twenty degrees centigrade below zero. Gutters and crevices in the roads were full of ice, which the midday sun could

The Devil's Bridge in the Cordillera before Potosí

Rooftops and the Cerro Rico, Potosí

Colonial Baroque—convent i
Sucre

Don Felipe chooses a hat

not melt. David went to the university, but found it quite empty, and thought it must be on strike until he discovered it was closed because of the cold. With no wood or coal for heating, everyone had simply gone home to shiver in bed.

The city looked bleaker and more forgotten than ever. The streets were empty, but for the occasional hurrying figure, bent and muffled against the cold, and the Indians wore scarves under their hats and over their mouths.

David did succeed in locating some of the university professors, who then invited us to dinner in Potosí. We were to meet at the house of a beautiful woman named Blanca, who sounded a little like the famous Doña Clara of the city's heyday. She had just parted from her fourth husband.

Blanca's father was very rich. He owned several mines which still worked, and had somehow managed to survive the revolution. He had been pointed out to us once as he drove his lorry up into Potosí, a wan little man with very large ears. He had seventeen children, of whom Blanca, aged forty, was the first and favourite, the others being scattered throughout Bolivia, and even in Caracas and North America. The old man, people said, took a great interest in all of them, seeing that they were properly brought up and educated.

Blanca was alarmingly attractive; she had flashing eyes and a torrent of black hair, and a heaving, expressive bosom. All the professors seemed to be passionately in love with her. Her declared ambition, however, was to leave the boredom of Potosí, and go to La Paz, where she would learn to become an interior decorator. Her *salón* was small and carefully arranged to show her books and pictures. One end was *intimo*, with sofas and chairs round a fire, the other end, to my surprise, was left empty. The fire was obviously a rarity and source of much discussion, its fuel being small knots of twigs, like dried heather, which had been brought up from lower valleys. Blanca, or some admirer, must have bought several donkey-loads, as the stuff flared up without the aid of much kerosene and was consumed almost within seconds. One of the professors kept leaping up to put more bundles on the fire; another darted out to bring in more bottles of whisky (*Escotch*), which we drank neat for

M

warmth. Blanca was a very good cook. We ate her chicken casserole with relish, sitting on the sofas by the fire.

The conversation was sedate. We discussed education in our respective countries, schools, universities, the British Council, travel in Europe, the English language and the Spanish. From time to time, Blanca, who seemed a trifle bored, would go to the door and look out, saying she was waiting for *"los chicos"*. Her son, she explained, was bringing some of his student friends, and they would play their guitars to us. We envisaged a small concert, but when they entered the atmosphere changed abruptly, and in excited haste Blanca moved us to the empty, colder side of the room.

"Do you know the Bolivian dances?" she asked us.

"No."

"Ah! You don't know the Cueca?"

"No!"

"AAH! We must show you."

So we sat by the wall, while Blanca chose a partner, and they took their places on the floor, facing each other, one hand on the hip, the other fluttering a white handkerchief.

"What's the handkerchief for?" I asked.

"Para coquetear," Blanca laughed ("for flirting"), and whirled her little square of white lace under her partner's nose. He shut his eyes in rapture—flaring his nostrils.

The boys struck up and Blanca drummed her heels on the floor, the men shouted and began to clap.

Blanca's son had her looks; his black eyelashes drooped, his voice sobbed in the tremulous lilt that all Bolivians sang in, breaking on the sad crescendoes,

> *"Soledad, soledad,*
> *Esta noche estoy muy triste . . .*
> *Soledad, soledad,*
> *En la soledad de mi alma*
> *Lloro de mi desventura . . ."*

Blanca danced like a gipsy, supple, suggestive, aloof, and all the men sang the chorus with an expressive rolling of each "r".

> "*Solo estoy aqui*
> *Sin querer vivir*
> *Si algun dia tu volvieras*
> *Al revuelver-r-r-r-me la calma,*
> *Lai la la laira . . .*"*

"But you must dance too," cried Blanca, swooping me on to the floor. So we watched and followed and circled and twirled our handkerchiefs, and the boys played on, one lovelorn thrumming song after another.

"Now you show us the twist," cried Blanca.

"Ah, yes, and the rock and roll," echoed the professors.

We gave a short, self-conscious exhibition, falling down several times, as the altitude and whisky had made us unsteady. Then they began to follow us, transforming these dances at once into an elegant Latin-American step, their backs bolt upright and stiff, chests stuck out, feet nipping about below. When we were all tired we sat drinking more whisky while the boys played on.

> "*Addios Oruro,*
> *Mi ciudad,*
> *Ciudad de mi sueño . . .*"

("Goodbye Oruro, my city, city of my dreams . . .") Songs about laziness, about carnival, about the mountains, many of them difficult to follow as the words came in such a torrent.

> "*Selva del infierno verde,*
> *Soy el prisonero del amor . . .*"

("Forest of green hell, I am the prisoner of love . . .")

The professors were tormented with love for Blanca. She began to dance again, calling us to join her, but we were too breathless still and were content to watch and clap as she tossed her head, swayed

* These songs mean roughly: "Alone, alone, tonight I am very sad; in the solitude of my soul I weep at my misfortune . . . Alone I am here, not wishing to live; if but one day you would return, Ah, then would calm return to me . . ."

and spun, and shook her handkerchief or drew it across her neck like a quick caress. The boys must have chosen the song for her:

> *"Nada no tengo yo,*
> *Ni nada me importa*
> *E! me n'importa de nadie*
> *Si o nadie me importa yo ..."*

And the dons sang together:

> *"Te quiero con pasión ..."*

("I have nothing, for nothing do I care; Eh! I matter to nobody if I care for nobody, I ..."
"I love you with passion! ...")

But Blanca was caught in the dance, and in her dreams, passionate dreams of La Paz perhaps, and the new life and loves awaiting her there.

Next day an English television team appeared in Potosí, pale and shaken after their journey up from Chile in an army plane. They were doing a survey of South America, and had come up here for some local colour and "Colonial background". But it was all so tumbledown, they complained, and the cameraman could not find any good shots. They were miserable and ill with the cold and the altitude. We tried to think of something exciting for them to film, but it was very difficult, the *Casa de Monedas*, the *Cerro Rico* and the alleys with their balconies and vistas not, apparently, being photogenic. Even a llama sacrifice was ruled out as likely to offend the R.S.P.C.A. But they cheered up at the news that there were to be miners' demonstrations the next day, and went off to see the *prefecto*, who was very amenable, but suggested that if the Señores could stay until Saturday they could see some real fighting. This, he explained, was the day of the annual fight between two Indian villages in the mountains. It was old, very old, this fight, and the object was to take a hostage from the enemy, who was not in fact a hostage at all but a victim, for he was then carried off to the village and ceremonially killed, cooked and eaten. At this point the Señores became mindful of the taste of the British public, as well as the cold and terrible discomfort of their hotel. They were not to be detained, and settled for a grandstand view of the miners.

In the afternoons I would go driving with Thornley's wife Laura, who was still shaken and diffident after her accident, and afraid to drive about alone. We went up and down the valley where Arofilla lay, and called on some of her friends.

"Doña Rosa's family once owned vast estates," said Laura as we drew up at a large stone gateway, with a crumbling coat of arms. "They had a couple of mines, and their lands stretched for twenty kilometres round this house." We went in through a courtyard where an old carriage stood under some trees. Behind it the stables and loose-boxes were empty. Doves cooed and strutted on the roof; a cat jumped out of the carriage window as we passed, and streaked off into the shadows.

Through an archway, in a second courtyard, a fountain stood empty on the stone paving beneath an almond tree in bloom. Various doorways led off into dark rooms, and ahead steps led up to a terrace. Some children, playing in a patch of sunlight, saw Laura and rushed across to her, explaining their game—and then suddenly eyed me in silence.

Laura's "Where's Granny?" brought a chorus of replies, and a small girl with pigtails scampered off.

"Doña Rosa was a great beauty once," explained Laura. "She was very wild, and half Bolivia was in love with her. Even now—she may be over seventy, but she still has looks . . ."

Doña Rosa greeted us with amiable surprise. Her figure had not weathered the years well and she complained of rheumatism, and hobbled somewhat. But her head was remarkable and her presence commanding. Her eyes were enormous, the pupils black, the whites almost blue, like those of children. Her hair tumbled in curls and ringlets past her shoulders with hardly a streak of grey, and gold hoop-rings dangled from her ear-lobes, shaking and glinting as she moved her head.

"*Chiquitita!*" she embraced Laura, who stood head and shoulders above her. "And your nice friend—Laura's friends are always *sympáticas*."

I was introduced to Doña Rosa's daughter Soledad, who stood behind her. I could not believe her the mother of all these wild ragged but attractive children. She was desperately thin and had a bird-like, haunted look.

"Soledad," commanded Doña Rosa, "go and find some drinks for our friends." And Soledad padded off across the court, while her mother took us into a sitting-room.

"Sit down, sit down. *Chico*, bring these ladies tables for their drinks," and a small boy staggered up to me with a marble-topped stool. Laura and I perched on a large window-seat covered in tapestry, and Doña Rosa settled into a low armchair with her knitting.

"Look, Laura! I am making a new jersey for Juanito. Here are his two old ones—grown out of—and I knit them up into a big one in two colours—very smart, don't you think?" She waved her needles in the air, and pulled at the two discarded garments which lay on the floor, matted and half unravelled, one a garish yellow, the other green. The new garment would be a mottled khaki.

Soledad came in with some beer, and we sat for a few seconds in silence, drinking. A shaft of sunlight slanted in through the door, and flies buzzed across it. Doña Rosa's hands, clutching the khaki knitting, lay still in her lap. On three fingers she wore enormous diamond rings that flashed in the sun. Her skirt stretched tightly over her plump knees, her thick lisle stockings had tiny holes in them, and on her feet were a pair of worn felt slippers.

The shadows beyond the sunny patch where Doña Rosa sat were deep. I gradually made out a high ceiling, stained and drooping like the folds of a tent after rain, with huge cobwebs spanning the corners. At one side a fireplace had been torn out, leaving a gaping space with ashes and rubble in it. Below the chair rail was a faded green wallpaper, above it, bare mud bricks, and through innumerable holes in the carpet, which was simply an underfelt, dust sifted up from the mud floor.

Laura leant across to me. "There were marvellous tapestries on the walls here until last year," she said softly. "They sold them to pay for a party."

Doña Rosa wanted to know all about my travels and the *Embajada*

Britanica, and Europe, and how the prospecting was going on the River Pilcomayo.

I asked if I could see her garden.

"The garden? Oh, see it if you wish—there is nothing left—no one to work it any more—the Indians all sit in their villages now, doing nothing but drink *chicha*."

Laura took me across the courtyard, and we peered into the family chapel, which was small and dark, with white plastic lilies in little brass vases. From a higher terrace, we reached the *salón*, "They keep it for parties," explained Laura, as we pushed the big double doors open. "Now look at all this: eighteenth-century French Provincial. They could make a fortune if they sold it, send all the children to school. But they won't. It stays like this, and the children run wild and speak more Quechua than Spanish. None of them will ever be able to read or write at this rate."

It was a large room with perfect proportions, and exquisite chairs, tables, cabinets, all in reasonable repair. Along the sides were window bays with seats in them and curtains to the floor in golden damask. On the walls between each window hung high, gilt-framed mirrors, reflecting the furniture, the grand piano with its cover of embroidered silk, and the glass chandeliers, so that wherever one looked there were extra rooms, strange angles and perspectives which the greyish colour of the glass made a little misty and uncertain.

But this very uncertainty, in that peculiar way of old glass, really blurred the imperfections, and heightened the golden colours of the room, and the brilliance of the crystal, so that the reflected world seemed the true one, and the freshness of a century ago was there. It was as though the people who had lived then would come in and walk about the room with us, saying, "This is the portrait of my mother in her dress she wore to meet the Viceroy . . . the President . . . here is Juan in his army uniform . . . Will you come tonight? There will be a fiesta . . ." I pictured the chandeliers lit and carriages rolling into the courtyard among the doves.

Laura, who had been struggling with a shutter, opened it with a bang, and sunlight burst in across the gilt and glass, filling the room with rainbows.

"I wish I could have seen it in the old days," she said. "They were famous for their parties. Fifty people would come to a fiesta here and stay a month." She strummed a few notes on the piano—but it was out of tune, and the spell of the room had broken.

We wandered through the garden, which must have been lovely, once, with orchards, flower borders, and lawns. There were hedges of roses, wild and bushy, threaded with brambles and creepers, and walled gardens for vegetables and vines, now filled with weeds. Chickens scratched about the paving, squawking when the children ran past, and a sow and her piglets rootled about what had once been a formal rose garden, rubbing their backs against the sundial.

"How is Carmencita?" Laura asked Doña Rosa on our return.

"Well enough—La Paz is better than Potosí still—the University keeps her busy—work, work, work. All those brains—and look at the children—a lot of wild animals." She shook her head and the earrings jingled.

She came out to say goodbye to us. I turned to look back from the archway, and she was still standing there beneath the almond tree. A quick gust of wind shuddered across the courtyard and she waved to us through a shower of petals.

"Who is Carmencita?" I asked Laura as we bumped away down the valley.

"She's the first daughter. I thought I wouldn't tell you until we'd been there, it's such an odd family. Doña Rosa had three daughters. No sons. That's why the place is in such a hopeless state, though I suppose even if there had been sons they wouldn't have done anything much. It's the curse of the Spanish pride—they won't do manual work."

I was haunted by the house and its ghosts, and sickened by the passive acceptance of all that hopeless decay. Was there nothing, I asked Laura, that had survived the revolution?

"Well, there is, at Callara," she said. "Tom McKinnon foresaw the Land Reform. He shared out his land to the Indians long before it happened, keeping only a small portion for himself, so when the revolution came they had nothing against him. The land he gave away has gone to ruin which is very sad for him, and he struggles away on his own bit, trying to make ends meet. He could never leave it. It has been in his mother's family since—well ever since Potosí existed."

The next day Laura took me to meet Tom McKinnon. His mother's family, who were of French origin, had once been great mining magnates. But they had sold out their assets years ago and moved away. The last remaining daughter had inherited the estate outside Potosí and by good fortune or good management married a Scot, who did not think hard work an undignified occupation for a gentleman.

The house Callara lay in the lap of a wooded hill looking down a valley of beautifully tilled fields. There were groves of poplars and cypresses, orchards in bloom, and the buildings were compact and well kept. Tom McKinnon had been one of the first landowners to mechanise his farm work—he had tractors now instead of oxen to do his ploughing. We visited the chapel and the family graveyard, and the estate offices, where he showed us the original title deeds of the place, inscribed in Latin on vellum.

The *salón* had an arched ceiling and magnificent Colonial furniture, silver and paintings, but McKinnon's real pride was his library. This was austere, almost like a monk's cell; but the walls were lined with a remarkable collection of books, works of reference, of Spanish and French literature, and centuries-old volumes on Spain and her Empire. It was clearly the sanctum of a cultured, scholarly man, who spent many hours here, reading, and perhaps writing. McKinnon's wife was away taking the children to school. His mother gave us tea, presiding over the table in a room whose arched windows framed a view of fields, cypresses and distant sunlit hills like a Florentine painting.

Already well into her seventies, Doña Maria was a strikingly beautiful old lady. Her hair though snow-white, was thick, and swept up on top of her head; her eyes were brilliant still, and she wore a long, soft grey dress. She spoke to us in French.

It seemed strange that these people, who appeared so sensitive, and deeply educated, had managed to survive a life which must subject them to violence, insecurity and appalling isolation. "They must," I thought, suddenly an outsider watching our group at the table, "they must have some rock-like inner strength, toughness and determination, which I do not at first sense. And a sort of nobility."

McKinnon was talking about the necessity for progress, and for sacrifices. It was so incredibly difficult, he said, to present the technological age to the primitive mind. How tragic it was that so many people, not merely the rich but the educated, had left the country after the revolution. After all, there had been so many revolutions, and this was bound not to be the last.

On one wall of the room hung a large portrait of a girl in *chola* dress, with ornately embroidered shawl, and heavy silver clasps and earrings. As I looked more carefully I saw she wore clogs on her feet, and could hardly in fact be an Indian, her skin was so fair.

"The portrait is of me, when I was a young girl," said the old lady. "It was very popular then to wear *chola* dress—for parties.

"I was born here you see—and educated. A tutor came out from Potosí. It was very different in those days—there were more people. The house was often full of visitors . . .

"I remember in the summer holidays my mother used to take us to Arica—(you know—on the Pacific Ocean?) for the sea air. We went by mule train, and —you see that leather chest—the one with the brass handles? Well, there was no paper money in those days— and no international exchanges and such like. My mother used to take that box, full of gold bars, to pay for everything. At night she just slept with it under her bed."

The plan for this trip had been to go on from Potosí down south to Tarija, and then back across the Eastern lowlands of the country to Santa Cruz. But time by now was running short. In La Paz the President was due to be re-inaugurated, and rumours of unrest everywhere were alarming. Once more the miners of Catavi were said to be planning to march on Oruro . . .

The road from Tarija to Santa Cruz was for the most part merely a track through the Chaco, best travelled in convoy, with compasses. One of the few towns on the route was caught in an epidemic of bubonic plague. Further on, in the huge *departamento* of Santa Cruz, there were two warlords (both members of the Bolivian senate) who each had a private army, and were at the moment skirmishing close to the town of Santa Cruz itself. And skipping about between them were guerilla groups of *falangistas* (neo-fascists, reputedly Cuban-supported) and Communists (also reputedly Cuban-supported), conducting some independent anti-government sabotage. A police patrol, led by an American adviser, whom we knew, was ambushed, and in the ensuing gunfight our friend was shot in the spine. He was flown back to the United States paralysed for life from the waist down. His replacement, who was rushed up at once from Brazil, had a heart attack on arriving at the *altiplano* airport, and died.

We gave up our tour plans, and, unconfident of the British Embassy Emergency Kit, drove warily back to La Paz.

XIV

Winter Politics

DESPITE THE CEASELESS rumours of unrest, the re-inauguration of the President took place in relative calm. Four days were declared national holidays, an excellent way of avoiding trouble by promoting *fiestas*, and the miners failed to march on Oruro.

However, on the morning of the great day itself, the ex-Vice-President (who had been so much in the public eye when we first arrived in Bolivia), declared publicly that he would "expose" the President in the Chamber of Deputies during the Inauguration Speech. La Paz at once became excited, awaiting the crisis, or the next move by either side.

That morning the entire Diplomatic Corps, and every Bolivian dignitary able to get a seat, went to the Cathedral for the Inauguration Mass. Morning dress, or uniform with decorations, was *de rigueur*. Women had to wear black from head to foot, and mantillas.

We filed in past ranks of armed troops. Long rows of chairs had been placed down the nave, facing each other, and the women were all herded together on one side near the chancel steps. Being very junior, I had a humble position several rows back, but when the President entered, flanked by armed guards amid the ministers and clerics, I found that my seat was immediately behind his wife's with the two thrones, one for him, and one for the Archbishop, facing us from across the aisle.

I had an excellent view. The President seemed tranquil but watchful. He shielded his eyes but did not close them while he prayed.

Beside him the Archbishop in full embroidered regalia, intoned the service, and twelve little choirboys sitting in a row up by the chancel steps sang the responses with their eyes raised to heaven, rebuked in loud whispers every time they shuffled by a *maestro* who sat behind them.

The acoustics were bad, the loudspeakers crackled, and the service was difficult to follow. Around us, in the shadowy aisles and side-chapel, knelt the silent crowds, behind rows of steel-helmeted soldiers. Far up in the gallery above the West door, a row of monks in dark habits sang the descants with a fervour as though they could see the heavenly gates. Behind them I could see little flashes of steel in the gloom where soldiers with machine-guns were keeping watch.

The President knelt at the feet of the Archbishop to be blessed, and he and his wife both received the sacrament. The crowds watched in silence. Even the little boys were still. There was an exalted tension about it all. Although the Cathedral was cold, I felt stifled.

At this moment, unbeknown to the kneeling crowds, the tactless ex-Vice-President was being summarily dealt with. The secret police scoured the town, found him and beat him up—not enough to kill him, that would have lacked finesse—just enough to ensure that he could not appear in Parliament.

Dignified and sure of himself, the President moved on to the high point of the service, the Washing of the Feet. The choirboys across the aisle, instructed by their hoarse *maestro*, one by one whipped up their long white surplices and removed their black boots and grey woollen socks. The smell of their feet billowed across us, hot and foetid like a breath from the jungle. The President's wife coughed into a lace handkerchief, and a symphony of coughing, sniffing and blowing broke out among the surrounding ladies. The French Ambassadress looked about to faint.

The President had either great self-control or no olfactory nerves. He moved slowly with a large gilt bowl of water up the row of grubby children, washing and drying each pair of feet.

We shuffled out, gasping and spluttering still, through the rows of soldiers and the trumpet blasts, into the square.

The Inaugural Speech in Parliament went without interruption. The ex-Vice-President was still lying safely unconscious in an expensive clinic. Doubtless he would have to foot the bill himself.

Rumours and reminiscences continued. Of course it was all typical tactics, people said. And was not the new Vice-President already beginning to fall out with his chief?

Not long after the Inauguration, the new Vice-President was driving down to Obrajes in his new Cadillac when he "smelt something burning". He stopped the car and got out to examine it, at which there was a violent explosion in the boot, and the car was blown to pieces. Rumour was conflicting: "Of course, that, too, was the work of the *control politico*."

"Nonsense, he arranged it himself—to arouse our excitement and sympathy."

"How can you smell a bomb burning before it goes off?"

The Vice-President said nothing to enlighten the public beyond making the obvious remark that he had had a lucky escape.

The only other event of the holiday was a railway accident. The train to Buenos Aires had left La Paz one morning along the sloping track to the south. An engine-driver in a nearby goods-yard had been doing some shunting, still in a celebration stupor, and failed to notice that one goods wagon had rolled on to the main line. It slipped slowly away then gained speed as the track began to slope. They were serving lunch on the Buenos Aires train when the goods wagon caught up with it. Several carriages telescoped together. Five people were killed, more died in hospital. Two English volunteers, on their way back to England, were alive but badly cut. One of them came to stay with us to convalesce. He resisted some of my attempts at nursing, as he wanted still to be suitably battered on his arrival home—to impress his family about the wildness and dangers of life in South America.

One of the highlights of the winter in David's section of the Chancery was La Paz's first International Book Exhibition. Originally planned to take place the year before we arrived, this exhibition had been postponed by the Bolivian Government "for technical reasons". It was due to take place in August. Then the date was put forward to June, "for further technical reasons", and in June it was postponed to July "for political reasons". Most of us thought it would never happen at all, but at last the finally-settled date, in

September, drew near, and caught almost everyone unprepared.

The exhibition was to be held in the Prado, the main boulevard of La Paz. The Bolivian government offered an official stand to hold a set number of books, at a set price. Some countries accepted this stand, others thought it not decorative enough.

The books for the British stand had been accumulated with a great deal of trouble: volumes carefully selected in subjects apt for Bolivia such as tropical agriculture, mining, engineering, economics, tropical diseases, veterinary science, dentistry, and how to teach English. There were about 700 of them, in English and Spanish, sent in from Madrid, Mexico, Buenos Aires and Montevideo as well as from London. The British Council had also supplied a quatro-centenary mountain of books on every aspect of Shakespeare scholarship. Clearly there were far too many books for the official stand, which was also too expensive.

David had the unenviable task of designing a stand which would take double the official rating of books and cost half the price. The result was an ingenious and hideous contraption which could later be taken to bits and sold to defray the expenses of its construction.

Two days before the exhibition was due to open, Mayori, a carpenter employed by the Embassy, with several *chicos* and Forgues to give him a hand, drove up to the Prado with a lorry-load of miscellaneous pieces of hardboard and iron railing, to join the bands of other workmen already struggling, shouting, and borrowing screwdrivers, paintbrushes or hatchets. It was not a tussle to see who could get done first, but a battle against the wind, which blew cease-lessly down the Prado as if it were a funnel. The workmen were like campers in a tempest; our hardboard and iron stand had to be pinned in place with wires tied like guy-ropes to nearby telegraph poles.

Inside, it was like a flimsy bus-shelter with a screen across the front. The walls shook and rattled deafeningly with every gust, and clouds of dust whipped in through the gap between them and the pavement. A moment of panic set in when it became clear that Mayori's steel railing which formed the shelves as well as the scaffolding frame-work, was one size too narrow to hold the books. They fell down in a thick clatter with each gust of wind. Forgues and I spent many hours drilling holes in the hardboard and threading hundreds of feet of nylon fishing-line to keep the books in place.

Not even two coats of white paint could make the stand look decorative—and a carefully selected group of posters of "Beautiful Scotland", and "Cornwall-in-the-Spring" only served to accentuate the bus-shelter look—but at least it housed the books, which were an intelligent and informative collection.

No one really believed that the exhibition would open on time. While Mayori shouted at his *chicos* and the stand swayed in the wind, David was locked in discussions at the Chancery as to whether we should take part at all.

The teachers were on strike all over the country, and staging violent demonstrations against the government. In protest against the Ministry of Education, which sponsored the exhibition, they might march into the Prado and tear down the foreign stands, or, worse, use the books as missiles against the police. But the final decision was to risk it.

Suddenly, with less than twenty-four hours to go, the Ministry announced that the opening of the exhibition would be at midday the following day instead of in the evening. This was a ruse to put the teachers off their stride. But it took the exhibitors quite unawares.

Mayori hammered and shouted and slapped on paint; Forgues and I threaded the fishing-line feverishly, but the newly appointed hour came before we had any books in the stand.

The opening speeches, relayed over loudspeakers strung to the trees, were inaudible above the wind. The President and his party toured the exhibition long before half of us had our books up, but somehow by the evening everything looked better, the Prado was half-heartedly floodlit, and crowds of people appeared to examine each stand.

No foreign publishers took part, but most countries were represented. The Americans had over 1,000 books, endless volumes on the White House and the Presidency, and a great many paper-back thrillers. France, Germany and Italy were crowded under one title, "*El Mercado Común*" with about sixty books each. Spain had a large stand of glossy volumes, most of them on art; at least a quarter of the Yugoslav stand was devoted to books entitled *Tito*, and the

Wise woman from Potosí

Tarabuco—man—and his wife

Wedding on the shores of Lake Titicaca—Feast of All Saints

Revolution Day in La Paz

Japanese had a huge, beautifully set out exhibition of lanterns, photographs, magazines and picture-books on flower arrangement. The
Republic of China (Formosa) whose Ambassador incongruously,
was an Anglican, and would come, unofficially, to our church
functions, had a beautiful little red pagoda with no books in it at all.

The whole city seemed quite excited that first evening, but next
day in the papers we read that the exhibition was a dismal failure,
and its failure the fault of the government. At least this kept the
teachers away from the Prado. They stayed up in the city, smashing
the windows of various ministries. We also read the opening speeches.
The Minister of Education, whose high chirping voice we had been
unable to follow, had said that the exhibition had been organised
"because we are conscious that the spiritual activity of the people
must develop in absolute freedom in an atmosphere in which the
writer is not subject to pressure and in such a way that the success of
an idea will not carry with it the blot of oppression and violence but
will be the result of a lofty ideological struggle".

Joaquín toured the exhibition the second day. "It is all so typical,"
he said. "This stand is typical of the British temperament: serious,
earnest, informed, useful, and dry."

I said, "What about Shakespeare—you like Shakespeare, don't
you?"

"Oh yes, he's wonderful—but all these books are technical."

"That's what we want—we want to show that English books are
some use, that it's important to know English. All these volumes on
medicine and so on—they're going to be donated to colleges and
universities. Surely that's a good thing?"

"Yes."

"Well, which stand do you think is best?"

"Oh the Spanish—all the books are so beautiful—not useful I
know, but lovely. I can go and look at them and think about the
things that glorify life like art and poetry and love. I come here and I
have to think about grammar and under-development and virus
diseases."

Two hundred books were stolen from the Spanish stand in the
first three days. Our losses did not exceed a dozen: we were more
vigilant, but our visitors were usually more serious. We all took

N

turns at minding the British stand, wrapped in coats and scarves against the weather. During one of my sessions, three books were stolen. I saw two youths examining a dictionary for some time, then one of them took another book down and came across to me asking if he could buy it. I told him not, and explained the books would be donated. He left the book on the table and moved out into the street. His friend had already disappeared, and so had the dictionary and two other volumes. I rushed to the door, but there was no sign of them by now, and I could not leave the stand. After this we had two people on duty.

The cold weather took its toll. Soon everyone seemed to be ill, and public interest waned, yet the exhibition was supposed to go on for a fortnight.

After a week, a deputation of cultural attachés from various embassies, David among them, went to call on the Minister of Education to say they wished to end the exhibition and take down the stands. The Minister refused to see them. Diligent persuasion got them an interview with the *Oficial Mayor* (the head Civil Servant at the Ministry). He said he could not give permission, he would have to ask the Minister. But it was contrary to etiquette for him to approach the Minister. He would have to wait for the Minister to speak to him, and this would not be for four days. Could he not write a note to the Minister, the dismayed attachés asked? No, there would be no point—the Minister did not read notes written on Ministry paper. The attachés, he suggested, should write a joint letter. But then someone remarked that there was no paper with the crests of all embassies on it, so this would not be possible. Could not, the *Oficial Mayor* asked, could not the senior representative of the attachés write the letter on behalf of all of them? But this again was not possible as the senior representative was the Chinese, and Britain did not officially recognise Nationalist China, and in any case the Chinese had little case for closing their pagoda as it had no books in it. So the meeting ended in deadlock.

The exhibition dragged on for a few days more, until one by one the cultural attachés or their assistants were officially ill, and the stands were summarily dismantled.

The teachers' strike also petered out, and no one remembered the Minister's stirring speech. Within a month, the government, having failed to get journalists to toe the party line, censored all newspapers and radios: the country became more tense than ever.

One day the government claimed to have discovered a plot to overthrow it and assassinate the President. It was allegedly instigated by an ex-president of the country, who had therefore been arrested that morning with thirty of his "accomplices". Argentina was asked to give them political asylum but refused. Paraguay, however, accepted them, and they were flown out forthwith to exile. Ninety days of martial law was declared, and La Paz was said to be "in a state of siege". Travel permits were made obligatory for any journey outside the city—meetings of more than five people were banned, and there was a curfew each night from eleven to six a.m.

Ramón was outwardly quite laconic about the national state of crisis. We went to dinner with him, just before the curfew was imposed, at his new house in Calcoto. He had furnished it delightfully with antiques and objets and a great many books in Spanish and English, and the whole atmosphere was more relaxed than the previous party at the palace. Here the guards stood outside the door, so we felt more at ease, and he felt less need for discretion. He was gay and indefatigable and whirled us all off to a night-club somewhere in the town, and promised, as always, that he would take us with him on one of his "trips".

None of these plans for weekend expeditions seemed likely to come to anything, but in the middle of the curfew-crisis he invited David to go down to the Argentine border with him.

Down in the south, near Bermejo, there were large sugar plantations, and the government was building a new refinery. But it was worried about the market for the sugar. Ramón was to look into the arrangement of outlets into northern Argentina.

They set off early one morning in an army plane.

Days later, Carver, the English volunteer in Tarija, came up to La Paz, and called to see me. He brought a letter from David, who had passed through Tarija with Ramón after leaving the sugar refineries and the Argentine border. Their expedition had, it seemed, been a remarkable success, socially. Whether or not the sugar market developed, I never quite discovered.

Carver told me that David had gone on from Tarija to visit Santa Cruz.

"He had to wait a couple of days for the plane to leave. The airways company kept delaying departure in the hope that more passengers would turn up.

"By the way," he added as he left, "don't expect David back too soon. I hear the airline has run out of money again. All flights have been cancelled."

Santa Cruz was Bolivia's boom town, the centre of an enormous province being developed by various groups of agriculturalists and industrialists. The town itself stood amid plantations of sugar-cane, and fields of rice and cotton. Oil had been discovered, and the area now supplied the whole country with motor fuel. At times when the airways company had not run out of money there were daily flights to La Paz, and within the last few years a modern tarred highway had been built to link the town with Cochabamba.

But it was still in a sense a "wild frontier". As little as ten years before, the only way of getting out of Santa Cruz had been a twenty-day mule trail to Cochabamba. Guerilla country was near, and so were primitive and wild Indian tribes, some said to be cannibal. It was still quite normal to walk about armed, and legal, I had been told, to shoot a Tanaigua Indian on sight—if by some lucky chance one saw him first.

With the country in such a state of unrest, and reports that guerilla bands were very near to Santa Cruz, I was far from happy at the thought of David being there at all. I confessed my misgivings to Joaquin one afternoon at the Chancery.

"I shouldn't worry if I were you," he said. "He seems to be quite all right. Look at this—a friend of mine brought it up from Cochabamba last night."

He handed me a folded newspaper. It was a copy of the Santa Cruz daily, *El Progreso*, days old, crumpled and torn. On one page a large ring had been drawn round an article entitled "*Grata Visita*".

"*Señor David de Caccia,*" I read, "is visiting Santa Cruz to look for the really important intellectuals so that he can get to know them personally. . . ." The writer went on to describe the impression my husband had made on him: "He showed, like a good Englishman, the fine culture of the United Kingdom . . . I was benevolently impressed by his candour and his extraordinary intelligence . . ."

XV

The Revolution

I N LA PAZ, meanwhile, life became increasingly tense. What dinner parties there were ended early because of the curfew, and no one wanted to be out late in any case, as you never knew whom you might meet; the police were on the lookout for anyone, the army were about, and so were groups of hooligans, all armed. Lying awake at nights, I would listen to police jeeps and gangs passing along the main road, and wonder what I should do if they came into our house. Unlike some of our neighbours we did not keep a gun. "Would I offer them all drinks?" I wondered. In my mind I conjured up ridiculous scenes where they sat in a circle, and I walked about in my dressing-gown with glasses and cakes. I wished the airways company would become solvent and resume its services.

By the time it did, and David had returned to La Paz, there had been some severe rioting. The teachers were still discontented and at large—at least some people said they were, but it was never quite clear who set mobs going, suddenly they were there, surging through the streets.

One day they rioted through Sopocachi, past the flat where our American friends Luz and Winifred lived. They tore up the cobbles to use as missiles against the police, flung them at the windows of houses, smashed up the Centro Boliviano-Americano, and even managed to break the panes in Luiz's flat on the third floor. Winifred was locked into her flat for several hours, while the mobs surged about below shouting and letting off firecrackers, and the police struggled for order, shouting and letting off tear-gas. We persuaded Winifred and Luiz to come to the comparative calm of Calacoto for a few days.

Through all this, life went on—women went marketing, foreign visitors came and went, diplomatic lunches, teas, dinners, still took place. Conversation, though, was of nothing but whether there would be a revolution and if so when and how. And everyone held different opinions, for it was very difficult, with all the different meshes of political intrigue, most of them unknown to us, to see clearly what shape events would take.

On one side the President seemed so securely entrenched. He was, after all, still the hero of the last revolution, and of the *Reforma Agraria* which had "given the Indians back their land". In theory he should still have the loyalty of a large section of the population. Moreover, he was, people admitted, clever, shrewd, and ruthless. His party had fortified its power by the use of a strong, armed police, and an ever alert secret police the *control politico*. Further, with his flawless English he had captured the confidence of the Americans, who were pouring dollars into the country. It was even rumoured that he had a hot line to Washington.

But on the other hand, the increasing strikes and riots, and the need to impose martial law and press censorship, were seen as signs of weakness. There were endless rumours of corruption and strife among the Cabinet, and so in the Party. The *control politico* was getting out of hand, beating up ex-Vice-Presidents and—so people said—trying to blow up air force generals. The failure to reform electoral law (each party had a different coloured ballot paper, so that the ruling party could confiscate the papers of its opponents at the vital moment of an election), and the "rigged" elections of the winter had made another black mark. Then there was the exiling of the ex-President, perhaps another admission of weakness. All in all the gossip went on, it encouraged people to think of violence.

"It must be coming soon," said Joaquín one day.

"Revolution?"

"Yes. I can't say I think it will solve anything—I mean I don't have much hope of the army preserving the rights of the people—and yet who else is going to get rid of this régime?"

"But have they got the power?" I asked. "After all, they lost to the miners and *obreros* [workers] in the last revolution."

He shrugged. "Maybe. But something must be done. They are all getting quite hysterical. Look at the *control politico*. It's all very well.

You may need one—but it should be discreet and not too efficient. This one—it's like the Gestapo. The Party—they are in everything. The rule of law? Pah! The judges are just party hacks, taking bribes from everyone. As for Congress—it's a farce. Where are the ideals, the speeches—'*retorica altosonante*?' Anything against the government is just shouted down by the *Control Politico*'s hecklers."

With the censorship in force, it was impossible to know definitely which way the wind was blowing. Everything depended on hearsay from "reliable sources" whatever these were. I pictured the town seething with diplomats slinking about the cafés and squares among the *politicos* and trades unionists and soldiers, trying desperately to eavesdrop without losing their dignity, and at the same time to avoid any chance of being caught in the next riot. Every time I went up to market there seemed to be road gangs putting down fresh cobbles where they had been last torn out.

Whichever side one was on, there seemed to be a great many people heavily armed: the army, the air force, the police, the *control politico*—these conventionally. Then the miners were a heady lot, with unlimited supplies of dynamite and home-made bombs. They had an armed trade union militia in Catavi, which consistently defied both army and government—no one had been able to get near them for four years. Whose side would they take, we all wondered? Perhaps, it was suggested, they might even march on La Paz, bring out the 10,000 factory workers to support them, over-throw the government, set up a Marxist or *Castristo* régime.

As if this were not enough, there were also the teachers, and, more passionate still, the students, who seemed constantly open to any suggestion of violent action, as if they longed to rush through the streets in a hail of machine-gun fire, waving flags in a dash of *heroismo*, throwing home-made bombs or dying for some stirring concept like *libertad*, all of which was naturally far more exciting than studying.

"Of course," said Joaquín, "you can rely on the students to create plenty of *violencia* at any time. They are longing for the chance."

"What about the professors?" I asked.

"Well, they are in a very difficult position. You see a few years ago the government broke the university *autonomía* and allowed half

the governing board of each university to be made up of students—
so all professors are partly appointed by students. If they try to go
against the students they may lose their jobs. They have to curry
favour all the time, and are elected because of their politics. Still, the
students are paid for by the local taxes—so you see the government
still has a whip hand."

"Well what are their politics?"

"Oh, anything—*Marxismo, Castrismo*, Catholic democratic socialism, neo-fascism—but always against the government. The main
thing is they are more interested in politics than work. They can
create plenty of chaos for whoever is doing the real fighting—still,
most people will try to be on the winning side . . ." he grinned.
"As soon as they can tell which side is winning!"

So we waited, and watched as the students seemed to be seizing
every opportunity to riot. They demonstrated for the teachers, and
against martial law, and against censorship, and even against a
change in the date of their examinations—and this went on outside
La Paz too, in Cochabamba and in Sucre. In some places lorry-loads
of armed *campesinos* were brought in from the country to deal with
them. And the police went on throwing tear-gas.

But one day in Cochabamba they ran out of tear-gas, and opened
fire. Some students were hit, and one later died of his wounds. This
set off more student riots throughout the country, and they became
rougher. In Oruro forty students were wounded and two killed.
Next day the bodies of the two students "lay in state" in Oruro
University in the hall where we had shown Hamlet. The following
morning the miners from the San José Mine came in to the funeral
in sympathy—one of the students had been the son of a miner. The
police also turned out. There was a clash, and they opened fire. There
were rumours that the mother of one student was killed in the mêlée.
Fighting, dynamiting and looting went on all night. The army
moved in to cordon off Oruro and try to isolate the trouble—at
which the miners' militia, organised, the reports said, by Trotskyites
from Huanuni, tried to break into Oruro. A prolonged battle
ensued, in which 100 miners were killed.

Next day David came down for lunch with news of a pitched
battle between the students and police up at the university. It had

started as a "March of Liberty" until the militia appeared, at which the students had barricaded the streets round the university in the Prado, using cars, boxes and torn up cobble-stones. At one moment they had surged out from their defences and made for the nearest ministry, which happened to be the Ministry of Health. This they soon set fire to, and looted.

"Think of it," he said, "tons of filing-cabinets and card indexes with irreplaceable *estadisticos* for TB, VD, birth-rates, death-rates, all being hurled out of the windows through the smoke."

The summer rains had already begun. In the middle of lunch a torrential storm broke.

"That should stop them," we said, as David churned back to the Chancery through the swirling water.

But the fighting went on. In the rain the police shot their way through the barriers into the university, where they rounded up and arrested over 1,000 people, many of them innocent passers-by who had run into shelter from the storm and the shooting. About twenty people died in this contretemps, the *control politico* started "interrogations" and everyone knew, grimly, what that meant.

Rumour had it that the students had expected the factory-workers and, indeed, the army, to take up arms in support of their "heroism"—and that they felt they had been grossly let down in their gesture for liberty.

That night we listened on the radio to the President broadcasting to the nation. He sounded firm, convinced, and very angry. He blamed Communists and extremists and said the government would prevail against subversion.

It was announced that a cache of Czech guns had been found in the university. At once diplomatic relations with Czechoslovakia were broken off and the Czechs expelled for "gun-running". Western diplomats had known of this for some considerable time and warned the Bolivians about it, but with no previous effect. Someone said the government was doing its best to fan the fear of a *Castristó coup*.

Everyone began to wonder how the army would react, whether or not it would remain loyal, as several generals had been critical of the Party.

At this dramatic point, however, there was a sudden lull. We woke next morning expecting gunfire—but there was a heavy silence. "Of course," we remembered, "it is a public holiday." And so were the next two days. We had All Saints and All Souls, and, politics or no, these were festivals.

David took a party of friends across the *altiplano* to Copacabana, leaving me in charge of house and baby just in case something should happen—though no one expected anything to happen at all, and in the event nothing did.

They drove to Copacabana, took a boat across the lake to the Island of the Sun, where Manco Capac, the first Inca, was created, and clambered up and down the wonderful Inca's steps. They wandered about Copacabana, and lit the two candles Juana (our cook) had given them, urgently, as they left La Paz, for the *Virgen de Copacabana* was Juana's *patrona*. There were a few pilgrims who had arrived by motor-bike and some Germans who had walked from La Paz (well over fifty miles) and were making their way on their knees up to the top of a little promontory above the lake. Wanting to get to the Island of the Moon, which was less easily reached, David made enquiries about hiring a boat and was sent to a Señora who had once looked after Eichmann's boat when he had lived in hiding in Copacabana. She described him as a "*caballero honorable*". After a good deal of haggling, she agreed to take the party to the Island of the Moon and they set off in the morning, with the Señora and a sullen, silent coca-chewing boatman. They never reached the island at all. The boat, old and decrepit and overloaded, puttered a good way out from land, and then the engine spluttered into silence. They lay becalmed all day, with the Señora shouting at the boatman, whose attempts with the engine failed utterly, and they ate their lunch-time sandwiches, and drank a few bottles of beer, and sat in the sun wondering what would happen. At dusk a very slight breeze drifted them slowly towards some cliffs. Leaving Eichmann's Señora, who refused to forsake her boat, they paddled ashore, climbed the precipice, and walked twelve miles back to Copacabana in the dark.

On the last day of the holiday, as they drove back across the plain, it seemed as if the whole population had taken to the roads: for miles they had to weave slowly through crowds of Indians, dancing, jogging, bicycling, reeling and tottering after three days or more of non-stop *fiestas*. Perhaps these people had set off for La Paz. Certainly they never got there. Outside every village the sides of the road were littered with prone bodies, asleep or unconscious.

La Paz during the holiday was very quiet. I sat at home, listening anxiously to the various radio stations, but the censorship was still in force—and if anything at all was happening, no news had a chance of penetrating the cacophony of rumbas, sambas and cuecas that blared ceaselessly over every wavelength.

Behind this curtain of inebriation and merrymaking, a drama was being played out, with intrigues of such duplicity and intricacy that it was never really possible later to discover exactly what had happened, or in what sequence, but at some stage the scales of fate finally swung against the Party.

Later reports held that the chief army general had spent a very busy holiday with a small Japanese tape recorder in his pocket: recording conversations with the President, and playing them back to his officers, then recording conversations with his officers and playing them back to the President. Only the General could have known which conversation was genuine and who was being duped at each moment. The situation must have held fascinating ironies for him. By this means, at any rate, the President was informed that the young army officers were about to hold a secret meeting. With no alternative but to trust his right-hand-man, he sent the General to attend this meeting and report to him what went on. In fact the General himself was to preside at the meeting. Perhaps he even had two different tape recorders for representing different views. The events of the meeting never became clear.

However, the morning after the holiday, the Ingavi regiment in La Paz mutinied. The President sent the General to treat with them. The regiment immediately seized the General and declared him hostage. It was not clear whether this was genuine, or part of a secret plot between the General and the regiment.

The Air-Force-General, who was in Cochabamba, was informed of this, but was also reported to believe that the General was being held, not by the regiment, but by the *Control Politico*. It was no more clear, either, whether this was genuine, or part of a plot between the two Generals. But it gave the air-force-General the excuse he wanted to take over the Cochabamba garrison, capture the city without a shot being fired, and declare for the rebel regiment.

The President's personal secretary flew down to Cochabamba to treat with the Air-Force-General—but to no avail, and soon the regiments in Oruro, and Viacha, declared that they would not march on La Paz and shoot their brothers.

Radio stations, suddenly less wary, began to announce a few tentative pieces of news. At home, we kept the wireless on constantly, switching from one station to the next. That afternoon the President took over all stations to broadcast. It was a speech lacking in the usual Spanish tautologies—curt, and quick, and uneasy. He was, he declared, still in complete control of the country, despite any vicious rumours we might hear to the contrary; he had been constitutionally elected, and the "*pueblo*" were still behind him.

The General had not been nicknamed "the fox" for nothing. He came on the air after the President. They must have been in the broadcasting studio together. The General spoke stirringly of his loyalty to the people (a safe remark which could be taken either way), denied that he had been arrested (had the hostage been let out—or had the officers planned to let him broadcast to thus gain time?), and implied his loyalty to the President very cleverly without actually saying it in so many words.

That evening we drove up to the town to see what was happening. Nothing, however, was. Very few people were about, and those who were were very quiet. Even in the Prado there was far from the usual everyday bustle and babble. People stood around on the pavements outside the cinemas and cafés, hardly talking. There were little groups of Indian men on corners, hunched against the cold wind, their mouths taut, their slit-eyed faces like masks. David thought the atmosphere extremely tense. I admitted that they all looked as though they were waiting for something to happen, but thought that as usual whatever it was, in that whimsical Latin-American way, probably would not happen. In the event he was right.

We awoke next day to one of those cloudless, dew-drenched

mornings when every colour in the valley seemed a radiant distillation. Trees, roofs and hillsides glistened magically and no sound
broke the spell—as if the world had caught its breath. We drove
early up to the Chancery, passing a couple of buses, one or two cars
—but none of the usual traffic. I dropped David, and drove on up into
the town, determined to do some shopping, as we had invited the
Ambassador to lunch and I had planned an ambitious meal.

But the main streets were deserted. In the Camacho, the area with
most well-to-do shops, and the expensive markets, everything was
closed. The markets higher up in the town were open, but there
were few goods on display. I drove up into the Indian town to buy
flour and sugar. Most of the shops were shuttered and barred, but
the one I always dealt with was open. I climbed down the steps (it
was like a cellar, this shop, piled high with enormous sacks of sugar
and flour), and bought an *aroba* (twenty-five lb.) of sugar, and half
a hundredweight of flour.

"Why's everything closed?" I asked the shopkeeper as we loaded
the sacks into the Land-Rover. "The whole town down there is
dead. Do they really think there will be fighting—or is it just another
holiday?"

He grinned. "I don't know, señora. Some are afraid, some like
any opportunity to stay at home. But if there is fighting—it's not
just the shooting they are afraid of. It's all the looting, you know.
They don't want their shops ransacked."

"And you? What about you?"

"I'm always open—I'll stay so till I really hear the trouble.
Anyway my stuff is quite difficult to steal, you know—too heavy."
Which was quite true, I noticed. Most of the large sacks must have
weighed over 200 lb.—hardly stuff for a mob to run off with.

I drove on to the German sausage factory, where I had ordered a
fillet of pork. (This I intended to stud with truffles and roast for
lunch in a slow oven.) The German owner was marching about in
his white overalls as usual, but few of his employees had turned up.
He groused and said it was typical—prolonging their holidays, and
that he was sure nothing would really happen—the *politicos* would
just all go on talking.

Halfway back to Calacoto I realised I had forgotten the wine. I turned back and raced crossly up the hill past the Chancery to the nearest German wineshop, bought two very expensive bottles of hock, and turned to go back, only to find my route blocked by soldiers. I wheeled off up the hill and drove quickly down some side streets to reach the pass to Obrajes lower down. This meant that the last thing David saw out of his office window before the shooting started was our Land-Rover dashing up towards the city.

I did not hear the first gunfire, but it must have begun as I turned into our valley and crossed the last bridge before our house. I could think of nothing but the urgency of cooking the lunch. I left the car in the street and ran into the house holding my purchases untidily in my arms. As I put the meat down, one of the precious bottles of hock slipped from my grasp and burst on the stone floor. I was furious. One bottle was not enough for our numbers. I could not have the lunch ruined like this.

"Start the pork," I called to Juana. "I'm going straight back to get another bottle." And I ran back to the car.

All this could not have taken more than two minutes. When I reached the street, there were three soldiers crouching outside the gate, machine-guns and bayonets at the ready. I looked up and down the valley. As far as I could see there was a soldier behind every tree, every lamp-post. The steel flashed in the sun, and far down at the bridge I could see lorries moving.

"What's going on?" I asked the nearest soldier. "I want to go up to the town. Will they let me get past?"

"No, señora. Go back into your house at once. This is a very dangerous business."

"Well, what's happened?"

"I don't know. They say the President has escaped. You must get out of the way. And put your jeep away—someone might think it's useful."

Though polite, they looked very threatening. My blood pounding with fear, I put the Land-Rover into the garage, locked the doors and the gates, and as I went into the house, I could hear the gunfire down the valley—probably from the President's house.

Juana, Magdalena and Chérie, our English nanny, were all in the kitchen listening to the wireless.

"Are they shooting the President?" I asked.

"No one knows, señora. It must be a revolution. But here—they say nothing." We switched from one station to another.

The electricity had been cut off. We started roasting the pork in a saucepan, and ran about filling baths with water. I tried telephoning the Embassy but the line was dead.

Lorry-loads of soldiers churned past outside. I wondered if any would try to break into the house. I pictured us in a state of siege, unable to get any food, unable to get out of the country—the airport was so far away up on the *altiplano*—and the only exit. Perhaps it would be bombed or broken up. Feeling stifled, I went back to the kitchen, where we sat tensely, turning the meat and changing from one radio station to another in search of news.

By chance we tuned in to Radio Continental, owned by the "Communist" factory workers' trade-union, and heard a passionate voice crackling across the air: "The President has escaped! He has escaped! He is driving up the town through Villa Victoria. People of Villa Victoria, run, run into the streets and stop him, lynch him here and now . . . " This was followed by a burst of martial music.

On another wavelength the cry was echoed. We switched fascinated from one station to another: "Follow the President, find him—he has escaped in a blue car . . . " "Catch the tyrant! He is fleeing across the *altiplano* to Titicaca. He is in a grey car, disguised as a woman. Stop him, stop him!" "Bolivians of Calamarca, Ayo Ayo, Tiahuanaco, Sica Sica, take up your arms, fill the roads, catch the traitor. We must bring him to justice." "Brothers of Pucarani, Brothers of Guaqui, now is your chance. Seize the dictator who has brought us all such misery." How quick and easy it was to voice this passion and hatred, I thought.

In fact the President was in no danger of being caught in blue or grey cars, in any disguise at all. By this time he was sitting comfortably in El Hotel Country Club in Lima. It was later revealed that he had sat up all night at the Palace in the city, with his Cabinet, who were fast losing confidence. The *milicianos* (the trade unionists and haphazard groups of the people's militia, armed but wayward) were thought still to be loyal, but due to the holidays, few of them were probably sober enough to respond to any call to arms. Only

the President's private secretary had the confidence to say he would
lead them into the streets and fight to the death. The rest of the
Cabinet were stonily unforthcoming, so much so that the private
secretary lost his own confidence, left the room and made a dash for
the street, where he quickly sought asylum in the house of the
papal Nuncio.

In the early hours of the morning, the Army General had arrived
at the Palace. In a private meeting with the President, he had
announced that he could no longer control his officers. He gave
the President two hours to leave the country. The President went
back to the Cabinet and told them that he was going out to inspect
the police and militia. He then went out through ranks of weeping
palace guards, and into a car with the General, who drove him up
to the airport, where an aeroplane was already waiting on the
runway. His wife and children had been brought up secretly in
another car. They were all hustled aboard and the plane took off:
the General wanted no lynching and martyrdom. In Peru, the President was given red-carpet treatment, met by a posse of Peruvian
politicians, put up in luxury, and before the day was over had given
his first press conference, denouncing the army, and declaring his
firm intention of returning, and belief that the people wanted him.

In La Paz, the news of his departure filtered out slowly at first,
then panic broke. In each ministry and government office the
ministers and their juniors dropped pen and paper and dashed out
into the streets, making for asylum in the nearest foreign embassy.
The shooting started as I was driving unwittingly downhill to
Calacoto. Up in the Camacho, crowds surged through the streets,
and the police and *milicianos* lost their heads, and stood on street
corners spraying everyone with machine-gun fire. Anyone who saw
a parked car or truck leapt into it and drove off downhill, but the
students had barricaded the *avenida* again, and the piles of cobble-
stones were soon jammed with vehicles, stuck on top with their
wheels spinning. The students joined the tide, shouting for *libertad*—
their moment of *heroismo* had come at last. They swept through the
streets, and stoned and sacked the offices of the *control politico*,
stormed every ministry building within reach, and smashed open
the prison, to let out scores of Communists, Fascists, bandits,

o

murderers and thieves, who joined in the fighting and sacking with gusto. The police, seeing which way the wind was blowing, stripped off their uniforms, handed over their thousands of dollars' worth of American-supplied guns to the mob, and disappeared. For the few stray people who just happened to be about and did not want to join the fighting, things were very difficult. No route home was safe to take, and shelter from gunfire almost impossible as all the shops were barred. Several American ladies made their way to different embassies. One tough English railway wife, hearing the mob approach, lifted the cover off the nearest drain, and climbed down into the sewer. Here she spent several hours, nauseated but safe.

The Chancery, being downhill from the Camacho, was an ideal refuge. Halls and offices were soon crammed with people. David, Drake and Fitzwarren stood at the windows, craning for signs of gunfire uphill, and watching bands of soldiers advancing up the road towards the fighting. One group crept stealthily along, bayonets at the ready, staring straight ahead.

"Where are you going?" Drake called to one soldier as he passed.

"*No se,*" was the curt reply—"I don't know."

"Who will you fight?"

"*No se,*" and the group moved on, the soldier slowly extracting a banana from his pocket, peeling and munching without averting his gaze from the man ahead.

David was convinced that I was still up in the town—he could only hope I had taken shelter somewhere. His worried efforts to telephone our house were useless, as all lines were dead.

Cut off in Calacoto, we could do nothing but watch the soldiers dashing past the door, and listen to the radio. Pablo, the gardener, was desperately excited. He revealed to me that he had been a *miliciano.*

"Give me permission to go, señora. I must go up to the town. I must fetch my uniform."

"But it's no use, Pablo. You can't fight for the President—he's gone. Who will you fight for? I don't want you to get shot."

"But they owe me money, señora. For four months now they have not paid me. I must go to the little offices at once, before they close, before all the people run away. Before there is no money left."

"No, no, no," I insisted. "Anyway, everything must be shut by now. I can't have a dead gardener. And you would never get past the guard on the bridge."

I sent him out into the street to look, and a soldier smartly pushed him back into the garden at bayonet point.

In the kitchen Juana was bending over the sizzling meat. She was still sure the Ambassador would come to lunch—and the Señor.

"He has to eat somewhere, *el pobrecito*," she said. I wondered if she thought he was taking part in the fighting.

We hovered about, laying the table, listening to the crackling radio voices. The *Señora Lavandera* came in from her wash-tub from time to time to follow events too.

The government radio station was broadcasting *"el rock en rol"*. Then suddenly the music was joined by sounds of shouting and scuffling—when the wavelength cleared, a passionate voice announced that the station had been taken over in the name of the Revolution. One by one, we heard other stations, even the Jesuit-run Radio Cruz del Sur, and the American Missions' radio station, capitulate. I imagined our friend Padre Montegut sitting quietly in his little studio, surrounded suddenly by hi-jacking soldiers (in fact this was exactly how it happened, as he later told us). Passionate announcements about *libertad, honor, heroismo* and hope for the future came torrenting out over every wavelength. Reports of the fighting were few, though we knew by now that the President had been forgotten, that the airport had fallen to the Revolution, and that fighting was fierce in the city where thousands of the brave were dying for the cause.

"*Atencion, Atencion! Pueblo de Bolivia,*" we heard. "Your hour is here, your hour has come. Seize your liberty," and strains of the Marseillaise would swell through the crackling atmospherics.

Up in the Chancery they had a fuller view of the fighting, and could soon see that the main conflict was centred on an escarpment that lay between the main town (the Camacho) and the suburb of Miraflores. This had a well-fortified garrison-point, with many sentry-boxes, and the hillside was riddled with underground passages. It had, indeed, a dominating position over the whole city, and was manned by a tight group of *milicianos* loyal to the President. These had evidently not heard of their leader's betrayal and flight. They were fighting to the death. The army had quickly seized other vantage points, including the penthouse restaurant of the main luxury hotel, and was blasting heavy fire at the *milicianos*, whose bodies could be seen from the Chancery, rolling down the steep slopes below their hide-out.

At this point, following the capture of the airport, the air force joined the fray, with all seven Mustangs in operation. They circled about over the town, then suddenly swooped down over the valley of Calacoto. The first pair came frighteningly low over our house and whirred off up the valley. It was really not at all clear what they were doing—showing off, doing close reconnaissance, or simply trying to frighten any waverers. I wondered if they were going to bomb or strafe us, and suddenly realised the vulnerability of our house, with the Minister of the Interior and the *Colegio Militar* (still said to be loyal too) so close by. When the second pair of aeroplanes came over, swooping directly over our house so low that the pine tree waved as if it had been brushed, I was convinced we were being singled out for attack. I rushed into the garden, snatched up Alexander who was chasing butterflies on the lawn, and ran inside. The *lavandera* followed me, wringing her soapy hands and wailing, "Oh señora, little mother, what shall we do?"

There was little I could think of. The only place in the house that could be safe from flying glass was the small larder under the stairs. I took the baby there, and sat on a sack of flour, waiting to hear the next plane, and bombs, or shelling. But it suddenly seemed a bit ridiculous to be there, and I could not leave him alone with all the sacks of flour and sugar, and we still had the lunch to see to. So I took him to the kitchen.

"The *Colegio Militar* has declared for the Revolution," said Juana. I felt relieved, and went outside. Another plane came over, more slowly, I could see the pilot, and half-believed he grinned and waved at me. He swooped away and I later saw him turn, join two others and wheel up to the escarpment above, to attack with a splatter of fire.

After an hour or so of this bombardment, the *milicianos*, whose numbers had been terribly decimated, surrendered, and the fighting subsided into sporadic bursts of shooting and mortar-fire.

By 2.30 p.m. the Ambassador saw no more reason to postpone lunch. He drove down the hill in his large black car with the flag flying, stopping every now and then to deposit members of staff or of the English colony who had been sheltering in the Chancery. The streets were full of stolen police trucks packed with students, heavily armed and waving bloodstained banners. In Obrajes, one of these trucks pulled up beside him with a jerk, and muttering *"Americanos"* the students started to train their rifles, and a bazooka. But the chauffeur bravely got out, saying *"Embajada Britanica"*—and they suddenly grinned and roared off up the hill shouting *"Viva Bolivia!"*

By the time we sat down to lunch, the worst of the Revolution seemed to be over. We all felt unbelievably exhilarated, relieved, even amused. The Ambassador brought a guest, another diplomat, from Panama, who had lived in Latin America many years. This was the eighth revolution he had actually witnessed. He thought it very well managed.

"A perfect army coup—well-timed, obviously very carefully planned—and it seems, really not very much bloodshed." He had been in Bogota in 1948, he said, "A terrible battle, when it had been estimated that 250,000 people, about a third of the city's population, had died in the conflict."

In the afternoon we listened to the radio stations again. The Communist one was urging the *obreros* to come out into the streets and set up a workers' government, but the army seemed to be well in control, and the *obreros* stayed at home. As Joaquín had predicted, most people were on the winning side as soon as they discovered who was winning. The students were still dashing about the streets, but by now in ambulances as much as armed lorries. The radios all began to appeal for blood donors and help for the wounded, and parties of students combed the suburbs asking for sheets, blankets and bandages. The hospitals were full.

At one stage the Communist ex-Vice-President made a bid for power, coming out of hiding to be carried to the Palace on the shoulders of his supporters. But the army was already securely installed here and the doors shut. The General said he would see the ex-Vice-President alone. In the ensuing argument, shooting started again, and four people were killed. But a torrential hailstorm put an end to the fighting.

In the evening a huge crowd gathered in the square outside the Palace. A military junta was declared. But the people shouted down the General. They were angry, it seemed, at his "weakness" in allowing the President to escape and thus depriving them of the revenge drama—a corpse on a lamp-post.

There was little shooting that night, and the next day dawned as beautiful and glistening as any before. The air of relief was extraordinary. People were walking arm in arm. There was not a policeman in sight. Traffic duty was being done by boy scouts. Soldiers in their grey-green uniforms lounged about, casually leaning on their guns chatting to passers-by. In the main square by the Palace people sat on the sunlit benches, reading newspapers, having their shoes polished as if nothing had happened, and no one appeared to notice the large bloodstains that still darkened the cobbles. The students had been busy overnight. The government radio station was now broadcasting under the name *Radio Universidad*, still the same impassioned speeches about liberty, and bursts of the Marseillaise. And the government's newspaper had appeared, now entitled *Tribuna Universitario*. They were also still very busy in the government offices, sacking everything they could enter, shouting and singing as they tipped files, cabinets, and showers of paper and pamphlets out into the streets. Occasionally the air would be splintered by machine-gun fire, and people would leap for cover or flatten themselves against the walls, but it was probably only someone emptying his magazine . . .

From the various radio stations we heard how the Revolution had gone in the Provinces. In Santa Cruz, Potosí, Sucre, they had smashed the offices of the U.S. Information Service. In Tarija, only one shot had been fired—at a pigeon.

The afternoon saw the final playing out of the performance: all day people waited in the square for the arrival of the Air-Force-General. When he appeared, it was soon made quite plain that he was their darling, and that the General, who had done all the work and not flinched at the nasty task of actually removing the President, was no longer in favour—he had not satisfied their taste for blood and drama and had been perhaps, too clever, too calculating.

Again the General was booed. When the Air-Force-General stood on the balcony the crowds went wild with excitement. Standing in the same position where only three months before he had declared passionately the merits of the President, and the glories of the Party, he now worked the people into a frenzy where they would have no other leader but himself. Not that he needed to say much—it was almost, though not quite, a foregone conclusion.

Most diplomats kept carefully away from this occasion. No one had recognised the revolutionaries and there might be more fighting, one could not be sure.

But we all heard it on our radios. The Air-Force-General spoke, inspired, for three-quarters of an hour, of "*la unidad de la familia Boliviana*," and "*los horizontes illimitados*" now opened by "*las grandes conquistas del pueblo*," of "*trabajo, disciplina y orden, libertad, legalidad, integridad, dignidad, y la grandesa de la patria marchando por el camino de la democracía . . .*" It was difficult to follow, the sound kept fading, and swelling, and his voice was often quite blotted out by the cheering. "We must demonstrate to the world!" he cried, "that we are a rebellious people, but that our rebelliousness is edifying not destructive."

They were his slaves by now, the weeping, cheering crowds. "*Viva, Viva!*" they shouted—"down with the General!" And so the General stood down, and the Air-Force-General was the new leader. There was to be a new government, a military one, but temporary, simply holding power until things settled down; until that Utopian state of affairs arrived when the country was really ready for proper elections.

And this, it seemed, was just what everyone wanted.

XVI

Aftermath

THE COUNTRY SETTLED down, refreshed, invigorated, with a new page in its history to write, all past mistakes written off, and only a few reprisals—(as much for general entertainment as anything else).

The President's house, and those of Cabinet Ministers, were thrown open to the public, which queued to see in what "disgraceful and lewd luxury" the fallen leaders had lived. Ramón was also subjected to this treatment, as he too had had to flee. The newspapers showed enormous pictures of his little house, with suggestive captions about his taste for loose living. It seemed a pathetic ending to his gay acceptance of life, and his genuine and intelligent attempt to do something for his country. And it also seemed a sinister pointer to his inevitable fate, enmeshed in the politics of this continent. He wrote to us later, from Spain, a long letter, characteristically trying to see it all in an amusing light, but in fact unable to conceal deep bitterness and disappointment about his own wasted potential. He had fallen on his feet, he admitted, and found a good job with a worldwide bank, but he was determined to come back one day. I found it hard, somehow, to envisage that day dawning.

A spate of little picture-book pamphlets now appeared for sale on all news stands, giving blow by blow accounts of the Revolution. They had titles like "*El Pueblo—ha Triunfado!*" The highlight of these was the capture and sacking of the *control politico* headquarters and an exposé of the scandalous goings-on within its walls: the luxurious apartments of the chief, the torture chambers downstairs, the graves in the garden, and an office filled with card indexes and the names of 90,000 people who had been watched. The queues to see this house stretched hundreds of yards down the street.

The people were after the chief's blood, but he had gone into hiding. For days the papers were full of conjecture as to where he could be: some said he was being harboured by foreigners, others that he was in the lowland jungles. Then one day word got out that he was hiding in the Paraguayan Embassy, which occupied the top floor of a small house next to the Crillon Hotel. I drove down from market that morning to find the roads blocked by soldiers. From a back route higher up the hill, I could see a large crowd in the plaza outside the suspected refuge. There was a great deal of shouting and even some shooting. Eventually a permanent military guard had to be mounted on the Embassy's steps. The *control politico* chief was said to be in great discomfort: the Embassy only consisted of about three rooms, and he spent most of his time hiding in terror under the kitchen table.

Countries in Latin America did not subscribe to international regulations about political asylum. France or Germany, for instance, had to hand over within three days anyone who had taken refuge on their premises whose whereabouts were known and presence wanted by the new government. Our friend the German *chargé* had sheltered a number of officials from the next door Ministry of Finance, who had dashed in at his door in panic at the first shooting on "Revolution Day". He had agreed only to harbour them until the shooting stopped. When it had, he went down to the cellar to find the officials had already gone out by the back door, leaving behind all their uniforms and guns. There must have been a moment in the day when the streets were full of high-ranking officials scampering home in their underclothes.

Between Latin American countries there was a most convenient reciprocal agreement about asylum, which provided that any politician in his hour of need could find somewhere to go. So every Latin American Embassy was filled with refugees. In that of Argentina whole families were camping in the hall. The Ambassador was said to be desperate at the expense, and complaining that he could not go on feeding all these people: they consumed a whole ox each day.

Gradually news filtered out that various deposed Ministers had found asylum, in Argentina, Chile, Paraguay. Perhaps they themselves had made provisions: the President was said to have taken more than forty million dollars from the national treasury, and to possess a large, comfortable house in one of the richer suburbs of Buenos Aires.

In the diplomatic sphere, everyone waited with interest for the reactions of the Americans.

Joaquín came round to see us. "So, it wasn't too bad at all—was it? A very quick take-over. Of course I can't think what they'll do in the long run—stay in until there's another coup I suppose. At least it means they'll get some able people back. You wait—all sorts of new faces will appear—old diplomats, *politicos* who have been living in exile."

"But what do the people really want?" I asked.

"Want? Do they know themselves?" he shrugged. "Well, it just seems this has to happen every now and then. It may be the altitude—but it's an emotional thing as well. They want a change— new faces, new ideas, a chance to discuss ideals instead of boring practical things like how to balance the economy. By the way, what about the Americans? It's very embarrassing for them after backing the régime so heavily. Their Ambassador will have to resign, won't he?"

But their Ambassador showed no sign of leaving. The White House apparently decided to back the new régime just as heavily, and after a while no more was said.

Diplomatic functions were suddenly filled with new faces: Señor Fulano Bermudes, who had once been an Ambassador, was now at the Foreign Ministry. Señor Moreno had just arrived back from Chile to "help" the Ministry of Finance... We were fascinated.

The British customs team, however, had a nasty shock. Of their nucleus of 200 men, only twenty-five remained. All the others had disappeared, taking with them their official arms, uniforms and vehicles.

"It's worse than going back to square one," groaned Allenby. "How on earth is Whitehall going to accept the story, let alone produce more money for replacements? You know how tight-fisted they all are. And what is much worse is to think where all

these fugitives are now. Where do you suppose? I'm sure I know—
they ran straight into the arms of the nearest *contrabandistas*. They'll
find all our equipment only too useful."

For the rest, life soon settled back to normal: the markets went on,
shops re-opened, visitors came and went, and even the courts now
began to function. Rain fell in torrents, landslides had to be dealt
with, power cuts continued . . .

Don Felipe wrote from Sucre. He was fairly satisfied with the
revolution, though it had not come soon enough, and was bound not
to be right-wing enough for him.

"By the way," he added, "it may surprise you to hear that,
after all these years, my wife and I are getting divorced. It is over the
marriage of my son Juan, with which I do not agree."

Isabella was not surprised to hear this.

"I expect Juan wants to marry an Indian girl," she said. "It's
ridiculous, isn't it? After all, Don Felipe's own mother was a *chola*.
I expect that's why he hates them so—and yet loves them too. He
knows he's one of them."

One day I saw the deposed President's famous car going up the
hill. It was inconspicuous and alone, without the old escort of
outriders. It had been painted a pale blue-grey, and inside, on the
back seat, I could see a row of men in smart uniforms. I felt the
Revolution had come full circle.

Lines from *Ode to the Andean Cordillera* by Pablo Neruda

En medio	Midway
de la tierra y del cielo	between earth and heaven
se interpuso	you thrust yourself, you planet-
tu nieve planetaria	ary snow,
Congelando la torres de la tierra.	freezing the turrets of the earth.

Volcanes, cicatrices, Volcanoes, cicatrices, caverns,
socavones, iron-rusted snows,
nieves ferruginosas, insolent titanic heights,
titanicas alturas heads of the mountains,
desolladas, feet of the sky,
cabezas de los montes, gulf of Hell,
pies del cielo, slashes that peel the terrestrial
abismo del abismo, rind.
cuchilladas And that coin the sun,
que cortaron at seven thousand metres' height
la cascara terrestre hard,
y el sol pure like a diamond above the
a siete mil veins,
metros de altura, above the ropes of shadow and
duros como un diamante snow,
sobre above the worlds' enraged tor-
las venas, los ramales ment
de la sombra y la nieve that imprisoned itself burning
sobre la enfurecida and in the vast silence
tormenta de los mundos imposed these seas of granite.
que se de tuvo hirviendo
y en el silencio
colosal
impuso
sus Mares de granito.

Cordillera, colegio
de piedra,
en esta hora
tu magnitud
celebro,
tu dureza,
el candelabrao frio
de tus altas
soledades de nieve,
la noche
estuario inmóvil,
navegando
sobre
la piedras de tu sueño,
el dia
transparente
en tu cabeza
y en ella, en la nevada
cabellera
del mundo,
el cóndor
levantando
sus alas
poderosas,
su vuelo
digno
de las acérrimas alturas.

Cordillera, school of stone,
at this hour I celebrate
your hard grandeur,
the cold candelabra
of your high solitudes of snow,
the night, a motionless estuary,
sailing above the stones of your
　　sleep,
the day transparent
about your head,
and upon her,
upon the snowy tresses of the
　　world,
the condor lifts his mighty
　　wings,
his flight
worthy
of these harshest heavens.

Acknowledgements

I am most grateful to Pablo Neruda for his kind permission to use the lines from his *Oda a la Cordillera Andina* on page 220; also to Ediciones Losada for permission to quote the song by Lorca on page 160; and to my husband, David Caccia, for allowing me to use passages he wrote in letters from Bolivia. The quotation on page 135 is from *The Imperial City of Potosí* by Lewis Hanke, and is his translation of a passage from the remarkable *Historia de la Villa Imperial de Potosí*, written in the early eighteenth century by Bartolomé Arzans de Orsua y Vela.